A Robin's Egg Renaissance:
Chicago Modernism & the Great War

Other Books by Robert Alexander

POETRY

Finding Token Creek: New and Selected Writing, 1975–2020
Richmond Burning
What the Raven Said
White Pine Sucker River, Poems 1970–1990

NONFICTION

The Northwest Ordinance: Constitutional Politics and the Theft of Native Land
Five Forks: Waterloo of the Confederacy

ANTHOLOGIES

Spring Phantoms:
Short Prose by 19th Century British & American Authors
ed. Robert Alexander

Nothing to Declare:
A Guide to the Flash Sequence
ed. Robert Alexander, Eric Braun, and Debra Marquart

Family Portrait:
American Prose Poetry, 1900–1950
ed. Robert Alexander

The House of Your Dream:
An International Collection of Prose Poetry
ed. Robert Alexander and Dennis Maloney

The Party Train:
A Collection of North American Prose Poetry
ed. Robert Alexander, Mark Vinz, and C. W. Truesdale

A Robin's Egg Renaissance:
Chicago Modernism & the Great War

Robert Alexander

WHITE PINE PRESS | BUFFALO | NEW YORK

White Pine Press
P.O. Box 236
Buffalo, NY 14201

Publication of this book was supported by public funds from the New York State Council on the Arts, with the support of Governor Kathy Hochul and the New York State Legislature, a State Agency.

Printed and bound in the United States of America.

Cover image: "Main Entrance of the Building." In *The Book of the Fine Arts Building*, by Elia W. Peattie. Chicago: Ralph Fletcher Seymour, 1911.

Photo credit: "Eugen Wiener, 1914." W. Gerlich's Photograph Studio, Neuruppin. *Eugen Wiener as a soldier in uniform, c. 1914.* Jewish Museum Berlin, Inv. No. 2000/285/94. Donated by Peter Sinclair, formerly Peter Jacob. Courtesy Jewish Museum, Berlin.

ISBN 978-1-945680-67-0

Library of Congress Control Number: 2022950767

—for Katie

Contents

Interlude: Ford Madox Ford & Ezra Pound in London

Part Two: And the War Came to Europe

Part Three: The War Saps All One's Energy

Epilogue: And the War Came to America

Coda

List of Narrators

Richard Aldington	# 90, 101, 121
Mildred Aldrich	# 81
Margaret Anderson	# 12, 29, 31, 39, 67, 73, 77, 99, 106
Sherwood Anderson	# 21
Ray Stannard Baker	# 6, 53
Johann von Bernstorff	# 111
E. Ashmead-Bartlett	# 84
Albert J. Beveridge	# 75
Henry N. Brailsford	# 59, 63
Randolph Bourne	# 107
Chicago Tribune	# 25
Irvin S. Cobb	# 71
John Cournos	# 57
Richard Harding Davis	# 77
Floyd Dell	# 11, 42
W. E. B. Du Bois	# 10
Robert Dunn	# 89
Max Eastman	#108
John Gould Fletcher	# 19
F. S. Flint	# 14, 17
Ford Madox Ford	# 20, 47, 49, 51, 52, 91
Florence Kiper Fran	# 74
Henri Gaudier-Brzeska	# 103
Emma Goldman	# 98, 99
Douglas Goldring	# 50
Robert Graves	# 102
Harry Hansen	# 2
Jane Heap	# 120
Ben Hecht	# 33, 34
Frederic C. Howe	# 8, 27, 64, 114
Inez Haynes Irwin	# 24
Mietzi Jacob	# 85
John Maynard Keynes	# 54
Julius Koettgen	# 58, 69, 78, 80, 82, 87

A Robin's Egg Renaissance

It was the time of a kind of renaissance in the arts, in literature, a Robin's Egg Renaissance I have called it in my mind since. It had perhaps a pale blue tinge. It fell out of the nest. It may be that we should all have stayed in Chicago.

—Sherwood Anderson[1]

We took as an office room 917 in the Fine Arts Building—one of the most delightful buildings in the world I thought, before having seen anything of the world. And still think so, having seen something of it. I went into 917 the moment we signed the lease and spent the first day there alone, staring at the blue walls and living the future of the *Little Review*.

—Margaret Anderson[2]

Author's Note

New York, London, and Paris are well known as centers of modernism in the first decades of the twentieth century, but Chicago not so much. More than forty years ago I was intrigued when I first came upon a series of memoirs that discussed the literary movement in Chicago in the years before the United States became involved in the First World War.

My initial impulse was to limit this study to the so-called Chicago Literary Renaissance and its crucial place in the development of Anglo-American poetry—crucial because of two seminal magazines edited by women, *Poetry* and the *Little Review*, which first introduced many modernist authors to a wide audience. Over time I realized how important it would be to place this literary moment in its broader historical context, which is to say progressivism, women's suffrage, and, above all—swallowing so much positive human endeavor in its appetite for death—the Great War.

By 1917, Anglophone poets had already produced many pieces now considered masterpieces—for example, T. S. Eliot's "Love Song of J. Alfred Prufrock," which first appeared in *Poetry* magazine in 1915. This achievement was in no small part due to the efforts of Ford Madox Ford, whose influence, in my estimation, has been vastly underrated. Modernism, in both politics and art, had in its early years an optimistic tone about it—characterized by what some critics, such as H. L. Mencken, referred to as "uplift." But when the horrors of war began to overwhelm the world, first in Europe and only later in America, this optimism gave way to the disillusionment and dislocation we've come to associate with twentieth-century literature.

The technique I employ uses a variety of original sources: letters, memoirs, speeches, newspapers. My purpose is to let the participants tell their own story; as the Nobel Prize winner Svetlana Alexievich explains, "I tried this and that and finally I chose a genre where human voices speak for themselves."

R. A.
Madison, Wisconsin
February 14, 2022

Preface

Then in 1900 everybody got down off his stilts; henceforth nobody drank absinthe with his black coffee; nobody went mad; nobody committed suicide; nobody joined the Catholic church; or if they did I have forgotten. Victorianism had been defeated.

—W. B. Yeats[3]

In July 1913 at Gettysburg, more than fifty thousand former soldiers turned out for a "Great Reunion of Blue and Gray." Graybeards enacted skirmishes at various sites on the battlefield, then shook hands in friendship. Also in 1913, for the first time, the moving assembly lines at Ford Motor Company turned out a thousand cars per day. America—and indeed the world—was at a time of transition. Just one year later a Great War would break out in Europe that would make the slaughter at Gettysburg look paltry by comparison. In Floyd Dell's words, the volcano was preparing to blow—but not quite yet. There was still a little time for the butterfly of Modernism to spread its dewy wings and taste the air.

✳   ✳   ✳

When my father died I inherited the cello he'd bought for me to play when I was in sixth grade, though—this being the sixties—when I went to college I switched over to guitar, and the cello stayed with my parents when they left Boston for New York City.

After the funeral I brought the cello back with me to Milwaukee, where I was in grad school, and one afternoon I took it down to Chicago, where I could get it appraised for insurance coverage. I walked into a downtown office building and took the creaky elevator to whichever floor it was—after forty years I've forgotten—and dropped it off at the musical instrument shop. In the meantime, I'd begun to have the strangest sensation that I'd been there before, that it was a very familiar place. But I hadn't, so far as I knew. I'd only been to Chicago a few times, and none of them involved this downtown location—and when I asked the counter salesman, he told me they had only the week before moved into the building. Yet leaving the office I looked down the hallway and was struck by how familiar it looked, music tinkling from some location and (so I recall) a small fountain playing in a restaurant.

I took the elevator back to the ground floor and walked out of the building. Right beside the door I saw a small plaque—Fine Arts Building—and I thought: Oh, the Fine Arts Building, that's why it seems so familiar! Yet right away I realized I'd never in my life been to the Fine Arts Building, and I wondered why that thought had popped so quickly into my mind.

I returned to Milwaukee that same day and didn't think much more about it. This sensation had happened to me a couple of times previously, though it had never lasted as long or been quite so intense.

A couple of years later I had moved back to Madison and was beginning work on my doctoral dissertation, which involved a rather obscure piece of modern American literature. For this I was doing research in the little magazine collection at the university's Memorial Library, and it wasn't long before I was going through the files of *Poetry* and the *Little Review*, and I began to realize what a central place the Fine Arts Building had in the Chicago literary world of the second decade of the twentieth century. I also began to read the work of many writers whose names, up to that time, were unfamiliar to me—though I'd been studying American poetry for fifteen years or more. This was a whole world I knew nothing about. Greenwich Village and its storied history were familiar to me—even in the sixties and seventies it retained some of the mystique it had first gathered half a century earlier— but the fact that there had been a modern literary movement in

Chicago was new to me. So I began to read memoirs of the era to find out who all these people were.

I was teaching part-time that year in an alternative high school, and I'd come home in the afternoons when I wasn't in the rare book department of Memorial Library and spend the time reading memoirs. Sometimes I'd fall asleep with the afternoon jazz radio program playing softly in the background. I began to have dreams where people in the memoirs were talking to me, vague but familiar faces out of the fog of time, telling me to be happy that I was still walking the earth.

I'd had a classmate in grad school who was writing a novel about three generations of a Viennese family, for which he was experimenting with past life regression, and he told me one day, "If you start to screw around with past lives, you really have to be grounded or you'll end up losing your mind." Suffice it to say that at that time I was anything but well centered, and I paid the price—though I did manage to keep it together long enough to get my degree. But that's another story altogether.

Fifteen years later my life had regained some semblance of order. I was working as an editor for a small literary press, and I attended a publisher's convention in Chicago. I stayed an extra day in the downtown hotel, and Monday morning I walked over to the Fine Arts Building on Michigan Avenue. By that time I knew that the *Little Review* had occupied an office on the ninth floor, and there I went. I found 917, and for some reason the door was open. The office was empty—between tenants, perhaps—so I walked in. It was a lot smaller than I had imagined, seeming much smaller than the living room of my own house, and there was a sink in one corner and, as I recall, a couple of windows along one wall. Otherwise the walls were bare white and the hardwood floor polished and clean. I stood there for a long while and summoned the ghosts whom I had gotten to know so well.

It is their story I will tell you now—or rather, using their own words, I will now let them tell you their story.

Introduction

As with most cultural "renaissances," it is difficult to find a point of origin for this one. Vincent Starrett has suggested, only half in jest, that the "first note of revolt" was sounded on the night of November 25, 1910, when Mary Garden's Dance of the Seven Veils in Salomé at the Auditorium Theatre was halted by the Chief of Police. Said Chief Steward, describing Miss Garden's performance, "she wallowed around like a cat in a bed of catnip."

—Jackson R. Bryer[4]

On March 4, 1913, Woodrow Wilson became the 28th president of the United States. Only the second Democrat to be elected to that august position since the Civil War, he was also the first Southerner since James K. Polk to move into the White House, excepting Andrew Johnson after Lincoln was assassinated. (Lincoln was born in Kentucky but raised in Illinois, and few Southerners outside of Kentucky would have claimed him as one of their own). The Republican Party had split in the summer of 1912 and spawned the Progressive or "Bull Moose" Party, named for its candidate Theodore Roosevelt, and the Electoral College had given Wilson the nod, though the combined popular vote for Taft and Roosevelt would easily have beaten him had circumstances been different.

It was a watershed moment for the country, as Wilson—known for his speech-making ability—duly noted in his inaugural comments:

There has been a change of government. It began two

years ago, when the House of Representatives became Democratic by a decisive majority. It has now been completed. The Senate about to assemble will also be Democratic. The offices of President and Vice-President have been put into the hands of Democrats. What does the change mean? . . .

It means much more than the mere success of a party. . . .

The great Government we loved has too often been made use of for private and selfish purposes, and those who used it had forgotten the people. . . .

Our duty is to cleanse, to reconsider, to restore, to correct the evil without impairing the good, to purify and humanize every process of our common life without weakening or sentimentalizing it. There has been something crude and heartless and unfeeling in our haste to succeed and be great. Our thought has been "Let every man look out for himself, let every generation look out for itself," while we reared giant machinery which made it impossible that any but those who stood at the levers of control should have a chance to look out for themselves. . . .

We have come now to the sober second thought. The scales of heedlessness have fallen from our eyes. We have made up our minds to square every process of our national life again with the standards we so proudly set up at the beginning and have always carried at our hearts. Our work is a work of restoration. . . .

Justice, and only justice, shall always be our motto.[5]

Meanwhile in Chicago, a forty-ish poet named Harriet Monroe was also beginning a new endeavor. During the previous August she had sent out a letter to poets in England and America whose work intrigued her, soliciting submissions to the magazine— *Poetry: A Magazine of Verse*—whose first issue she would bring out in October 1912, shortly before the election which brought Wilson to the White House. Arthur Ficke, a lawyer and poet from Davenport, Iowa, responded to Monroe's message: "Your letter of yesterday has deeply interested me, and I shall be very glad to do anything I can to assist you. The project has a fine ring to it—I rejoice to see that the Bull Moose movement is not confined to politics."[6]

In his speech accepting the nomination as the Progressive candidate for president of the United States, Teddy Roosevelt said that "the time is ripe, and overripe, for a genuine Progressive movement, nation-wide and justice-loving . . . representing all that is best in the hopes, beliefs, and aspirations of the plain people who make up the immense majority of the rank and file of both the old parties." Roosevelt ended his speech with the famous words, "We stand at Armageddon, and we battle for the Lord."[7]

Arthur Ficke was prescient in conjoining the two movements—one which was attempting to remake the politics of the nation, and the other which would be successful in remaking the established poetic idiom. While Progressivism, both Republican and Democratic, would falter and die in the face of the Great War—and the U.S. involvement in it—Anglo-American modernism would transform contemporary poetry and set the stage for the rest of the century's work. Two Chicago magazines, *Poetry* and the *Little Review*, were instrumental in this endeavor.

Five years later, in a retrospective essay, Monroe outlined what that endeavor consisted of:

> What is the new poetry? and wherein does it differ from the old? The difference is not in mere details of form. . . . It is not merely in diction, though the truly modern poet rejects the so-called "poetic" shifts of language—the *deems, 'neaths, forsooths,* etc., the inversions and high-sounding rotundities, familiar to his predecessors. . . . These things are important, but the difference goes deeper than details of form, strikes through them to fundamental integrities.
>
> The new poetry strives for a concrete and immediate realization of life; it would discard the theory, the abstraction, the remoteness, found in all classics not of the first order. It is less vague, less verbose, less eloquent, than most poetry of the Victorian period and much work

of earlier periods. It has set before itself an ideal of absolute simplicity and sincerity—an ideal which implies an individual, unstereotyped diction; and an individual, unstereotyped rhythm. . . . In presenting the concrete object or the concrete environment, whether these be beautiful or ugly, it seeks to give more precisely the emotion arising from them, and thus widens immeasurably the scope of the art. . . .

Great poetry has always been written in the language of contemporary speech, and its theme, even when legendary, has always borne a direct relation with contemporary thought, contemporary imaginative and spiritual life. It is this direct relation which the more progressive modern poets are trying to restore.[8]

We should note here Monroe's use of the word "progressive," a term also used to describe the change-oriented politics of the era. The growth of this poetic movement in the five years between 1912 and 1917—and the political context within which it flourished—is what this book is about. New York and London are well known as places where modernist literature developed—but Chicago, the City on the Lake, also played a central role in those years, in large part because of two women, Harriet Monroe and Margaret Anderson, who conceived and nurtured two of the most important literary magazines of the era. The world of bohemian Chicago in those days is not so well known as New York or London—and a century later, it still deserves our attention.

I.

H. L. Mencken

Civilized Chicago

The most civilized city in America? Chicago, of course! And per corollary the most thoroughly American, at least among the big ones. A culture is bogus unless it be honest, which means unless it be truly national—the naif and untinctured expression of a national mind and soul.

That of Boston is as bogus as a set of false teeth. The Bostonian is simply a fourth rate colonial snob. Even in his preposterous speech he tries to conceal the damnable fact that he was hatched a Yankee. Take him at his best and he is still ashamed of his nationality. Run a Manchester commercial gent through Harvard and you would have a Back Bay intellectual.

The trouble with New York is that it has no nationality at all. It is simply a sort of free port—a place where the raw materials of civilization are received, sorted out, and sent further on.

In the arts it is a mere wholesaler. It prints two-thirds of the books of the country—and can't show a single author worth printing. It has the world's largest warehouse of artistic fossils—and never produces a picture worth hanging. Its social pushers pour out millions for music—and even Boston has a better orchestra.

Philadelphia? A Sunday school with a family entrance up the alley. An old maid with the Decameron under her pillow. An intellectual slum. A Devil's Island for both artists and gentlemen. A first rate book or symphony coming out of Philadelphia would astonish the world almost as much as an ostrich coming out of a hen's egg.

San Francisco? Dead, done, extinct, kaput, murdered by the New Thought and an act of God.

Pittsburgh, Baltimore, St. Louis, New Orleans, Washington, Cleveland, Detroit, Newark? *O, mon Doo!* My word, my word! . . .

But in Chicago there is the mysterious something; in Chicago a spirit broods upon the face of the waters. Find me a writer who is indubitably an American and who has something new and interesting to say, and who says it with an air, and nine times out of ten I will show you that he has some sort of connection with the abattoir by the lake—that he was bred there, or got his start there, or passed through there during the days when he was tender.

*   *   *

One hears a vast hullabaloo in New York about Little Theaters. They become a fashionable diversion, and hence mere boob traps. The first and best Little Theater in America was set up in Chicago. It ran for years before New York ever heard of it. When New York heard of it at last New York made fun of it.

And now every alley in New York has a Little Theater, and all the ideas tried out in Chicago years ago are set before the oafs of Broadway as great novelties, and the New York critics hail them as revolutionary, and the pockets of many a wondering tripe seller of Forty-Second Street are agreeably stuffed.

Art? Progress? The theater of the future? The future your grandmother! The theater of four or five years before last. There was more real music in the old Thomaskirche at Leipzig, says James Huneker, than in all your modern opera houses and concert halls put together. There was more serious purpose and honest striving and sound understanding in Maurice Brown's little playhouse in Chicago than in all the Demi-Tasse theaters and half-portion theaters and MacDougal Alley theaters between Fourth Street and the Harlem River.

Another matter that kicks up a vast pother among the

newly intellectual is the new poetry movement.

Go to Boston and you will find various eminent composers of *vers libre* pointed out on the street with the same awe that New Yorkers used to show in pointing out Diamond Jim Brady and Bim the Button Man. Go down into Greenwich Village and you will find others publicly exhibiting themselves at $2 a peep at nightly balls in Webster Hall.

But out in Chicago you will still find the first magazine ever devoted to this new verse, and either the actual corpse or the plain tracks or four-fifths of its best professors, from Vachel Lindsay to Carl Sandburg, and from Harriet Monroe to Edgar Lee Masters. In brief, all American literary movements that have youth in them, and a fresh point of view, and the authentic bounce and verve of the country and the true character and philosophy of its people— all these come out of Chicago.

It was Chicago, and not New York, that launched the *Chap-Book* saturnalia of the nineties—the first of her endless efforts to break down formalism in the national letters and let in the national spirit. It was Chicago that produced the *Little Review*. It was Chicago that turned out Ring Lardner, the first American author to write in the American language.

There was a time when San Francisco seemed likely to take this first place. Mark Twain and Bret Harte were given their starts out there; such fellows as Frank Norris and Jack London felt the spell of the town; there was in it a certain tolerant and expansive spirit that undoubtedly had a charm for men of ideas.

But the earthquake finished San Francisco. The old romance was blown up overnight—and on the ruins the Philistines planted their dullness. Today San Francisco is simply a third rate American town—a town full of vice crusaders and other such prehensile messiahs, but as empty of artiste as Hoboken.

*   *   *

But Chicago, so far at least, has escaped any such flattening. The sharp winds from the lake seem to be a perpetual antidote to that Puritan mugginess of soul which wars with civilization in all American cities. In Chicago originality still appears to be put above conformity. The idea out there is not to do what others do, but to do something they can't do. This idea is the foundation of all artistic endeavor. The artist is either an anarchist or he is not worth a hoot. One may either train for the Union League club or one may train for Parnassus: one cannot train for both.

The trouble with New York, intellectually, is just here. The curse of the town lies in the fact that it seems to foster the spirit of the pusher and bounder—that it puts much higher values upon conformity, acceptance, intellectual respectability, than it puts upon actual ideas.

The typical New Yorker is forever trying to get into something; to be recognized in this or that circle; to be accepted grudgingly by someone he envies—usually some cad. He lives in the place, not where ideas are hatched, but where rewards are distributed—and any system of distributing definite rewards is bound to encourage the usual, the acknowledged, the tried and found harmless.

This deadening spirit shows itself not only in the ludicrous horde of social climbers who infest the town, wildly trying to buy their way into a codfish aristocracy through opera houses, picture galleries, and various pecksniffian philanthropies, but also in actual artists.

A writer, let us say, begins in Chicago. His aim out there is to do something new, to express himself fully, to pump his writing full of the breath of life. Then he comes to New York—and immediately he begins to write as if his main object were to get a favorable notice in the *Nation*, or even *The New York Times*. In other words, he takes the veil. Once a producer of ideas, he is now merely a producer of platitudes. . . .

I give you Chicago. It is not London-and-Harvard. It is not Paris-and-buttermilk. It is American in every chitlin' and sparerib, and it is alive from snout to tail.[9]

2.

Harry Hansen

from *Midwest Portraits*

Time has dealt gently with the landmarks that are associated, however remotely, with the World's Fair of 1893, from which
Chicago dates its artistic and commercial awakening, and here
and there near Jackson Park survive buildings that trace their lin-
eage back thirty years—a long time in a city like Chicago, where
the increasing ground values have laid houses low long before
their usefulness as habitations was ended. I have wandered along
these streets and stood before these houses as I might before an
inn of Pickwick's time, wondering what scenes they had beheld
and what sort of men and women had passed through their doors.
A different generation, surely, from our own, was there in 1893, a
generation still engrossed with talk of "home folks," with a love
for pies and griddle cakes, with surreys and puff sleeves and anti-
macassars, a generation which believed that art, both in painting
and in literature, meant pictorial representation of innocently
beautiful things, and which bought for its education large albums
of "art views" containing the sugary, well-modeled, and wholly un-
inspired paintings of contemporary masters. Even now, when we
glance toward the park, we get a glimpse through the trees of the
very building that housed the original paintings from all over the
world—a crumbling ruin of counterfeit stone, imparting, in its
glorious decay, something of its forlorn, exotic grandeur; a Greek
symphony that turned the thoughts of thousands from rococo and

late Victorian to the beauty that lives in simple lines.

But an industrial age demands its tithe; the solid masonry of a railroad embankment obscures the view; we must pass under its gloomy trestles before the stone pavements of the city yield to the less formal drives of the park. And just before the thoroughfare ends we observe on either hand rows of one-story frame structures that now shelter popcorn venders, photographers, and restaurateurs, or have their windows screened with long green curtains that permit a glimpse of studio life within. Just opposite, where clumps of dense shrubbery and iron chains mark the conventional entrance of an American public park, stood the flamboyant gate of the exposition, and in that remote day these storerooms were occupied by vendors of all sorts. When the fair ended these Arabs flitted away; the doors of the houses were boarded up and life lapsed as on a desert isle for a period, for the residents who lived nearby did their trading to the westward and no one bothered about these isolated survivors of the great days.

Slowly, one by one, artists and writers sought these ancient buildings and found here hospitable and inexpensive shelter. In time a little colony gathered here and friends and fellow craftsmen followed and made these haunts their rendezvous. And so they take their place in the literary history of Chicago and in the story that I tell, and although the years have scattered many of those who once came here as fledglings and whose names have since become widely known, reminiscences of those days flower whenever two or three are gathered together. Most of the time they met in Margery Currey's big rooms, once the habitat of Thorstein Veblen—perhaps they were even called "studio," for in that day, ten years ago, the word had not yet fallen into disfavor through commercialization—and Margery was the hostess whose gift for hospitality, for friendship, was as genuine and effective as that of Madame Nodier or Madame Adam or the Marquise du Deffand in Paris of other days.

If you have wandered down the narrow passage of the rue Visconti and let your imagination people it again with Racine and Balzac and the merry groups that met for controversy or for mutual laudation in the Café Rochefoucauld, you may have experienced a regret for the passing of the years; no less do these ancient store-rooms house a shrine, and one wishes that time could be turned back and afford us once more a glimpse of America's younger writers before they reached maturity. . . .

Glorious days those—rich, tempestuous, capricious, extraordinary. Tremendous days. And unforgettable nights. Out of the past dimly come these pictures:

Long past midnight and silence outside, save for the dull boom of the university bells to the west, marking the hours. Moonlight dimly flooding the walks seen through the half-drawn curtains. Tall candles throwing long, black shadows against the walls. A group sitting in silence, motionless, in easy attitudes. And near the candles Arthur Davison Ficke chants the ancient lines:

How beautiful are thy feet with shoes O prince's daughter! Thy joints of thy thighs are like jewels, the work of the hands of a cunning workman.

Thy navel is like a round goblet witch wanteth its liquor, thy belly is like an heap of wheat set about with lilies.

Thy two breasts are like two young roes that are twins.

Steps approach without and a shadow falls upon the ivory curtains. The big form of a policeman stands motionless before the window.

Thy neck is as a tower of ivory . . . thy nose is as the tower of Lebanon. . . . How fair and how pleasant are thou, O love, for delights!

The figure moves on. Within, the voice, chanting the ancient melody. Without, the slow, receding footsteps.[10]

Part One: Before the War

The World War had not yet come. It was to scatter us, shatter us.

—Sherwood Anderson[11]

Something was in the air. Something was happening, about to happen—in politics, in literature, in art. The atmosphere became electric with it.

—Floyd Dell[12]

Vernal Equinox

The scent of hyacinths, like a pale mist, lies between me
       and my book;
And the South Wind, washing through the room,
Makes the candles quiver.
My nerves sting at a spatter of rain on the shutter,
And I am uneasy with the thrusting of green shoots
Outside, in the night.
Why are you not here to overpower me with your tense
       and urgent love?

—Amy Lowell[13]

3.

Edgar Lee Masters

from *Across Spoon River*

I took a seat in the chair-car, as I had no money for a sleeper. Anyway I wanted to see the country from the window; I did not want to sleep. I wanted to think. Above all I had made up my mind to see the first traces of Chicago, to see how and where it began. So all night long I sat looking out at the prairie, an expanse of blurs and darkness, and at the stars which looked like splotches of running grease in the hot sky. When the sun came up like a fireman who has slept, all refreshed for more stoking, we were still many miles from Chicago. There were hours ahead of enduring the stifling atmosphere of the car impregnated with the hot breaths of sleeping men, women, and children slumped down in the seats. . . .

It was difficult to tell when we left the prairie, where the Illinois and Michigan Canal ceased, where it was that we first bumped over the tracks of the outlying belt lines, where there was still farming country and widely separated houses. Then came the truck gardens of the city with houses closer together along half-made streets which stretched into vanishing distances of flat country. Then there were the new subdivisions springing up all around, with newly built and half-finished apartment buildings and houses . . . along plowed strips soon to be streets or boulevards, and already half-curbed, where newly planted trees were making a desperate effort to grow. Factories, lumberyards, coal-yards, grain elevators, tugs, sailing vessels, steamboats on the river and the canal swam into view as we rattled over the switch tracks; and all around was the increasing density of the illimitable city, formed of miles of frame houses, lying cooked by the July sun and smothered in smoke and gas and smell, and in exhalations from the breweries, and in reeks from the stockyards. This was not Minneapolis with its flouring mills and its comparative quiet by the shores of the Mississippi. Now there were noises from a thousand engines, the crash of switching trains, the yells of laborers, and now and then the dull thunder of dynamite; for already the Drainage Canal was being dug to connect Chicago with the Gulf, and thus purify the drinking water of the city. Chicago thus began for me as a mist rising from the sea, in a sense without a beginning. . . .

And then the train drew under the dark shed of the Polk Street station.

*　　*　　*

I took my first glances of Chicago now, noting the countless saloons, and near at hand a whole street which looked suspiciously wanton, like streets I had seen in Peoria, and which turned out to be one of the brothel sections of Chicago. North along Dearborn Street, as we hurried on, I could see the city of the Loop district, not then called the Loop. The Monadnock Block, the Owings Building, and some other sixteen-story structures were then standing in that street. Crossing State Street at Polk we were in the midst of saloons, dives, flophouses, cheap hotels, sordid places of assignation. The streets swarmed with people of every clime: Chinese, Poles, Negroes, and at doorways the ubiquitous Jew was selling clothes. The great trucks made the cobblestones rattle. The air was suffocating with smoke and gas. And the heat! It seemed to me I had never before experienced anything like it.[14]

4.

Ralph Fletcher Seymour

Harriet Monroe & *Poetry*

It was on a summer's morning in the year 1912 that a thin, quiet mannered, bespectacled lady, Harriet Monroe by name, walked into my office and placed a bulky bundle of manuscript on my desk. Looking sharply at me through shining glasses she said, "Here are the poems and editorials for the first issue of *Poetry* magazine. Give it your most careful consideration. It is my child and I have brought it to you to dress and help care for." Then her enthusiasm for her child swept her reticence away. She leaned closer, looked hard into my face, with a characteristic, nervous gesture put her had on my arm and exclaimed; "Oh, Ralph, you will do your best for our magazine? It does mean so much for all of us! We must have it here, in this city, but there is no reason why it should not stand for the best thing of its sort in the world."

Thus I became the publisher of this incorruptible magazine, which has done so much to overcome the commonplace and "practical realities" in the field of poetry. For four years it was produced, at great pains, through this office. Miss Monroe, Henry Fuller, and Eunice Tietjens did most of the editorial and proof-reading work, and kept me in continual trouble trying to make each issue "perfect," get it out on time and yet stay in business....

In the year 1938 a banquet in honor of Harriet Monroe was given at the University of Chicago in Hutchinson Commons, and to mark the dedication of a Foundation for the support of modern poetry which she had started with the gift of her unusual collection of volumes pertaining to that subject. After the dinner Ford Madox Ford told this story:—"Ezra Pound was acting as my secretary at a period just predating the Great War. We were seated on opposite sides at a large library table, Ezra had been occupied for some time in trying to write a poem. He finally pushed it away from him and despondently exclaimed, 'Damn it! why should I try to make a poem? No one cares if it is made and no one reads the stuff!' I sat quietly and said nothing. Presently Ezra reached for the uncompleted manuscript, exclaiming as he did so, 'I think I will finish it. After all, there is always Harriet'!"[15]

5.

Harriet Monroe

from *A Poet's Life*

In 1910, at age 49, Harriet Monroe embarked on a round-the-world journey.

I remember the thrill which shook me as I bought at Cook's a ticket "from Chicago to Chicago"—for six hundred and fifty dollars which I had raked and scraped and borrowed to finance the adventurous trip. . . .

In London began a friendship with May Sinclair, the quiet little spinster novelist whose *Divine Fire* I had admired when it was first published. She introduced me to Elkin Mathews, the publisher, who was vividly enthusiastic about the work of a young American in London, Ezra Pound. "That is real poetry!" he exclaimed, as he showed me the *Personae and Exultations*; so I bought the tiny volumes, and later beguiled the long Siberian journey with the strange and beautiful rhythms of this new poet, my self-exiled compatriot.

＊　＊　＊

It was on the eleventh of January, 1911, that I finished circling the world at the Santa Fe station in Chicago. I found the city surging with art activities and aspirations beneath its commercial surface. . . .

As time went on the slight attention and meagre (if any) compensation granted to poets by publishers and the public made me more and more indignant. My mind contrasted the nothing done for them with the large endowment (partly by taxation) which supported the Art Institute of Chicago; and with the liberal gifts which endowed large prizes for painters and sculptors at its annual exhibitions, and many scholarships for its school. . . .

Why this difference between the respectful attitude of donors and press and public toward painting and sculpture, also to a certain degree music and architecture, and the general contemptuous indifference of all these powers toward the poet and the beautiful art he practices or aims at, the art which, more than any other, has passed on the "tale of the tribe" to succeeding generations? . . .

Gradually, during the half-year after my return, I became convinced that something must be done; and since nobody else was doing anything, it might be "up to me" to try to stir up the sluggish situation. . . .

My confidence gradually gained headway, and a talk with my Little Room friend Hobart C. Chatfield-Taylor—novelist, lover of the arts, man of culture, wealth, and social prominence— gave shape and purpose to it, and brought forth a definite plan. . . .

He thought that I could get one hundred men in Chicago to subscribe fifty dollars a year for five years to try out the hazardous experiment, providing I was willing to go to their offices and make the plea in person. . . .

From September until the beginning of June, 1912, I devoted my spare time to the project, gaining faith and momentum with each new name. . . .

By early June there were more than one hundred signatures on the little printed five-year pledges; a few of these promising $100 a year, and a few others $25, instead of the usual $50. More than $5200, besides a few outright presents, was ready for the new magazine when I ceased my soliciting. One of the last men I saw was Edward L. Ryerson, who said: "You don't need me now, so I won't join your regular list, but you will surely face emergencies in the future when a little extra money will be necessary, and then you may feel free to call on me." (He spoke truly; four or five times during the next fifteen years [before his death in 1928] he gave me two hundred and fifty dollars to meet such emergencies.)[16]

Poetry's guarantors included some of the richest and most well-known men and women of the city—bankers, lawyers, industrialists, as well as their spouses—names such as McCormick, Palmer, Dawes, Crane, and Insull—evidence of both Monroe's persuasiveness and of the motivation of these men and women to prove that the image of Chicago as "porkopolis"— a cultural wasteland—was in error.[17]

For years it had become increasingly evident that the present-day poets needed stirring up. Most of them were doing the same old thing in the same old academic way. . . . The well of American poetry seemed to be thinning out and drying up, and the worst of it was that nobody seemed to care.

It was this indifference that I started out to combat, this dry conservatism that I wished to refresh with living water from a new spring. Here and there were hints of freshness—I had tasted one in reading Ezra Pound's first books on my way around the world. Could I find and follow these traces of a new vitality in the art? There must be poets—could I search them out and assemble them, and find the necessary public for them?

*   *   *

Through June and July of that summer of 1912 I spent many hours at the public library reading not only recent books by the better poets, but also all the verse in American and English magazines of the previous five years. To the poets I thought interesting was sent, in August and early September, a "poets' circular," which, after explaining the financial basis on which the new magazine was founded, continued as follows:

The success of this first American effort to encourage the production and appreciation of poetry, as the other arts are encouraged, by endowment, now depends on the poets. We offer them:

First, a chance to be heard in their own place, without the limitations imposed by the popular magazine. In other words, while the ordinary magazines must minister to a large public little interested in poetry, this magazine will appeal to, and it may be hoped, will develop, a public primarily interested in poetry as an art, as the highest, most complete human expression of truth and beauty.

Second, within space limitations imposed at present by the small size of our monthly sheaf—from sixteen to twenty-four pages the size of this—we hope to print poems of greater length and of more intimate and serious character than the other magazines can afford to use. All kinds of verse will be considered—narrative, dramatic, lyric—quality alone being the test of acceptance. Certain numbers may be devoted entirely to a single poem, or a group of poems by one person; except for a few editorial pages of comment and review.

Third, besides the prize or prizes above mentioned, we shall pay contributors. The rate will depend on the subscription list, and will increase as the receipts increase, for this magazine is not intended as a money-maker but as a public-spirited effort to gather together and enlarge the poet's public and to increase his earnings. If we can raise the rate paid for verse until it equals that paid for paintings, etchings, statuary, representing as much ability, time and reputation, we shall feel that we have done something to make it possible for poets to practice their art and be heard. In addition, we should like to secure as many prizes, and as large, as are offered to painters and sculptors at the annual exhibitions in our various cities.

In order that this effort may be recognized as just and necessary, and may develop for this art a responsive public, we ask the poets to send us their best verse. We promise to refuse nothing because it is too good, whatever be the nature of its excellence. . . .

A personal letter was sent with most of these circulars, referring individually to the poet's work or to something I had heard or felt about it. . . . Answers expressing sympathetic interest and inclosing or promising poems came promptly.[18]

At this point Monroe was not alone in her endeavor:

In early August [1912], while I was staying in Lake Forest, I talked over the scheme with Alice Corbin Henderson, who lived in Lake Bluff, the next suburb to the north, where the Hendersons—painter, writer, and small daughter—had a studio home. A fine poet and intelligent critic, she was keen as a whip in those days, and seemed the one fit person available to assist in my project. By the end of September she had accepted the associate editorship at the munificent half-time salary of forty dollars a month. . . .

Alice was usually the "first reader" of the many poems from far and near which soon began to weigh down our mail. I could trust her to detect the keen note, the original style, and to pass on to me for discussion anything which offered a hint of promise.[19]

*   *   *

The most dynamic and stimulating of our early correspondents was [Ezra Pound], whose early small books, *Personae and Exultations*, I had read with delight on the Siberian journey. . . . His letter [in response to the circular] spoke with a fresh voice, and promised inestimable values to the magazine, for at that time he was the dynamic center of the keenest young literary group in England:

I am interested, and your scheme, as far as I understand it, seems not only sound, but the only possible method. . . .

If you conceive verse as a living medium, on a par with paint, marble, and music, you may announce, if it's any good to you, that for the present such of my work as appears in America (barring my own books) will appear exclusively in your magazine. . . .

If I can be of any use in keeping you or the magazine in touch with whatever is most dynamic in artistic thought, either here or in Paris—as much of it comes to me and I do see nearly everyone that matters—I shall be glad to do so.

—*and in a postscript he added*: Any agonizing that tends to hurry what I believe in the end to be inevitable, our American Risorgimento, is dear to me. That awakening will make the Italian Renaissance look like a tempest in a teapot!

I sent Pound an enthusiastic answer, asking him to represent *Poetry* abroad as Foreign Correspondent, and to send us his poems and prose articles and such British contributions as he approved of. On September 21st he wrote accepting the unsalaried job.

*   *   *

During our first year or two, Ezra's pungent and provocative letters were falling thick as snowflakes. Thus began the rather violent, but on the whole salutary, discipline under the lash of which the editor of the new magazine felt herself being rapidly educated, while all incrustations of habit and prejudice were ruthlessly swept away.[20]

The Progressives

At the turn of the a century a great progressive movement swept the country from coast to coast, calling to its colors all that was best in America. People looked on injustices and inequities with new eyes, and strove mightily against the greeds and cruelties that had crept into our national life.

—George Creel[21]

The whole political question in America seems one of making the poor man richer and the rich man poorer. That is all there is to it.

—Amos Pinchot[22]

6.

Ray Stannard Baker

from *American Chronicle*

Toward the end of Theodore Roosevelt's administration I attended a little dinner at the City Club in New York at which a group of us, who called ourselves Progressives or Independents in politics, discussed what we should do, whom we should support in the coming election. . . . It was not a mere question as to whom we should vote for in 1908, whether Taft the Republican or Bryan the Democrat, but how to strengthen the non-partisan liberal movement in which we were deeply interested and which we saw, or thought we saw, rapidly developing. . . .

[Roosevelt] had become the hope of the young liberals, the "insurgents" and progressives of that period. In the beginning we had great faith in him . . . [but] not a few younger men, of whom I was one, began toward the end of his administration, to question not only his objectives but also his method as a progressive leader. Was it enough to dispense moral judgments? Or balance these judgments between, say, the "good" trust and the "bad" trust? It began to seem a little like Bryan's comment that the financial problems of the country could be easily solved if "our hearts were in the right place. . . ."

Roosevelt himself had confessed that he was not primarily interested in the great economic and social questions that were confronting the nation. He had even said that so far as the tariff question was concerned he was an "agnostic"; in short, he had neither strong principles, nor any real program for meeting the most troublesome issues then facing the people. . . .

When it came to the election of 1908 I voted for Taft with hope rather than with confidence. The plain fact was that the country knew next to nothing at all about the real Mr. Taft until after his election. . . .

Taft was a lawyer whose ambition it was to sit on the Supreme Court. His approach to public questions from the first was that of the legalist. He seemed to believe that Roosevelt and the reformers had gone far enough. This was just the program that the "stand-patters" wanted. . . . At a dinner on April 30, only a few weeks after Taft's inauguration, Joseph H. Choate, the most notable lawyer of his time, spoke with fine sarcasm of the legal activities of the Roosevelt administration.

"Corporation lawyers," he said, "were universally condemned only about twelve months ago. It is time they had their inning."

But the Progressives believed that only a start had been made during Roosevelt's administration; that the real battle was yet to come, and it was soon evident that their efforts to understand and solve the important problems of the railroads, water power, trusts, the tariff, and the like, were to find small encouragement at Washington. . . .

The next year or two was to see a tremendous outbreak of political revolt, and the appearance of an Insurgent Movement without precedent in the country. It was, significantly, most strongly evident in Taft's own supposedly conservative party. The National Progressive Republican League soon had among its signers eight United States senators, among them such powerful leaders and campaigners as LaFollette of Wisconsin, Bristow of Kansas, Norris of Nebraska, and Cummins and Dolliver of Iowa. Besides these Senators, the list included sixteen members of the House of Representatives, six governors of states, and nineteen other active public men, including several well-known writers.

A similar insurgency was rapidly developing in the Democratic party. Woodrow Wilson was overturning the powerful New Jersey machine, and a vigorous young man named Franklin D. Roosevelt, then a state senator, was organizing the insurgent Democrats in the New York legislature. Judge Lindsey in Colorado and Brand Whitlock in Ohio were vigorous supporters of the new movement.

"An insurgent," remarked Theodore Roosevelt, who viewed the movement with some anxiety, "is a Progressive who is exceeding the speed limit."

What made the movement especially alarming to the conservatives was that there was little or no difference in their objectives between the insurgents of the two old parties. Governor Woodrow Wilson said in a public speech:

"If somebody could draw together the liberal elements of both parties in this country he could build up a party which could not be beaten in a generation, for the very reason that we would all join it." The movement was not socialist; although the Socialists were then stronger in the country, probably, than ever before. In an article I wrote at the time I tried to define and contrast the two movements. "The emphasis of the Insurgent Movement," I wrote, "was upon the development first of strong and honest political machinery; that of the Socialists, upon immediate economic reforms.

"The Insurgent believes," I went on to say, "that once the people get the power they can be trusted to use it properly. If the people wish then to adopt any part or all of the Socialist economic program, well and good. If, on the other hand, the people turn out to be economically more conservative than some of the extreme radicals desire, also well and good. It is a people's government, and this is the democratic spirit."

In seeking better political machinery, the Insurgents advocated various new devices of democratic control: direct nominations, the initiative and referendum, simpler forms of controlling City governments, direct election of United States Senators, and stringent new laws to prevent corrupt political practices.

But the Insurgents, even if they often differed among themselves, also had a program of economic reform calling for lower tariffs, conservation of natural resources, a parcel-post system, a national income tax, pure-food legislation, a Federal Reserve System, and stringent governmental control of all public utilities.[23]

7.

William Allen White

from *The Autobiography of William Allen White*

Politically the people were feeling for new weapons of democracy: the secret ballot, called "the Australian ballot"; the primary; the direct election of United States Senators; the initiative, referendum, and recall; a commission form of government in the cities; and other laws amending the registration laws which brought down part of the control of the citizen. In the economic field the movement which Theodore Roosevelt was calling "a square deal" advocated an income tax amendment, postal savings banks, parcel post, regulation of the railroads, prosecution and breaking of the trusts, a pure-food-and-drug law, with state laws to support it, extension of laws promoting public health and hygiene, shorter hours for labor, collective bargaining—and this was the catch phrase, "with representatives of their own choosing"—workingmen's compensation laws, state and national extension of the civil service, the movement for good roads, the regulation and control of insurance companies, banks, and savings institutions. . . .

The American people were melting down old heroes and recasting the mold in which heroes were made. Newspapers, magazines, books—every representative outlet for public opinion in the United States was turned definitely away from the scoundrels who had in the last third or quarter of the old century cast themselves in monumental brass as heroes. . . . The people were questioning the way every rich man got his money. They were ready to believe—and too often they were justified in the belief—that he was a scamp who had pinched pennies out of the teacups of the poor by various shenanigans, who was distributing his largess to divert attention from his rascality.

Reform was in the air.[24]

8.

Frederic C. Howe

Greenwich Village

We moved down to West Twelfth Street, on the edge of Greenwich Village, and began in earnest our New York life. Brilliant young people, full of vitality, ardent about saving the world, floated in and out of our apartment. The Hotel Brevoort was our neighborhood club. Socialism was the vogue, also woman suffrage. Graduates of Harvard, Columbia, and Vassar, concerned for the well-being of society but not for its conventions, formed an American youth movement. They protested against industrial conditions, suffered vicariously with the poor, hated injustice. Greenwich Village was a Mecca that called to itself poets, budding novelists, newspaper men. Girls exchanged the dullness of social work in the settlements for something more fundamental. Young men challenged the stagnation of home and university. There was a splendid enthusiasm among these emotional rebels, a generous willingness to make sacrifices. And a demand for immediate change. They started radical periodicals for the expression of their ideas. Muckrakers, it seemed, had had their day. Mere uplift was inadequate. Constructive change was demanded.

There were leaders among these leaders. Max Eastman, handsome, eloquent, winning, was associate professor of philosophy at Columbia. Poet and dreamer of better conditions, he was drawn from the university into life. Crystal Eastman, a graduate of Vassar and later admitted to the bar, held an important position as secretary of the Workmen's Compensation Commission, to which she had been appointed by Governor Hughes as the result of a brilliant investigation of housing and industrial conditions in Pittsburgh. This brother and sister became the center of a group of writers, artists, and poets, who started the *Masses* in 1912 and carried on its publication until 1917, when it was discontinued as a result of the war. Art Young, the cartoonist, loved for his genial personality, appeared from no one knew where and disappeared, and seemed as much at home in one place as another. Floyd Dell came on from Chicago, where he had been literary editor of the Chicago Evening Post. Jack Reed, recently from Harvard, was beginning that tempestuous career as poet, magazine writer, war reporter, and finally revolutionary agitator which led him first to Mexico with Villa and then to Russia, where he died, honored by a monument erected by the revolutionists. Boardman Robinson and John Sloan, the artists, Mary Heaton Vorse and Inez Haynes Irwin, the well-known fiction-writers, formed part of the group that contributed to the *Masses* as a forum for the expression of their ideas in art and literature.

Inez Milholland stood out in the group of women as a beautiful and commanding personality. Educated at Vassar, with the widest social opportunities, easily first in every field, she chose to give her wonderful vitality to the neediest claimants on her sympathy. For distress arising from the miscarriage of justice she was willing to make any personal sacrifice. We were neighbors in the country and I have known her to leave home on a moment's notice to rush about the state, following up some clue that might lead to the reprieve of a criminal whom she believed to have been unjustly condemned to the chair. She would stand by the telephone for hours appealing to the governor, to judges, to persons of influence to aid in the release of someone she thought innocent. Few people whom I have known controlled their lives as completely as did she; few lived in more complete indifference to public opinion, and none gave themselves more joyously to friends and the things they believed in. Persistence in a speaking campaign for suffrage when her strength was not equal to it cost Inez Milholland her life. . . .

Emma Goldman, deported to Russia in 1920, took part in

discussions in those more confident days from the floor of Cooper Union. She presented her ideas with a brutal frankness and disregard for conventions that suggested the advocacy of force. Had she been staged in some more conventional activity she might easily have been recognized as a remarkable person. She was an excellent dramatic critic and gave lectures in uptown halls before sympathetic audiences. A trained nurse, she would work under an assumed name at her profession until she had money enough to pay for the cost of printing her magazine, *Mother Earth*. She was indifferent to material comfort, generous to the last degree. Tolerant of people, but intolerant of institutions, she denounced the latter unsparingly, and dramatized her own radicalism, partly to secure a hearing, partly because she felt the necessity of becoming a martyr to her beliefs, as were other revolutionists in Russia. It was her ideas quite as much as herself that she insisted on exhibiting. And her ideas were always unusual and unashamed.

On one occasion the speaker was [W. E. B.] Du Bois, the editor of *The Crisis*. His manner was modest and dispassionate, without the slightest incitement to antagonism. At the close of his address a hot-headed Southerner arose from the audience, and, shaking his fist at the speaker, shouted: "Have you the effrontery to assume that the day may come when a Negro might hope to be elected the President of these United States?"

There was a long pause, a tension was felt in the audience, and everybody got ready for a good race row.

Mr. Du Bois waited for perfect silence, and then quietly, almost sweetly, he let fall one little word: "Yes," he said casually, and added promptly:

"Are there any other questions?"

There were other questions, but they were friendly. I have always remembered this incident as a masterly example of poise and self-control.[25]

9.

Ida B. Wells

Lynching: Our National Crime

The lynching record for a quarter of a century merits the thoughtful study of the American people. It presents three salient facts:

First: Lynching is color-line murder.

Second: Crimes against women is the excuse, not the cause.

Third: It is a national crime and requires a national remedy.

Proof that lynching follows the color-line is to be found in the statistics which have been kept for the past twenty-five years. During the few years preceding this period and while frontier lynch law existed, the executions showed a majority of white victims. Later, however, as law courts and authorized judiciary extended into the far West, lynch law rapidly abated and its white victims became few and far between.

Just as the lynch law regime came to a close in the West, a new mob movement started in the South. This was wholly political, its purpose being to suppress the colored vote by intimidation and murder. Thousands of assassins, banded together under the name of Ku Klux Klans, "Midnight Raiders," "Knights of the Golden Circle," etc., spread a reign of terror, by beating, shooting and killing colored people by the thousands. In a few years, the purpose was accomplished and the black vote was suppressed. But mob murder continued.

From 1882, in which year 52 were lynched, down to the present, lynching has been along the color-line. Mob murder increased yearly until in 1892 more than 200 victims were lynched and statistics show that 3,284 men, women, and children have been put to death in this quarter of a century. During the last ten years, from 1899 to 1908 inclusive, the number lynched was 959. Of this number, 102 were white while the colored victims numbered 857. No other nation, civilized or savage, burns its criminals; only under the Stars and Stripes is this human holocaust possible. Twenty-eight human beings burned at the stake, one of them a woman and two of them children, is the awful indictment against American civilization—the gruesome tribute which the nation pays to the color-line.

Why is mob murder permitted by a Christian nation? What is the cause of this awful slaughter? This question is answered almost daily—always the same shameless falsehood that "Negroes are lynched to protect womanhood."

Standing before a Chautauqua assemblage, John Temple Graves, at once champion of lynching and apologist for lynchers, said: "The mob stands today as the most potent bulwark between the women of the South and such a carnival of crime as would infuriate the world and precipitate the annihilation of the Negro race." This is the never-varying answer of lynchers and their apologists. All know that it is untrue. The cowardly lyncher revels in murder, then seeks to shield himself from public execration by claiming devotion to woman. But truth is mighty and the lynching record discloses the hypocrisy of the lyncher as well as his crime.

The Springfield, Illinois, mob rioted for two days, the militia of the entire state was called out, two men were lynched, hundreds of people driven from their homes, all because a white woman said a Negro had assaulted her. A mad mob went to the jail, tried to lynch the victim of her charge and, not being able to find him, proceeded to pillage and burn the town and to lynch two innocent men. Later, after the police had found that the woman's charge was false, she published a retraction, the indictment was dismissed, and the intended victim discharged. But the lynched victims were dead. Hundreds went homeless and Illinois was disgraced.

As a final and complete refutation of the charge that lynching is occasioned by crimes against women, a partial record of lynchings is cited; 285 persons were lynched for causes as follow:

Unknown cause, 92; no cause, 10; race prejudice, 49; miscegenation, 7; informing, 12; making threats, 11; keeping saloon, 3; practicing fraud, 5; practicing voodooism, 2; bad reputation, 8; unpopularity, 3; mistaken identity, 5; using improper language, 3; violation of contract, 1; writing insulting letter, 2; eloping, 2; poisoning horse, 1; poisoning well, 2; by white caps, 9; vigilantes, 14; Indians, 1; moonshining, 1; refusing evidence, 2 ; political causes, 5; disputing, 1; disobeying quarantine regulations, 2; slapping a child, 1; turning state's evidence, 3; protecting a Negro, 1; to prevent giving evidence, 1; knowledge of larceny, 1; writing letter to white woman, 1; asking white woman to marry, 1; jilting girl, 1; having smallpox, 1; concealing a criminal, 2; threatening political exposure, 1; self-defense, 6; cruelty, 1; insulting language to woman, 5; quarreling with white man, 2; colonizing Negroes, 1; throwing stones, 1; quarreling, 1; gambling, 1.

Is there a remedy, or will the nation confess that it cannot protect its protectors at home as well as abroad? Various remedies have been suggested to abolish the lynching infamy, but year after year the butchery of men, women, and children continues in spite of plea and protest. Education is suggested as a preventive, but it is as grave a crime to murder an ignorant man as it is a scholar. True, few educated men have been lynched, but the hue and cry once started stops at no bounds, as was clearly shown by the lynchings in Atlanta, and in Springfield, Illinois.

Agitation, though helpful, will not alone stop the crime. Year after year statistics are published, meetings are held, resolutions are adopted, and yet lynchings go on. Public sentiment does measurably decrease the sway of mob law, but the irresponsible blood-thirsty criminals who swept through the streets of Springfield, beating an inoffensive law-abiding citizen to death in one part of the town, and in another torturing and shooting to death a man who, for threescore years, had made a reputation for honesty, integrity and sobriety, had raised a family and had accumulated property, was not deterred from its heinous crimes by either education or agitation.

The only certain remedy is an appeal to law. Law-breakers must be made to know that human life is sacred and that every citizen of this country is first a citizen of the United States and secondly a citizen of the state in which he belongs. This nation must assert itself and defend its federal citizenship at home as well as abroad. The strong arm of the government must reach across state lines whenever unbridled lawlessness defies state laws and must give to the individual citizen under the Stars and Stripes the same measure of protection which it gives to him when he travels in foreign lands. . . .

As a final word, it would be a beginning in the right direction if this conference can see its way clear to establish a bureau for the investigation and publication of the details of every lynching, so that the public know that an influential body of citizens has made it a duty to give the widest publicity to the facts in each case; that it will make an effort to secure expressions of opinion all over the country against lynching for the sake of the country's fair name; and lastly, but by no means least, to try to influence the daily papers of the country to refuse to become accessory to mobs either before or after the fact. Several of the greatest riots and most brutal burnt offerings of the mobs have been suggested and incited by the daily papers of the offending community. If the newspaper which suggests lynching in its accounts of "threats of lynching were heard"; or, "It is feared that if the guilty one is caught, he will be lynched"; or, "There were cries of 'lynch him,' and the only reason that threat was not carried out was because no leader appeared," a long step toward a remedy will have been taken. . . .

Time was when lynching appeared to be sectional, but now it is national—a blight upon our nation, mocking our laws and disgracing our Christianity. "With malice toward none but with charity for all," let us undertake the work of making the "law of the land" effective and supreme upon every foot of American soil —a shield to the innocent and to the guilty a punishment swift and sure.[26]

10.

W. E. B. Du Bois

from *The Souls of Black Folk*

The passing of a great human institution before its work is done, like the untimely passing of a single soul, but leaves a legacy of striving for other men. The legacy of the Freedmen's Bureau is the heavy heritage of this generation. Today, when new and vaster problems are destined to strain every fiber of the national mind and soul, would it not be well to count this legacy honestly and carefully? For this much all men know: despite compromise, war, and struggle, the Negro is not free. In the backwoods of the Gulf States, for miles and miles, he may not leave the plantation of his birth; in well-nigh the whole rural South the black farmers are bound by law and custom to an economic slavery, from which the only escape is death or the penitentiary. In the most cultured sections and cities of the South the Negroes are a segregated servile caste, with restricted rights and privileges. Before the courts, both in law and custom, they stand on a different and peculiar basis. Taxation without representation is the rule of their political life. And the result of all this is, and in nature must have been, lawlessness and crime. That is the large legacy of the Freedmen's Bureau, the work it did not do because it could not.

I have seen a land right merry with the sun, where children sing, and rolling hills lie like passioned women wanton with harvest. And there in the King's Highway sat and sits a figure veiled and bowed, by which the traveler's footsteps hasten as they go. On the tainted air broods fear. Three centuries' thought has been the raising and unveiling of that bowed human heart, and now behold a century new for the duty and the deed. The problem of the twentieth century is the problem of the color-line.

* * *

A resistless feeling of depression falls slowly upon us, despite the gaudy sunshine and the green cotton-fields. This, then, is the Cotton Kingdom—the shadow of a marvelous dream. And where is the King? Perhaps this is he—the sweating plough-man, tilling his eighty acres with two lean mules, and fighting a hard battle with debt. So we sit musing, until, as we turn a corner on the sandy road, there comes a fairer scene suddenly in view—a neat cottage snugly ensconced by the road, and near it a little store. A tall bronzed man rises from the porch as we hail him, and comes out to our carriage. He is six feet in height, with a sober face that smiles gravely. He walks too straight to be a tenant—yes, he owns two hundred and forty acres. "The land is run down since the boom-days of eighteen hundred and fifty," he explains, and cotton is low. Three black tenants live on his place, and in his little store he keeps a small stock of tobacco, snuff, soap, and soda, for the neighborhood. Here is his gin-house with new machinery just installed. Three hundred bales of cotton went through it last year. Two children he has sent away to school. Yes, he says sadly, he is getting on, but cotton is down to four cents; I know how Debt sits staring at him.

Wherever the King may be, the parks and palaces of the Cotton Kingdom have not wholly disappeared. We plunge even now into great groves of oak and towering pine, with an undergrowth of myrtle and shrubbery. This was the "home-house" of the Thompsons—slave-barons who drove their coach and four in the merry past. All is silence now, and ashes, and tangled weeds. The owner put his whole fortune into the rising cotton industry of the fifties, and with the falling prices of the eighties he packed up and stole away. Yonder is another grove, with unkempt lawn, great magnolias, and grass-grown paths. The Big House stands in half-ruin, its great front door staring blankly at the street, and the back part grotesquely restored for its black tenant. A shabby, well-built Negro he is, unlucky and irresolute. He digs hard to pay rent to the white girl who owns the remnant of the place. She married a policeman, and lives in Savannah.

*   *   *

This was indeed the Egypt of the Confederacy—the rich granary whence potatoes and corn and cotton poured out to the famished and ragged Confederate troops as they battled for a cause lost long before 1861. Sheltered and secure, it became the place of refuge for families, wealth, and slaves. Yet even then the hard ruthless rape of the land began to toll. The red-clay sub-soil already had begun to peer above the loam. The harder the slaves were driven the more careless and fatal was their farming. Then came the revolution of war and Emancipation, the bewilderment of Reconstruction—and now, what is the Egypt of the Confederacy, and what meaning has it for the nation's weal or woe?

It is a land of rapid contrasts and of curiously mingled hope and pain. Here sits a pretty blue-eyed quadroon hiding her bare feet; she was married only last week, and yonder in the field is her dark young husband, hoeing to support her, at thirty cents a day without board. Across the way is Gatesby, brown and tall, lord of two thousand acres shrewdly won and held. There is a store conducted by his black son, a blacksmith shop, and a ginnery. Five miles below here is a town owned and controlled by one white New Englander. He owns almost a Rhode Island county, with thousands of acres and hundreds of black laborers. Their cabins look better than most, and the farm, with machinery and fertilizers, is much more business-like than any in the county, although the manager drives hard bargains in wages. When now we turn and look five miles above, there on the edge of town are five houses of prostitutes, two of blacks and three of whites; and in one of the houses of the whites a worthless black boy was harbored too openly two years ago; so he was hanged for rape. And here, too, is the high white-washed fence of the "stockade," as the county prison is called;

the white folks say it is ever full of black criminals—the black folks say that only colored boys are sent to jail, and they not because they are guilty, but because the State needs criminals to eke out its income by their forced labor.[27]

11.

Floyd Dell

First Days in Chicago

In the days of which he writes and in which I knew him Floyd Dell
was a lean lad with a bit of fuzz on his cheeks, rather negligent of
his clothes and somewhat diffident in his manner; unobtrusive in a
group, with a sort of smile that might be half interest, half disdain.
And yet he was the best and most fluent talker of all if you hit his
subject.

—Harry Hansen[28]

[In 1908], after casting my vote for the Future, as represented politically by that perennial candidate, Eugene V. Debs, I
went to Chicago.

∗ ∗ ∗

Margery [Currey's] letters and conversation . . . had a
graceful lightness of their own; the image which it had called up
to my mind was that of the butterfly shimmering in a sunny landscape which has a smoking volcano in the background. The world
was, to my mind, the volcano, though I had no notion at all of the
way in which it was presently to prove itself such—a volcano, in
my thoughts, merely as a vague general promise of hell to pay; and
the butterfly was the way the mind could, in thought and talk,

66

catch and reflect in an idle winged dance the glints of sunshine in that landscape. That was the way her mind worked, and it fascinated me.

∗   ∗   ∗

When I took the El in the mornings and emerged from one of the stations just over some railroad tracks, with the air full of clouds of steam, Chicago seemed mysterious and romantic, and I myself in a dream. "Am I really here?" I would ask myself. Did I have a job, a salary, a future in newspaper literary criticism? Did I have a wife, and an apartment in Rogers Park? Or was it just a dream, and would I wake up to find myself back in Davenport, fired from a job?

∗   ∗   ∗

The year 1912 was really an extraordinary year, in America as well as in Europe. It was the year of the election of Wilson, a symptom of immense political discontent. It was a year of intense woman-suffragist activity. In the arts it marked a new era. Color was everywhere—even in neckties. *The Lyric Year*, published in New York, contained Edna St. Vincent Millay's "Renascence." In Chicago, Harriet Monroe founded *Poetry*. . . . Maurice Browne started the Little Theatre. One could go on with the evidence of a New Spirit come suddenly to birth in America. . . .

Something was happening—no doubt of that. But what it was seems now less certain. Looking back now, it seems almost as if the world had had an icy premonition of its impending doom, and was seeking feverishly to live in the last days still vouchsafed to it.

12.

Margaret Anderson

from *My Thirty Years' War*

Someone has said that Margaret Anderson had two enthusiasms, the *Little Review* and the Mason & Hamlin piano; for both she worked and sacrificed. She gloried in oriental rugs—it was known that there were always beautiful objects about her.

An intimate sketches this portrait of her: "She was always exquisite, as if emerging from a scented boudoir, not from a mildewed tent or a camp where frying bacon was scenting the atmosphere. She was always vivid, is yet, and beautiful to look upon, and lovely in her mind. There is a sort of high, wind-blown beauty about her; her fluffy hair blows marvelously, her eyes are in Lake Michigan's best blue. And she is valiant, always."

—Harry Hansen[30]

Chicago: enchanted ground to me from the moment Lake Michigan entered the train windows. I would make my beautiful life here. A city without a lake wouldn't have done.

As usual I felt I had only to decide something and it would happen. I have a single superstition—that the gods are for me and that anything I want will happen if I play at it hard enough. I can't say work at it because anything I work at never seems to come out right.

* * *

Michigan Boulevard had a smell of water across its asphalt and a soft gray light over its shops. The doorman at the Annex— black, white-gloved, white-toothed—was resplendent in red, blue and gold and almost hysterical in his efforts to make you like his hotel. I went at once into the flower shop and had white lilacs sent up to my room. I put them against the lake which became more blue than it has ever been since. . . .

Back in my hotel room I could hear the beat of the orchestras where I sat by the lilacs looking out at the lake. There was a lighthouse that sent its searchlight hypnotically into my window. I began to repeat a vow to the rhythm of the light: I will become something beautiful. I swear it.

*   *   *

The next day at eleven I went to Clara Laughlin's office in Randolph Street. She was the literary editor of a religious weekly called the *Interior*, financed by Cyrus McCormick. Her affiliations with it were social rather than religious, for she knew everyone and was invaluable for literary gossip.

I loved the section of Randolph and Clark Streets—dark, high, depressing. I went up a stairway and was shown into an office where a stout, vigorous and smiling woman waited to receive me. She looked like Melba. She seemed surprised by me—agreeably, may I say without vanity. It would be unbecoming of me not to know that I was extravagantly pretty in those days—extravagantly and disgustingly pretty. I looked like a composite of all the most offensive magazine covers. . . .

No stage celebrities were in town at the moment, so she asked me if I had ever reviewed books. Naturally not. Would I like to? Naturally. Did I know how to go about it? Not at all. But I had read lots of them and if she would criticize my first effort I was sure I could learn. I needn't worry, she said, she had broken in any number of good reviewers. My first effort would probably be bad but she would be ruthlessly frank. She gave me Stephen Phillips' *Herod*.

I had read his *Marpessa* (and am sorry to say thought it excellent). I read *Herod* carefully that afternoon and spent the next morning carefully reviewing it. The care was to assemble every platitude that has ever been incorporated in a book review. Of the two I liked *Marpessa* better, so I talked rather of it than of *Herod*. I couldn't help feeling that I was rather good—that is, I thought the platitudes good, but I couldn't imagine how I had got to know them all. It sounded learned. Still, I was a little unconfident and hadn't the courage to present myself with the review and wait for the ruthless frankness. I sent it by messenger and followed an hour later.

Clara Laughlin's face was beaming and tender when I went in.

But, my dear, I haven't a word to say, not a word to blue-pencil. No one ever sent me in a first review like this. It's perfect. I might have written it myself. You can take all the books you want.

Which only shows what platitudes will do for you.

* * *

In those days books were published at lower prices. All novels sold for a dollar and a half. When you finished reviewing them you took them to McClurg's and sold them for seventy-five cents each. This was your salary.

I began reviewing too for the *Chicago Evening Post*. Francis Hackett was literary editor and had already gained the reputation of publishing the liveliest book page in the Middle West. One day after I had been reviewing for him for perhaps two weeks, Francis wrote me a letter.

Why all the big words? I have to cut half of them out. A little simplicity, please, and at intervals a great word for beauty.

I tried, but I was too proud of my vocabulary and my clichés to renounce them suddenly. When I finally woke to the horror of what I was doing I made such an effort to be simple that I lost my vocabulary forever.

Sometimes Clara Laughlin would telephone me on Saturday morning.

I've fifty books that must be reviewed by Monday. Can you do it?

Naturally.

And I never missed the Chicago Symphony on Saturday night nor the Sunday afternoon concert. Monday morning the reviews were always ready.

*   *   *

Then the necessary accident happened. . . . I became a book clerk. At eight dollars a week.

Not so bad as it seems. Chicago had a unique bookshop. In the Fine Arts Building, Michigan Boulevard, Frank Lloyd Wright (the architect known for his construction of Japanese houses in America and million-dollar American hotels in Japan) had built the most beautiful bookshop in the world. The walls were rough cement, sand color; the bookshelves, shoulder high, were in the form of stalls, each containing a long reading table and easy chairs. This was on the seventh floor of the building, looking into the lake at one end and, at the other, into the shaded Italian inner court from which tinkled always the sound of pianos . . . and a fountain. Still I'm not sure about the fountain. I have remembered a fountain. There may not have been one.

An L of the shop with a higher ceiling—long, dark, reposing, with an enormous fireplace and great armchairs—housed the rare bindings. Here tea was served and everyone was very smart. All Chicago society came to Browne's Bookstore.

The fine-binding room gave onto the offices of the *Dial*, a literary review founded by Edgar Allen Poe, which at this time was edited by Francis F. Browne.[31] His two sons were associated with him and also directed the bookshop, which was under the financial patronage of Mrs. Cooney Ward and Mrs. Wilmarth. I was soon taken on the staff of the *Dial* and initiated into the secrets of the printing room—composition (monotype and linotype), proofreading, make-up. This practical knowledge was indispensable when I began the *Little Review*.

It all happened by the grace of poetry. Francis Browne knew by heart all the lyric poetry of the world. He and John Burroughs and John Muir spent summer nights on the peaks of the

Rockies, gazing at the stars and saying poems in a sort of memory contest—each having the right to go on until he forgot a line. Mr. Browne, I believe, never stopped before dawn. . . . One day he walked into the bookshop in distress, murmuring Matthew Arnold's "eyes too expressive to be gray, too something to be brown." He had forgotten "lovely" and I supplied it. This made a friendship: I became his chief assistant—chiefly poetic.

But June and July—before the poetry episode—took all my courage. The heat was unimaginable, my living quarters unbearable, clerking unthinkable—my snobbism suffered rather more than I like to admit. The family had just moved to another town into a castle: meaning a marvelous old house of turrets and towers, rambling rooms on different levels, a river, bridges, rose arbors, cypress trees, a hoot owl in the pines at night . . . I could barely resist this. I lived on the photographs [my sister] Lois sent me. Cartloads of new furniture, a red and white living room, a long blue music room. . . . Quiet and cool and fragrant. Chicago was on fire. Lois came up to visit me for two days. She walked into the bookshop unexpectedly and handed me a yellow rose. . . .

I am either profligate—or I can be miserly. I knew if I didn't rush to extremes my heritage would swamp me. So I lived without roses. Out of my eight dollars a week I had to pay five and a half for room and board. Every Saturday I committed my one extravagance: fifty cents for a box of chocolates at Guth's in the Annex. This left two dollars for concerts, laundry, emergencies. Of course I could have bought more and cheaper candy, but the box was handsome and satisfied my hunger for luxury. It was the one link with past glory.

No, there was another. At five-thirty when the bookshop closed I used to walk from the Fine Arts Building through the second floor of the Auditorium Hotel, follow the corridor under Congress Street which led into the Annex and stroll down Peacock Alley to the gorgeous Elizabethan Room. I regarded this as my right: except for its size—it was as big as the New York Central Terminal—it was like home: soft davenports, low lights, rich hangings. I wrote letters here, read, and steeped myself in my proper atmosphere before going back to that narrow room so tragically turned away from the lake. . . . The maids who came in to restore order treated me with every consideration; they assumed I was living in the hotel.[32]

13.

Eunice Tietjens

from *The World at My Shoulder*

And then another picture: of Eunice Tietjens . . . clad in a lovely Japanese robe, moving gracefully, marvelously, through the postures of a Noh dance, suggesting again and again the prints of the eastern masters.

—Harry Hansen[33]

I was then twenty-seven, I think, though my time sense is hopelessly inadequate. Not many people surely remember with such absorbing accuracy as I can the exact moment of their awakening. Many of course never come to any second birth at all, and for those who do it must take place in various ways; but though for me it naturally took several years to reach completion, it began in a sudden and definite blaze.

I remember the room in which it took place with almost painful distinctness. It was a very small room in an apartment in Rogers Park, Chicago, and it was lined on all sides with books which reached to the ceiling. In the space between bookshelves there was room only for a couch, a chair or two, and a few feet of space in which to move about.

This room was in the apartment of Margery Currey and her then husband Floyd Dell, at that time literary editor of the *Chicago Evening Post*. I had met the Dells through Martha Baker, the miniature painter, and cottoned to Margery at once. She is another person with a genius for friendship—she and Harry Webster and Mary Mowbray-Clarke of the late Sunwise Turn bookshop in New York being the three most gifted people in that line whom I have known. Now she had invited me to dinner and to meet George Cram Cook, then assistant to Floyd on the *Post*.

George, or Jig Cook as his friends called him, had at that time not yet become the leader of the Provincetown Theatre in New York, nor yet come to his most fitting end as a Greek peasant on the slopes above Delphi. He was just short of forty, with a remnant of the great beauty of his youth; a somber personality much of the time yet lit at moments with an almost cosmic gayety; a good male drinker, as Susan Glaspell has so understandingly pointed out in her *Road to the Temple*, and with a queer ability to cast out shadows.

After dinner on this vital evening we repaired to the little room which was Floyd Dell's study. There Margery and Floyd curled up on the sofa, Jig alternately sat or paced the step or two of free space, with a pipe in his mouth and an inalienable dignity about him, and I sat translated.

For the talk ran on poetry. For the first time in the many years of my long sleep I heard what had been like a secret vice with me brought out boldly into the open, with no apology, as though it were indeed one of the great facts of existence.

"Here," said Floyd, "do you remember this?" And he put up a lazy hand, without otherwise moving, plucked down Swinburne, and began to read in a rather light but beautiful voice the chorus from "Atalanta in Calydon":

When the hounds of spring are on winter's traces . . .

"And here," said George Cook, taking a book from a high shelf. And he too read in a deep voice full of shadows, this time the part about death from Whitman's "When Lilacs Last in the Dooryard Bloom'd":

Come, lovely and soothing death . . .

And Margery added Middleton, whom few now remember, and we had out Richard Hovey and Byron and Shelley and so many others that we could hardly have moved in the tiny room had not Margery, who is very tidy, risen to put them back in their places.

So we sat till two o'clock.

Afterwards I walked home through the dark streets of Evanston. And I walked on air, like one warm with champagne, though I had had no alcohol except of the spirit. Poetry, I cried to myself, is not a dead thing, something that is shut in books to dress library shelves and is taught to schoolchildren, something to be given away at Christmas or bought shyly and never spoken of because nobody cares. Poetry is a live thing. I am not alone in the world today, nor am I touched by the sun. Poetry is alive! And I danced in the streets and sang to myself, thereby causing a most unpleasant person to speak to me. But from that evening some floodgate had broken in me and I was beginning to be awake.

It is odd, now I think of it, that this should have happened to me in just this way, but it did.

Afterwards I took my own feeble efforts at verse to these people and asked for help. It was George Cook who said the thing that released me, as the right thing said at the right moment has the power to do. "You have been too much preoccupied with technique and with little things," he said. "Your technique is good enough, but you are afraid. Take a great theme and attack it boldly. You will manage."

So I did, and in my degree I managed, and I began to have an inner vital life. It did not of course concern only poetry. A year or two later Edgar Lee Masters gave me a copy of the *Bhagavad Gita* and so changed the whole course of my spiritual existence. Yet in the main beauty, as exemplified in poetry, provided the mainspring.[34]

Imagism & Vers Libre

Poetry should be burned to the bone by austere fires and washed white with rains of affliction: the poet should love nakedness and the thought of the skeleton under the flesh.

—Rebecca West[35]

The great aim is accurate, precise and definite description.

—T. E. Hulme[36]

14.

from *Poetry: A Magazine of Verse*

F. S. Flint

Imagisme

Editor's Note—In response to many requests for information regarding *Imagism* and the *Imagistes*, we publish this note by Mr. Flint, supplementing it with further exemplification by Mr. Pound. It will be seen from these that *Imagism* is not necessarily associated with Hellenic subjects, or with vers libre as a prescribed form.

Some curiosity has been aroused concerning *Imagisme*, and as I was unable to find anything definite about it in print, I sought out an *imagiste*, with intent to discover whether the group itself knew anything about the "movement." I gleaned these facts.

The *imagistes* admitted that they were contemporaries of the Post-Impressionists and the Futurists; but they had nothing in common with these schools. They had not published a manifesto. They were not a revolutionary school; their only endeavor was to write in accordance with the best tradition, as they found it in the best writers of all time—in Sappho, Catullus, Villon. They seemed to be absolutely intolerant of all poetry that was not written in such endeavor, ignorance of the best tradition forming no excuse. They had a few rules, drawn up for their own satisfaction only, and they had not published them. They were:

1. Direct treatment of the "thing," whether subjective or objective.

2. To use absolutely no word that did not contribute to the presentation.

3. As regarding rhythm: to compose in sequence of the musical phrase, not in sequence of a metronome.

By these standards they judged all poetry, and found most of it wanting. They held also a certain "Doctrine of the Image," which they had not committed to writing; they said that it did not concern the public, and would provoke useless discussion. . . .

I found among them an earnestness that is amazing to one accustomed to the usual London air of poetic dilettantism. They consider that Art is all science, all religion, philosophy, and metaphysic. It is true that *snobisme* may be urged against them; but it is at least snobisme in its most dynamic form, with a great deal of sound sense and energy behind it; and they are stricter with themselves than with any outsider.[37]

15.

from *Poetry: A Magazine of Verse*

Ezra Pound

A Few Don'ts by an *Imagiste*

An "Image" is that which presents an intellectual and emotional complex in an instant of time. I use the term "complex" rather in the technical sense employed by the newer psychologists, such as Hart, though we might not agree absolutely in our application.

It is the presentation of such a "complex" instantaneously which gives that sense of sudden liberation; that sense of freedom from time limits and space limits; that sense of sudden growth, which we experience in the presence of the greatest works of art. It is better to present one Image in a lifetime than to produce voluminous works.

All this, however, some may consider open to debate. The immediate necessity is to tabulate a list of don'ts for those beginning to write verses. But I cannot put all of them into Mosaic negative.

To begin with, consider the three rules recorded by Mr. Flint, not as dogma—never consider anything as dogma—but as the result of long contemplation, which, even if it is someone else's contemplation, may be worth consideration.

Pay no attention to the criticism of men who have never themselves written a notable work. Consider the discrepancies between the actual writing of the Greek poets and dramatists, and the theories of the Graeco-Roman grammarians, concocted to explain their meters.

Language

Use no superfluous word, no adjective, which does not reveal something.

Don't use such an expression as "dim lands of *peace*."[38] It dulls the image. It mixes an abstraction with the concrete. It comes from the writer's not realizing that the natural object is always the *adequate* symbol.

Go in fear of abstractions. Don't retell in mediocre verse what has already been done in good prose. Don't think any intelligent person is going to be deceived when you try to shirk all the difficulties of the unspeakably difficult art of good prose by chopping your composition into line lengths.

What the expert is tired of today the public will be tired of tomorrow.

Don't imagine that the art of poetry is any simpler than the art of music, or that you can please the expert before you have spent at least as much effort on the art of verse as the average piano teacher spends on the art of music.

Be influenced by as many great artists as you can, but have the decency either to acknowledge the debt outright, or to try to conceal it.

Don't allow "influence" to mean merely that you mop up the particular decorative vocabulary of some one or two poets whom you happen to admire. A Turkish war correspondent was recently caught red-handed babbling in his dispatches of "dove-gray" hills, or else it was "pearl-pale," I cannot remember.
Use either no ornament or good ornament.

Rhythm and Rhyme

Let the candidate fill his mind with the finest cadences he can discover, preferably in a foreign language so that the meaning of the words may be less likely to divert his attention from the movement; e. g., Saxon charms, Hebridean Folk Songs, the verse of Dante, and the lyrics of Shakespeare—if he can dissociate the vocabulary from the cadence. Let him dissect the lyrics of Goethe coldly into their component sound values, syllables long and short, stressed and unstressed, into vowels and consonants.

It is not necessary that a poem should rely on its music, but if it does rely on its music that music must be such as will delight the expert.

Let the neophyte know assonance and alliteration, rhyme immediate and delayed, simple and polyphonic, as a musician would expect to know harmony and counterpoint and all the minutiae of his craft. No time is too great to give to these matters or to any one of them, even if the artist seldom have need of them.

Don't imagine that a thing will "go" in verse just because it's too dull to go in prose.

Don't be "viewy"—leave that to the writers of pretty little philosophic essays. Don't be descriptive; remember that the painter can describe a landscape much better than you can, and that he has to know a deal more about it.

When Shakespeare talks of the "Dawn in russet mantle clad" he presents something which the painter does not present. There is in this line of his nothing that one can call description; he presents.

Consider the way of the scientists rather than the way of an advertising agent for a new soap. The scientist does not expect to be acclaimed as a great scientist until he has *discovered* something. He begins by learning what has been discovered already. He goes from that point onward. He does not bank on being a charming fellow personally. He does not expect his friends to applaud the results of his freshman class work. Freshmen in poetry are unfortunately not confined to a definite and recognizable classroom. They are "all over the shop." Is it any wonder "the public is indifferent to poetry"?

Don't chop your stuff into separate *iambs*. Don't make each line stop dead at the end, and then begin every next line with a heave. Let the beginning of the next line catch the rise of the rhythm wave, unless you want a definite longish pause.

In short, behave as a musician, a good musician, when

dealing with that phase of your art which has exact parallels in music. The same laws govern, and you are bound by no others.

Naturally, your rhythmic structure should not destroy the shape of your words, or their natural sound, or their meaning. It is improbable that, at the start, you will be able to get a rhythm-structure strong enough to affect them very much, though you may fall a victim to all sorts of false stopping due to line ends and caesurae. . . .

A rhyme must have in it some slight element of surprise if it is to give pleasure; it need not be bizarre or curious, but it must be well used if used at all. . . .

Good prose will do you no harm, and there is good discipline to be had by trying to write it.[39]

16.

Edward Storer

Vers Libre

Form there must be, we know, for without form there is no inspiration possible. Form even stimulates thought, as Flaubert said, but form must not be allowed to domineer over thought. Form should take its shape from the vital, inherent necessities of the matter, not be, as it were, a kind of rigid mold into which the poetry is to be poured, to accommodate itself as best it can. There is no absolute virtue in iambic pentameter as such. . . . There is no immediate virtue in rhythm or rhyme even. These things are merely means to an end. Judged by themselves, they are monstrosities of childish virtuosity and needless iteration. Indeed, rhythm and rhyme are often destructive of thought, lulling the mind into a drowsy kind of stupor with their everlasting, regular cadences and stiff, mechanical lilts. . . . Their employment in serious poetry must only be secondary and subsidiary.

So far, it seems to me that most of the good poetry of the world has been written, as it were, by accident, in spite of colossal self-imposed difficulties and constrictions, such as the employment of forms in which it is practically impossible to write poetry at all except at the rate of about one really fine thought a page, if as much as that. Such difficult and precious forms as the *ballade*, the *triolet*, the *villanelle*, and to a less degree the sonnet—charming as they often are—were originally the work of word-tricksters rather than poets, the results of the pleasant labors of elegant dilettante French and Italian gentlemen, who emulated each other in this kind of dexterity, more as a species of gallantry than as serious art. . . .

Hitherto, among all verse forms in English, perhaps the most limpid and amorphous known is that of blank verse, which generally means verses of five feet in iambs, and it is by a poet's blank verse that he stands or falls. If he is only a trickster, a Cinquevalli of syllables and rhymes, he will not be able to disguise this fact in his blank verse. For this reason, the very best and the very worst poetry in our language is written in this form. Here a poet is on his mettle to write poetry, and if he has not got it in him, nothing in the form will help him. If he has, he suffers no insane constriction of a "wine" or a "love" or a "sky" by reason of which he must keep his inspiration within the radius—necessarily a limited one—afforded by phrases which contain a rhyme to these or similar words.

The artist, the great poet, triumphs over this difficulty; the rhyme seems inevitable and not conventional, you say. Yes; he triumphs over the obstacle he has himself raised and—loses energy and force of expression in the process. That is necessary, is it not? It is a result of the law of energy. If blank verse, however, is cut up and spaced, so that the lines are not always of equal length, but rise and fall with the swell of thought and imagery, a still more plastic and more natural form is obtained even than blank verse of unfailingly regular lines. The eye, too, does not suffer that hopeless sense of weariness and labor that a great solid chunk of verse is apt to inspire. It is relieved at once. That is, perhaps, more a matter of subediting than of poetry, but it is nevertheless true. Such a method also serves to "phrase" the poetry in a way that mere punctuation can never do. It becomes clearer, steps more easily into the eye and ear than verse for which this office has to be performed by the reader at the same time as he gathers up the meaning.

This is, of course, only the *vers libre*, supposed to be the invention of M. Gustave Khan, and since then, adopted by French poets like Verhaeren, Vielé-Griffin, Henri de Regnier . . . and English poets like Henley and Francis Thompson. As a matter of fact, however, we were using *vers libre* in England without making any fuss about it, long before it rose to the eminence of a movement in France. Sydney Dobell, Alexander Smith—Coleridge even—all used it at times. In a sense, nearly all the English poets have been vers-librists, for we never insisted on such rigidity of form as the French did, until their traditions were shaken by the decadents, symbolists and vers-librists of the last twenty or thirty years. Still, to do a thing without saying anything about it, and to do it, make a principle of it, and defend it, are two different things in England. You can do almost anything you like in this country, provided it is not against the law, so long as you do not propound any reason, any philosophy for doing it. But as soon as you attempt to show that your behavior has an origin in common sense, you make a great many people very angry. Intellectual honesty is a thing with a very small market in England.[40]

17.

F. S. Flint

The History of Imagism

Somewhere in the gloom of the year 1908, Mr. T. E. Hulme, now in the trenches of Ypres, but excited then by the propinquity, at a half-a-crown dance, of the other sex (if, as Remy de Gourmont avers, the passage from the aesthetic to the sexual emotion, *n'est qu'un pas*, the reverse is surely also true), proposed to a companion that they should found a Poets' Club. The thing was done, there and then. The Club began to dine; and its members to read their verses. At the end of the year they published a small plaquette of them, called *For Christmas MDCCCCVIII*. In this plaquette was printed one of the first "Imagist" poems, by T. E. Hulme:

Autumn

A touch of cold in the autumn night
I walked abroad,
And saw the ruddy moon lean over a hedge,
Like a red-faced farmer.
I did not stop to talk, but nodded;
And round about were the wistful stars
With white faces like town children.

In November of the same year, Edward Storer, author already of *Inclinations*, much of which is in the "Imagist" manner, published his *Mirrors of Illusion*, the first book of "Imagist" poems, with an essay at the end attacking poetic conventions. The first poem in the book was called "Image"; here it is:

> Forsaken lovers,
> Burning to a chaste white moon,
> Upon strange pyres of loneliness and drought.

Mr. Storer, who has recanted much since, was in favor then of a poetry which I described, in reference to his book, as "a form of expression, like the Japanese, in which an image is the resonant heart of an exquisite moment." . . . I have always wished that Storer, in his after work, had brought more art to the exploitation of the temperament he displayed in *Mirrors*, which, for me, is a book of poetry. But he changed his manner completely.

At that time, I had been advocating in the course of a series of articles on recent books of verse a poetry in *vers libre*, akin in spirit to the Japanese. An attack on the Poets' Club brought me into correspondence and acquaintance with T. E. Hulme; and, later on, after Hulme had violently disagreed with the Poets' Club and had left it, he proposed that he should get together a few congenial spirits, and that we should have weekly meetings in a Soho restaurant. The first of these meetings, which were really the successors of certain Wednesday evening meetings, took place on Thursday, March 25, 1909. There were present, so far as I recall, T. E. Hulme, Edward Storer, F. W. Tancred, Joseph Campbell, Miss Florence Farr, one or two other men, mere vaguements in my memory, and myself. I think that what brought the real nucleus of this group together was a dissatisfaction with English poetry as it was then (and is still, alas!) being written. We proposed at various times to replace it by pure *vers libre*; by the Japanese *tanka* and *haikai*; we all wrote dozens of the latter as an amusement; by poems in a sacred Hebrew form, of which "This is the House that Jack Built" is a perfect model; Joseph Campbell produced two good specimens of this, one of which, "The Dark," is printed in *The Mountainy Singer*; by rhymeless poems like Hulme's

"Autumn," and so on. In all this Hulme was ringleader. He insisted too on absolutely accurate presentation and no verbiage; and he and F. W. Tancred, a poet too little known, perhaps because his production is precious and small, used to spend hours each day in the search for the right phrase. Tancred does it still; while Hulme reads German philosophy in the trenches, waiting for the general advance. There was also a lot of talk and practice among us, Storer leading it chiefly, of what we called the Image. We were very much influenced by modern French symbolist poetry.

On April 22, 1909, Ezra Pound, whose book, *Personae*, had been published on the previous Friday, joined the group, introduced, I believe, by Miss Farr and my friend T. D. FitzGerald. Ezra Pound used to boast in those days that he was *Nil praeter Villon et doctus cantare Catullum* [loosely put: nothing but Villon who's learned to sing like Catullus], and he could not be made to believe that there was any French poetry after Ronsard. He was very full of his *troubadours*; but I do not remember that he did more than attempt to illustrate (or refute) our theories occasionally with their example. The group died a lingering death at the end of its second winter. But its discussions had a sequel. In 1912 Mr. Pound published, at the end of his book *Ripostes*, the complete poetical works of T. E. Hulme, five poems, thirty-three lines, with a preface in which these words occur: "As for the future, *Les Imagistes*, the descendants of the forgotten school of 1909 (previously referred to as the 'School of Images') have that in their keeping." In that year, Pound had become interested in modern French poetry; he had broken away from his old manner; and he invented the term "Imagisme" to designate the aesthetic of "Les Imagistes." In March 1913, an "interview," over my signature, of an "imagiste" appeared in the American review *Poetry*, followed by "A Few Don'ts by an Imagiste" by Ezra Pound. . . .

Towards the end of the year Pound collected together a number of poems by different writers, Richard Aldington, H. D., F. S. Flint. Skipwith Cannell, Amy Lowell, William Carlos Williams, James Joyce, John Cournos, Ezra Pound, Ford Madox Hueffer, and Allan Upward, and in February-March 1914 they were published in America and England as *Des Imagistes: An*

Anthology, which, though it did not set the Thames, seems to have set America, on fire. . . . There is no difference, except that which springs from difference of temperament and talent, between an imagist poem of today and those written by Edward Storer and T. E. Hulme.[41]

18.

Ezra Pound

A Retrospect

There has been so much scribbling about a new fashion in poetry, that I may perhaps be pardoned this brief recapitulation and retrospect.

In the spring or early summer of 1912, H. D., Richard Aldington and myself decided that we were agreed upon the three principles following:

1. Direct treatment of the "thing" whether subjective or objective.

2. To use absolutely no word that does not contribute to the presentation.

3. As regarding rhythm: to compose in the sequence of the musical phrase, not in sequence of a metronome.

Upon many points of taste and of predilection we differed, but agreeing upon these three positions we thought we had as much right to a group name, at least as much right, as a number of French "schools" proclaimed by Mr. Flint in the August number of Harold Munro's magazine for 1911.

This school has since been "joined" or "followed" by numerous people who, whatever their merits, do not show any signs of agreeing with the second specification. Indeed vers libre has become as prolix and as verbose as any of the flaccid varieties that preceded it. It has brought faults of its own. The actual language and phrasing is often as bad as that of our elders without even the excuse that the words are shoveled in to fill a metric pattern or to complete the noise of a rhyme-sound. Whether or not the phrases followed by the followers are musical must be left to the reader's decision. At times I can find a marked meter in "vers libres" as stale and hackneyed as any pseudo-Swinburnian, at times the writers seem to follow no musical structure whatever. But it is, on the whole, good that the field should be ploughed. Perhaps a few good poems have come from the new method, and if so it is justified. . .

.

The first use of the word "Imagiste" was in my note to T. E. Hulme's five poems, printed at the end of my *Ripostes* in the autumn of 1912.[42]

19.

from the *Little Review*

John Gould Fletcher

Vers Libre and Advertisements

In common with all the judicious readers of American magazines and newspapers, I have learned to look on the advertising pages for the best examples of news the journalist can offer. It is only reasonable that this should be the case. Advertisement writers are the best-paid, least rewarded, and best-trained authors that America possesses. Compared to these, even the income of a Robert Chambers pales into insignificance. Moreover, they understand the public thoroughly and do not attempt to overstrain its attention by over-seriousness, or exhaust its nerves by sentimentality. That is, the best ones do not. There may be some exceptions, but in the main I have found American advertisements refreshingly readable.

It had never occurred to me, however, that there might be gems of poetic ability hidden away in these tantalizing concoctions— these cocktails of prose. But I must revise my estimate. Without wishing to boom or discourage anyone's products I cannot resist quoting some recent advertisements that I and I alone have discovered, seized, and gloated upon. After all, I approach the subject purely from the angle of form. What student of poetic form could afford to ignore the following:

SERVE A HOT MUFFIN SUPPER

Light flaky muffins, *oven hot* and *golden topped*, a supper-time goody that certainly will strike that hungry spot. Serve them with the finest, richest syrup you can buy anywhere. That's "Velva," with the best of flavor, nourishing goodness and the satisfying elements that put real strength into growing children. Give them Velva three times a day. They'll say, "*Great,*" when they eat it on your *flaky* hot biscuits or on *waffles* or *batter cakes*.

I hope the unknown author of this little masterpiece will excuse my italics. The public simply will not see beauties that are not pushed under its nose. If the public could realize how much more difficult as well as more musical this style of writing, with its rich assonances and rhymes on *day, say, great, flaky, cakes*, is, than the insipid tinklings of the lyrists who feebly strum in pathetically threadbare meters through the pages of most magazines, then we would have a revolution in verse-writing. That we have not yet arrived at the revolution is proved by the fact that a talent of this order confines itself to writing syrup advertisements. . . .

Gentlemen of the poets' profession, be ashamed of yourselves! How can you expect to find readers by lazily sticking to your antiquated formulas, when even the advertisement writers in the very magazines you do your work for, are getting quite up-to-date?[43]

20.

Ford Madox Ford

Vers Libre

I wish I could take for granted the reader's acceptance of the doctrine that Poetry is a matter of the writer's attitude towards life, and has nothing in the world to do—nothing whatever in the world to do—with whether the lines in which this attitude is put before him be long or short; rhymed or unrhymed; cadenced or interrupted by alliterations or assonances. One cannot expect to dictate the use of words to a race; but it would be of immense service to humanity if the Anglo-Saxon world could agree that all creative literature is Poetry; that prose is a form as well adapted for the utterance of poetry as verse. It would be a good thing, because then Anglo-Saxondom would come at last into the comity of all other nations. . . .

For who in his senses will deny that, between the entrenched lines of Prosaists and Versificators lies a No Man's Land that is the territory of Neither-Prose-Nor-Verse? And few who have given the matter any attention will deny that this is the oldest, the most primitive, the least sophisticated form of all literature. It is the form of incised writing, of marmoreal inscription, of the prophets—rhythm!

*   *   *

I had to make for myself the discovery that verse must be

at least as well written as prose if it is to be poetry. Its sentences must be as well constructed; its thoughts as close; its language as nervous. The Victorians killed the verse side of poetry because, intent on the contemplation of their own moral importance, they allowed their sentences to become intolerably long, backboneless, and without construction. (They called that poetic license.) Being too lazy to think out their words, they adopted a sesquipedalian and obsolescent vocabulary, hoping to attract to their verse the glamour of Spenser or Malory. The men of the nineties had "sensed this out." They wrote. On the whole their sentences, when they wrote in verse, were as well constructed as prose sentences. They aimed at a nervous style and a compact form; they tried to distill picturesqueness from the life that was around them.

So that, although their actual leavings are small and of little attraction today, literature, when it again comes into its own in these islands, will owe them a great debt of gratitude. Material circumstances drove them out of the world; but they were not in any backwater, they were in the mainstream of letters.

For myself, as I have said, I did not learn anything from them. I wish I had. But I had shynesses and I had distastes. And, in a sense, I had carried, even then, my logical progression further than they had carried theirs. Their ideal of what I will call the surface of their poems, whether in prose or in verse, was, for me, too hard and too brilliant. Too self-assertive, and leaving too much the marks of coruscating chisels! And I had been too much hammered by the Pre-Raphaelites. So that my troubled mind took refuge in an almost passionate desire for self-effacement. I remember telling Mr. Edward Garnett—or I ought to put it that my telling Mr. Garnett so shocked him that twenty years afterwards he recalled the fact to me—at any rate, I must have told Mr. Garnett in 1898 or so that my one ambition was to pass unnoticed in a crowd. I do not know that my ambition has ever changed.

But, in those days, that ambition was difficult, or at least arduous of attainment. If, as a young littérateur, you desired any of the society at all of your fellow young littérateurs—and one could not be human and not desire it!—you had to wear some parts of a sort of uniform. You might or might not wear a red tie;

might or might not wear a blue linen, turned-down collar, an inverness, a virgin beard, a slouch hat. . . . But, if you did not wear at least one of these regimental badges you would be ostracized by the intellectuals. I remember being approached by a formal deputation from a colony on the outskirts of which I lived. I had had my slouch hat blown off on Waterloo Bridge, and had purchased at a Smith's bookstall a cloth cap, such as golfers wear. The cloth cap, by the colony, was regarded as antisocial, and I was requested to scrap it. I could not afford in those days a new uniform head-covering every other day, and I am afraid I remained anti-social, and have so remained to this day.

The incident was symbolic. I resented the sartorial tyranny, but still more bitterly did I resent the tyranny of the intellect. It is perfectly true that humanity divides itself into the stuff to fill graveyards and the creative artists who carry forward the work of the world. But it seemed to me then, as it seems to me now, that it is difficult to be certain into which division oneself falls. So that no one man should intellectually browbeat his fellows all the time—or, indeed, ever, except in moments of heated personal controversy. And my aspiration to pass unnoticed in a crowd was intellectual far more than sartorial. I did not then care how I was dressed, and I never have cared how I was dressed, except on parades social or military. But I have always passionately desired to avoid, either in my person or my work, anything approaching what it is convenient to call a highbrow attitude.

That appears to me to be plain commonsense for the poet. His poetry must come from his observation of surrounding humanity. If he browbeats his surrounding humanity so that it sits up and, in the effort to live up to its company, behaves pompously, our poet will never see a human being. He will be like a doctor who never sees men's homes at their most sordid, or like a solicitor who is always hampered in court because his clients persist during preliminary consultations in representing themselves as suffering angels. . . .

And the truth remains that, if we are to get back ever again into the mainstream of literature, our attitude must be other. I mean that, just as in our persons we poets must pass in a crowd, so must our verses—our poems. Just as we must sit in bar-parlors and railway offices as the unsuspected great, so must our poems slip into the readings of common men amongst the outpourings of the Yellow Presses and commercial fiction. Only—they must remain in the heart. That is what makes it so difficult.

*   *   *

[By 1898] I had pretty well worked out my formula, which was that a poem must be compounded of observation of the everyday life that surrounded us; that it must be written in exactly the same vocabulary as that which one used for one's prose; that, if it were to be in verse, it must attack some subject that needed a slightly more marmoreal treatment than is expedient for the paragraph of a novel; that, if it were to be rhymed, the rhyme must never lead to the introduction of unnecessary thought; and, lastly, that no exigency of meter must interfere with the personal cadence of the writer's mind or the pressure of the recorded emotion. . . .

For no man's views are worth very much; the facts that any man can collect during his short pilgrimage through life are ludicrously or pitifully few, and the only empire over which we can for certain reign, or for which we can assuredly speak, is the heart of man. And one's own heart is the heart that one knows best!

I don't mean to say that there is no room in the world for rhetorical expression; rhetorical expressions are, as a rule, the expressions of a man's emotions as he would like to feel them—or as he would like the world to believe that he feels them. There is plenty of room for that, and the room has been well filled. But of gentle, unaffected, and intimate expression there has been very little. And the difficulty is simply that of getting down to oneself—but that is a very great one. For it is hard for a man to see that the writing of himself small is his job, and that he must not swell himself, as if pneumatically, until for a time at least he shall cast on some stage or other a shadow as large as that of the Colossus of Rhodes. Yet, having as a boy seen many such colossi, I had no other ambition than that of avoiding the colossus expression. I tried to imagine myself keeping up a little, intimate warble amongst the hurricanes and the detonations. I remember writing a poem twenty-five years ago as a preface to some volume or other. It was never printed, because Mr. Garnett said it was not poetry, and I dare say it was not. But it ended:

> Like poor Dan Robin, thankful for your crumb
> Whilst larger birds sing mortal loud, like swearing,
> When the wind lulls I try to get a hearing.

And that seems to sum the matter up. Later, I arrived at the definite theory that what I was trying to attain to was verse that was like one's intimate conversation with someone one loved very much. One would try to render what one was like when, on a long winter's night before the fire, one talked, and just talked. No doubt, when one talks to someone one likes very much, one renders oneself, sometimes, a shade more virtuous or more picturesque than one actually is. But then, if the person to whom you are talking loves you very much, or knows you very well, they will know you for the odd creature that you are. . . .

That is to say that, supposing the poet accepts as his my ambition, and desires that his verse shall exhibit him as he really is, whether he be merely talking to a friend, flying in an aeroplane, or indulging in any intermediary activities—the poet then must seek to reproduce his actual vocabulary, his own characteristic turns of phrase, the exact cadence of his own usual sentences. . . .
That will be no easy task[44].

21.

Sherwood Anderson

from *Sherwood Anderson's Memoirs*

Into this alert and colorful atmosphere came Sherwood Anderson, dreamer, philosopher, corn-fed mystic, a man who gathered into himself all the torment of life, who suffered, to some extent voluntarily, all its pangs and ecstasies.

—Harry Hansen[45]

Something was stirring at that time in the world of arts in America. I think everyone felt it. Little magazines with several of which I was to have connections broke out like measles in that period. There was the *Little Review* in Chicago. The *New Republic*, the *Seven Arts* and also what is now known as the old *Masses* got under way in New York. In Chicago the old Dial changed hands— later on moving to New York. The impulse reached out over the country. There was a Midwestern magazine called the *Midland*. In New Orleans another called the *Double Dealer*.

It was the time of the struggle for woman's suffrage, women parading, picketing the White House, going to jail. . . .

To Chicago from New York came the fabulous exhibit of modernist paintings known as the Armory Show. For the first time we saw the gorgeous work of Van Gogh, Gauguin, Cezanne, and the rest of the French moderns. Thousands of citizens stood waiting at the door of the Art Institute of Chicago when the show opened. One of the paintings which roused a great clamor in the newspapers—it was called *Nude Descending a Staircase*—one of the first of the abstract cubist paintings—was bought I believe by Mr. Sherwood Eddy.

It was a kind of outburst of energy and penetrated even to the copy department of the advertising agency where I was employed.

*   *   *

I am trying to give here an impression of what was to me a gay happy time, the gayest and happiest I have ever known, a feeling of brotherhood and sisterhood with men and women whose interests were my own. As yet I had not begun to face what every practitioner of any art must face, the terrible times of bitter dissatisfaction with the work done, often the difficulty of making a living at your chosen work, the facing of the petty jealousies that pop up among fellow craftsmen, the temptation, always present, to try to get into the big money by attempting to give them what you think they want, the times when the ink will not flow, when you have worked, perhaps for weeks and months, on some project only to have to face the fact on some sad morning that it is all no good, that what you have attempted hasn't come off and must be thrown away.[46]

Suffrage

Forward, Out Of Darkness,
Leave Behind The Night.
Forward Out Of Error,
Forward Into Light.

—Inez Milholland[47]

22.

Suffrage Army out on Parade

Perhaps 10,000 Women and Men Sympathizers March for the Cause

Ten thousand strong, the army of those who believe in the cause of woman's suffrage marched up Fifth Avenue at sundown yesterday in a parade the like of which New York never knew before. Dusty and weary, the marchers went to their homes last night satisfied that their year of hard work in preparing for the demonstration had borne good fruit. . . .

Women, young and old, rich and poor, were all banded into a great sisterhood by the cause that they hold dear. Gowned for the most part in simple white, the line of march was gay with bright banners, bright sashes, and bright pennants. And a perfect weather blessed the undertaking.

Women who toiled in the earliest and most unpromising days of the cause, years and years before such a demonstration as yesterday's would have been possible, were not forgotten in the hour of celebration. Julia Ward Howe, Elizabeth Cady Stanton, and Susan B. Anthony are dead, but their names, written large on huge banners, were carried reverently by another generation of suffragists.

There were close to a thousand men in yesterday's parade. Jeered from the sidewalks but unabashed in their convictions, they marched four abreast . . . and a cluster of college sympathizers brought up the rear. . . .

Promptly at 5 o'clock, as the late afternoon shadows were beginning to slant across the green of Washington Square, the order to start the parade came. Sharp whistles from the traffic policemen were followed by a muffled cheer from the spectators packed thick upon the sidewalk and banked high up the steps of all the houses. A ripple of anticipation passed through the groups of suffragettes assembled in the cross streets. Then a company of women on horseback trotted around the east side of Washington Arch, and the great suffrage parade had begun. At 7:20 o'clock, with the streets ablaze with the flare of shaking torches, the scarlet-banded Socialist division, chanting the Marseillaise with such fervor that its strains were caught up by the densely packed crowd of spectators, marched by Carnegie Hall and disbanded. The great parade was over.

For it was a great parade. There is probably no one in this city today who knows just how many persons swung into line on Fifth Avenue yesterday in the cause of woman suffrage, but one estimate, arrived at by counting sections of the parade, put the number at ten thousand. . . .

It was a parade of contrasts—contrasts among women. There were women of every occupation and profession, and women of all ages, from those so advanced in years that they had to ride in carriages, down to suffragettes so small that they were pushed along in perambulators. There were women whose faces bore traces of a life of hard work and many worries. There were young girls, lovely of face and fashionably gowned. There were motherly looking women, and others with the confident bearing obtained from contact with the business world.

There were women who smiled in a preoccupied way as though they had just put the roast into the oven, whipped off their aprons and hurried out to be in the parade. They were plainly worried at leaving their household cares for so long yet they were determined to show their loyalty to the cause. There were women who marched those weary miles who had large bank accounts. There were slender girls, tired after long hours of factory work. There were nurses, teachers, cooks, writers, social workers, librarians, school girls, laundry workers. There were women who work with their heads and women who work with their hands and women who never work at all. And they all marched for suffrage.

The weather was perfect. The May sunshine made it pleasant to be out of doors, and a cool breeze kept the marchers from being uncomfortable.

—*New York Times*, May 5, 1912

23.

Belle Case La Follette

One Woman's View of the Parade

My knowledge of the great suffrage parade which took place in New York, on May 4, was gained as a participant rather than as a spectator, for I walked from Eleventh Street to Fifth Avenue, where the representatives of the non-suffrage states other than New York gathered, to Carnegie Hall on the corner of Fifty-Seventh Street and Seventh Avenue. I did, however, get a chance to look on for a time, for I did not get into the hall to attend the meeting, but stepping aside from the procession found a place on the steps of a nearby house. From this point I saw the ovation which was given to the one thousand men in the parade as they came into Fifty-Seventh Street where suffrage enthusiasm was greatest. They deserved the ovation, and were doubtless glad of it, for while they had not been "guyed" in lower New York as were the eighty men who marched last year, they had braved no small measure of ridicule.

One remarkable thing about the parade was that in spite of its size, variously estimated at from ten to twenty thousand people, it started on time. Having found my place shortly before five o'clock when the procession was scheduled to leave Washington Square, I had settled myself for a long wait on the principle that processions never started on time. Suddenly, a very few moments after the hour the sound of music was heard, and the women on horseback who headed the procession came into view.

They had left Washington Square on the moment. They were fifteen minutes late in reaching Carnegie Hall; not their own fault, but that of the police.

Where uniformity of dress had been adopted as it was by most of the marching clubs, the spectacle was most beautiful. White dresses were worn for the most part, and a regulation hat of white straw. Yellow sashes and scarfs were worn by some of the clubs, green and purple by others, and blue by one of the particularly well-drilled and dignified delegations from upstate. But even where there was no uniformity of dress, it was an impressive sight, not only because of floating banners and waving flags but because of the seriousness and moral fervor of the marchers.

Some of the inscriptions on the banners were:

WE PREPARE CHILDREN FOR THE WORLD;
WE ASK TO PREPARE THE WORLD FOR OUR CHILDREN.

MORE BALLOTS, LESS BULLETS.

WOMEN VOTE IN CHINA, BUT ARE CLASSED WITH
CRIMINALS AND PAUPERS IN NEW YORK.

Dr. Anna Shaw carried a flag with the inscription:

WE ARE TRYING TO CATCH UP WITH CHINA.

Best of all was a banner carried by The Men's Equal Suffrage League of New Jersey which bore this legend:

WOMAN SUFFRAGE HAS PASSED THE STAGE OF ARGUMENT;
YOU COULD NOT STOP IT IF YOU WOULD,
AND IN A FEW YEARS YOU WILL BE ASHAMED
THAT YOU EVER OPPOSED IT.[48]

24.

Inez Haynes Irwin

from *The Story of the Woman's Party*

In 1912 the situation in the United States in regard to the enfranchisement of women was as follows:

Agitation for an amendment to the National Constitution had virtually ceased. Before the death of Susan B. Anthony in 1906, Suffragists had turned their attention to the States. Suffrage agitation there was persistent, vigorous, and untiring; in Washington, it was merely perfunctory. The National American Woman Suffrage Association maintained a Congressional Committee in Washington, but no headquarters. This committee arranged for one formal hearing before the Senate and House Committees of each Congress. The speeches were used as propaganda mailed on a Congressman's frank. The suffrage amendment had never in the history of the country been brought to a vote in the national House of Representatives, and had only once, in 1887, been voted upon in the Senate. It had not received a favorable report from a committee in either House since 1892 and had not received a report of any kind since 1896. Suffrage had not been debated on the floor of either House since 1887. In addition, the incoming President, Woodrow Wilson, if not actually opposed to the enfranchisement of women, gave no appearance of favoring it; the great political parties were against it. Political leaders generally were unwilling to be connected with it. Congress lacked—it is scarcely an exaggeration to say—several hundred of the votes necessary to pass the amendment. Last of all, the majority of Suffragists did not think the federal amendment a practical possibility. They were entirely engrossed in state campaigns.

On the other hand, the Suffrage movement, itself, was virile and vital. The fourth generation of women to espouse this cause were throwing themselves into the work with all the power and force of their able, aroused, and emancipated generation. The franchise had been granted in six states: Wyoming, Colorado, Utah, Idaho, Washington, California.

With the winning of Oregon, Kansas, and Arizona in 1912, the movement assumed a new importance in the national field. These victories meant that there were approximately two million women voters in the United States, that one-fifth of the Senate, one-seventh of the House, and one-sixth of the electoral vote came from Suffrage States.

It was in December, 1912, as Chairman of the Congressional Committee of the National American Woman Suffrage Association, that Alice Paul came to Washington.

In the next eight years, this young woman was to bring into existence a new political party of fifty thousand members. She was to raise over three-quarters of a million dollars. She was to establish a headquarters in Washington that became the focus of the liberal forces of the country. She was to gather into her organization hundreds of devoted workers; some without pay and others with less pay than they could command at other work or with other organizations. She was to introduce into Suffrage agitation in the United States a policy which, though not new in the political arena, was new to Suffrage—the policy of holding the party in power responsible. She was to institute a Suffrage campaign so swift, so intensive, so compelling—and at the same time so varied, interesting, and picturesque—that again and again it pushed the war-news out of the preferred position on the front pages of the newspapers of the United States. She was to see her party blaze a purple, white, and gold trail from the east to the west of the United States, and from the north to the south. She was to see the Susan B. Anthony Amendment pass first the House and then the Senate.

She was to see thirty-seven States ratify the amendment in less than a year and a half thereafter. She was to see the President of the United States move from a position of what seemed definite opposition to the Suffrage cause to an open espousal of it; move slowly at first but with a progress which gradually accelerated until he, himself, obtained the last Senatorial vote necessary to pass the amendment.[49]

25.

Woman's Party, First in World, Born in Chicago

"One Flag, No Candidate, One Plank," and That:
U.S. Suffrage Amendment

With the assembling of more than 1,000 women—1200 to be exact—from all parts of the United States there was born last night at the Blackstone theater the first woman's party in the world.

As Miss Maude Younger of California, the temporary chairman, said in her "keynote" speech, it is a party "with one flag, no candidate, and one plank—the enfranchisement of women by an amendment to the federal Constitution."

President Wilson and the Democratic administration leaders in congress were openly unpopular at the convention. Mrs. O. H. P. Belmont in her address classed President Wilson as "the leader in the flimsy pretext that the freeing of women is a local and not a national affair."

—*Chicago Tribune*, June 6, 1916

26.

Doris Stevens

from *Jailed for Freedom*

When all suffrage controversy has died away it will be the little army of women with their purple, white, and gold banners, going to prison for their political freedom, that will be remembered. They dramatized to victory the long suffrage fight in America. The challenge of the picket line roused the government out of its half-century sleep of indifference. It stirred the country to hot controversy. It made zealous friends and violent enemies. It produced the sharply-drawn contest which forced the surrender of the government in the second administration of President Wilson.

* * *

A sweet old veteran of the Civil War said to one of my comrades: "Youse all right; you gotta fight for your rights in this world, and now that we are about to plunge into another war, I want to tell you women there'll be no end to it unless you women get power. We can't save ourselves and we need you. . . . I am 84 years old, and I have watched this fight since I was a young man. Anything I can do to help, I want to do. I am living at the Old Soldiers' Home and I ain't got much money, but here's something for your campaign. It's all I got, and God bless you, you've gotta win." He spoke the last sentence almost with desperation as he shoved a crumpled $2.00 bill into her hand.[50]

27.

Frederic C. Howe

from *The Confessions of a Reformer*

After graduating from the Meadville Theological Seminary, my wife [Marie Jenney Howe] had gone to Iowa, where she became the "Little Minister" in the pulpit of the Unitarian church in Des Moines. The church grew, she had a devoted following; when we married there was a loud protest from her friends. I had ended her career. Her achievements when she came to Cleveland were greater than my own; she was widely known as a speaker, as a leader in the Suffrage movement, and in social activities. She was eager to continue her work, work which was life to her. But I wanted my old-fashioned picture of a wife rather than an equal partner. Women did not take part in things in Cleveland; only a few had gone to college at that time; there were but few activities open to women. They did not earn their own living. That was a public admission of failure by the husband. I found reasons for deciding against each suggested activity in turn.

It did not occur to me that there was anything illogical in my position, anything unjust in it or out of keeping with what I believed in. My mind simply held fast to assumptions of my boyhood, which social prejudices seemed to justify. And as I look back over those years I realize that I never honestly faced what I was doing or the rightfulness of my wife's claims. It was not until we came to New York, where the Suffrage movement was claiming women of distinction, where no more notice was taken of a woman in work than a man, that I recast my prejudices. My mind did not do it, new standards did. Then I was as eager for her to find her work as I had been loath to have her do so in Cleveland. And she rapidly found opportunities to her liking. She arranged meetings at Cooper Union on various subjects, she developed dramatic activities in connection with her work as chairman of the Twenty-Fifth District, and rose rapidly in the many activities with which women were connected. But I had taken many years out of her life, had denied her the opportunity to pioneer, which she feared rather less than did I, and many of the enthusiasms that had been denied her in Cleveland could not be warmed into life again.

She had aided me greatly in public speaking and writing and gave me generous freedom to do as I chose with my life. She had consented to the abandonment of the law for the uncertainties of literature, the assured life of Cleveland for the hazards of the metropolis. All this fitted in quite naturally with my domestic picture at the time.

As I reflect on this evolution in my opinions, I see again the resistance of the mind to facts that involve sacrifice or personal discomfort, that involve disapproval by one's class or the society in which one lives. There was every reason why I should have allowed my wife any right which I enjoyed, should have given her every freedom which I took for myself, should have encouraged her to express her talents, which I recognized were of an unusual sort. I was proud of these qualities, and my belief in freedom should have made me the first to insist that she use them as she willed. Instead, I discouraged them, because I preferred my early picture of a wife, a picture that fell in with the current assumption of the period that a woman should quite literally "serve," quite literally "obey," her husband. Property rights die hard. Up to very recently a woman was property. Social mores die harder. They relate to the herd in which one lives. And social standing is as much prized as property.

As to women, I followed the changing *mores*. I spoke for women's suffrage without much wanting it. And I urged freedom for women without liking it. My mind gave way, but not my instincts. One can be a hard-boiled monopolist in personal relations, just as in property; and as unwilling to permit individuals to change as the Constitution of the land. I hated privilege in the world of economics; I chose it in my own home.

And I have sometimes doubted whether many of the men who spoke and worked for the equality of women really desired it. Intellectually yes, but instinctively no; they clung as did I to the propertied instinct, to economic supremacy, to the old idea of marriage, in which all that a woman got she got through petitioning for it. There is something so jagged about our convictions; they do not run a hundred percent true. My own unwillingness to abdicate masculine power made me better understand men's unwillingness to abdicate economic power.

And in the woman movement, as in other social movements, equality had to be seized by the class that had it not. I remember a saying of Tolstoy's that the "rich would do anything for the poor but get off their backs." That seemed to be as true in the relation of sexes as it was in the relations of classes.[51]

28.

Eunice Tietjens

I Join *Poetry: A Magazine of Verse*

Beginning in 1912 with the appearance of Harriet Monroe's magazine, *Poetry: A Magazine of Verse*, Chicago became for a few years the functional center, the fountainhead, of the art of poetry in this country, indeed in the English-speaking world.

The beginnings of course were tentative, but in the short space of a year or two it had found or helped develop a group of poets headed by the great Middle Western triumvirate Carl Sandburg, Edgar Lee Masters, and Vachel Lindsay. Others were Arthur Davison Ficke who, though he lived in Davenport, Iowa, was much in Chicago and belonged in spirit with the group, Alice Corbin Henderson, Harriet Monroe herself, Agnes Lee, Helen Hoyt, Cloyd Head, Maxwell Bodenheim, Frances Shaw, Edith Wyatt, Florence Kiper Frank, from time to time Alfred Kreymborg, occasionally Sherwood Anderson, and others, besides myself.

It was a great creative period, and we knew it at the time for what it was. A new vitality was being born in American poetry after a long winter of lying fallow. There were isolated voices elsewhere which presaged the movement, which belonged with it. There was Edwin Arlington Robinson, whose wise human penetrating voice, speaking in its quiet cadence, had paved the way; there was Robert Frost, who at about this time had published *A Boy's Will* in England, but whose more mature work, then beginning, had found no American audience; there was sturdy obstreperous Amy Lowell, breathing forth revolt as the mares of Diomedes breathed fire, and Sara Teasdale, a beautiful, frail, but deeply human spirit, then beginning to find her true voice; there was Rabindranath Tagore, whose first poems in English were sent us by Ezra Pound from London and printed in *Poetry*, and who soon after appeared in person in Chicago for many fertile months; and there were always the passionately devoted, passionately scolding letters from Ezra Pound in England, letters that seemed to me to be part pure genius, part naughty little boy, and part charlatan.

All these people, and many more, rallied to us at once and were with us, either by letter or from time to time in person.

But the Chicago group was the focal point. It had the united vitality that a strong local movement has always had in the arts. And *Poetry* was at once the clearing house, the Mother in Israel, and the magnet which held it all together. Life at the magazine office was a spiritual adventure and sometimes a physical one.

For myself, I came on the staff as office girl and general nuisance about a year after the magazine started. None of us can quite remember just when it was, though I dare say my first paycheck, appallingly small, would be recorded in the old checkbooks if they still exist. Harriet Monroe always tried to engage only accepted poets on the staff, even in minor capacities, and it was because she had accepted one or two poems of mine, the first fruits of my rebirth, that I was admitted. I succeeded Helen Hoyt in the very small position I then occupied. Now, after twenty-three years or so of being connected with the magazine in one capacity or another, I am the oldest member of the staff, the only one left from the early days. All the others who were in at the beginning have been blown away by the winds of circumstance.[52]

29.

Margaret Anderson

from *My Thirty Years' War*

And I came to love Chicago as one only loves chosen—or lost—cities.

I knew it in every aspect—dirt, smoke, noise, heat, cold, wind, mist, rain, sleet, snow. I walked on Michigan Boulevard on winter afternoons when the wind was such a tempest and the snow so icy that ropes were stretched along the buildings to keep pedestrians from falling. Only half a dozen ventured out in a day and they at once sat down like bathers in a high surf. On white misty winter mornings at six o'clock, I used to walk the ten miles from Wilson Avenue to Congress Street for the simple pleasure in the exercise and the hot chocolate at Child's afterward. I was always pretending that I was a poor-working-girl, always forgetting that I was really poor—also a working girl. . . .

And I was in love. My first love—I should say, my first real love. And it was a great love—great in everything including disappointment. But oh, how I was in love.

*   *   *

The *Little Review*

I was now twenty-one. And I felt it was time to confer upon life that inspiration without which life is meaningless.

Often in the night I wake with the sensation that something is wrong, that something must be done to give life form. Sometimes it is merely a matter of changing the furniture in a room. I imagine the whole operation, decide each change with precision, feel suddenly healthy and fall into deep sleep. In the morning I arrange the furniture accordingly, and it's always a great success.

So it was for the *Little Review*. I had been curiously depressed all day. In the night I wakened. First precise thought: I know why I'm depressed—nothing inspired is going on. Second: I demand that life be inspired every moment. Third: the only way to guarantee this is to have inspired conversation every moment. Fourth: most people never get so far as conversation; they haven't the stamina, and there is no time. Fifth: if I had a magazine I could spend my time filling it up with the best conversation the world has to offer. Sixth: marvelous idea—salvation. Seventh: decision to do it. Deep sleep.

In the morning I thought no more about it. I didn't need to think. To me it was already an accomplished fact. I began announcing to everyone that I was about to publish the most interesting magazine that had ever been launched. They found me vague as to why it was going to be so interesting, nebulous as to how it was going to be published, unconcerned about the necessary money, optimistic about manuscripts. Where any sane person would have explained that, sensing the modern literary movement which was about to declare itself, a review to sponsor it was a logical necessity, I only accused people of being unimaginative because they couldn't follow my élan. They really must be blind! As I remember, I never stated one basic reason why a *Little Review*, devoted to the seven arts, was necessary and inevitable. All this seemed so unimportant compared to the divine afflatus necessary to start it. I never said anything, I believe, except: It will be marvelous. I never say basic things. I forget to. They're so obvious.

I knew that someone would give the money. This is one kind of natural law I always see in operation. Someone would have to. Of course someone did.

During my year as literary editor Floyd Dell had become

literary editor of the *Chicago Evening Post*—a position arrived at through an extraordinary article he had written, as a reporter, about the telephone directory. His Friday book section was even more personal and brilliant than Francis Hackett's had been. Floyd's injunctions to his reviewers were invariably interesting: Here is a book on China. Now don't send me an article about China but one about yourself.

Floyd Dell was surrounded by a literary group that gave promise of being the only one of interest in Chicago. I have always felt a horror, a fear, and a complete lack of attraction for any group, of any kind, for any purpose. But I was willing sometimes to see this one because Floyd Dell was in it—was it, rather. I liked Floyd—which means I liked his conversation. Liked it enormously. On the *Post* he was chiefly engaged in pointing out to a naive but willing public the essential differences between Dostoyevsky and Kate Douglas Wiggin. In private he would engage you for hours in the most satisfying polemic on the current Browning discussions, trying to discover through what depravity of the public mind Browning had earned the title of philosopher, considering that "the shallow optimism of 'God's in his heaven, all's right with the world' has never been equaled by anyone with a pretension to thinking."

I often dined with the Dells. Mrs. Dell (Margery Currey) had created a sort of salon for Floyd who was so timid he would never have spoken to anyone if she hadn't relieved him of all social responsibility and presented him as an impersonal being whose only function in life was to talk. He used to stand before the fire, looking like Shelley or Keats (why do we always feel they looked alike?) and prove to his dinner guests that democracy and individualism were synonymous terms. Naturally. You can't be of any value to the world (be a good democrat) unless you're a great individual, and you can't be a great individual without being of value to the world.

Other people since famous came to the Floyd Dells: Theodore Dreiser, Sherwood Anderson, John Cowper Powys with his manias of interest and his: How extraordinary! for topics that failed to interest him; critics whose names I have forgotten; also

Jerome Blum, George Cram Cook, Susan Glaspell, Edna Kenton, Llewellyn Jones—and Arthur Davison Ficke who was concerned about English prose.

Do you really know English prose well enough to found a magazine of criticism?

I know great classic and romantic prose and I can sense a great deal about a new prose which is already forming.

Great prose is great prose—one doesn't talk of new prose, said Ficke.

Floyd and I talked of Pater and of living like the hard gem-like flame. Sherwood Anderson used to listen to us in a certain amazement (resembling fear) and indicating clearly that nothing would induce him into such fancy realms. But I liked Sherwood—because he, too, was a talker and of a highly special type. He didn't talk ideas—he told stories. (It sounds bad but the stories were good. So was the telling.) He said to everyone: You don't mind if I use that story you've just told, do you? No one minded. Sherwood's story never bore any relation to the original. He read us the manuscript of *Windy McPherson's Son*. Floyd was passionate about it—I, a little less so. It was a new prose but I knew by Sherwood's look that he would do something even better. I asked him to give me an article for the first number of the *Little Review*.[53]

30.

from the *Little Review*

Sherwood Anderson

The New Note

In the trade of writing the so-called new note is as old as the world. Simply stated, it is a cry for the reinjection of truth and honesty into the craft; it is an appeal from the standards set up by money-making magazine and book publishers in Europe and America to the older, sweeter standards of the craft itself; it is the voice of the new man, come into a new world, proclaiming his right to speak out of the body and soul of youth, rather than through the bodies and souls of the master craftsmen who are gone.

In all the world there is no such thing as an old sunrise, an old wind upon the cheeks, or an old kiss from the lips of your beloved: and in the craft of writing there can be no such thing as age in the souls of the young poets and novelists who demand for themselves the right to stand up and be counted among the soldiers of the new. That there are such youths is brother to the fact that there are ardent young cubists and futurists, anarchists, socialists, and feminists; it is the promise of a perpetual sweet new birth of the world; it is as a strong wind come out of the virgin west.

One does not talk of his beloved even among the friends of his beloved; and so the talk of the new note in writing will be heard coming from the mouths of the aged and from the lips of oily ones who do not know of what they talk, but run about in circles, making noise and clamor. Do not be confused by them. They but follow the customs of their kind. They are the stript priests of the falling temples, piling stone on stone to build a new temple, that they may exact tribute as before.

Something has happened in the world of men. Old standards and old ideas tumble about our heads. In the dust and confusion of the falling of the timbers of the temple many voices are raised. Among the voices of the old priests who weep are raised also the voices of the many who cry, "Look at us! We are the new! We are the prophets; follow us!"

Something has happened in the world of men. Temples have been wrecked before only to be rebuilt, and destroying youth has danced only to become in turn a builder and in time a priest, muttering old words. Nothing in all of this new is new except this—that beside the youth dancing in the dust of the falling timbers is a maiden also dancing and proclaiming herself.

"We will have a world not half new but all new!" cry the youth and the maiden, dancing together.[54]

31.

Margaret Anderson

from *My Thirty Years' War*

I had also met at the Floyd Dells' a man named—well, perhaps he would prefer to remain anonymous. His first name was DeWitt which I didn't at all like. I called him Dick.[55] He was one of those civilized men (to be found exclusively in America it seems) who are more interested in an idea than in a woman. If this isn't quite true at least Dick always made it seem true, which was all that was necessary. It would be difficult for me to express to what point I appreciate this attitude. I may of course be wrong (and of course I don't for a moment think so), but I have always had so little need of the humanity of people. Their humanity is always the same—in bad people (that is, bad-natured because they are always trying to compensate for some lack or hurt) and in good people (those who are on to themselves and who live without fictitious goals). But good or bad they all react in the same way to the great human dramas—love, ambition . . . (are there others?). People's humanity is either bad and boring or good and boring. In both cases one is dragged along the entire gamut of everyday life with them. It is this—the human drama—that has always been unnecessary to me. I don't seem to function in it. At twenty I didn't know as much about it as I do today but I knew it wasn't for me. I have always had something to live besides a personal life. And I suspected very early that to live merely in an experience of, in an expression of, in a positive delight in the human clichés could be no business of mine. I have learned nothing from living the humanities. I have learned a great deal from talking about them. With Dick I never had to live a moment of the redundant human exchange. With practically everyone else—men or women—I have had to. I will come to this later—and in case you don't feel it, the tone is grim.

Dick and I talked ideas. Of course we talked monstrously—rather like Oswald Spengler or Evelyn Scott. But this curse can be gradually overcome. By the time I conceived the *Little Review* my conversation had already become more supportable—I spoke only in gasps, gaps, and gestures. Dick understood the code and could supply all the words I never had time to stop for. When I hurriedly told him that I was going to publish the best art magazine in the world, he saw the idea perfectly. I was most grateful. People were always telling me that I "saw" their ideas without necessity for formulation on their part. I felt I deserved one friend who could perform this function for me. Dick was the only person who really "saw" the *Little Review*.

He hadn't much money—he was on the staff of an agricultural journal—but he said: You must have that magazine. I can put enough aside each month to pay the printing bill. And office rent. The rest will undoubtedly take care of itself in accordance with those miracles you seem to believe in.

So we dined at the Annex in the white and gold room where Steindhal played Chopin waltzes brilliantly on the piano while reading the newspapers, and we talked of how good the *Little Review* would be. Dick thought it might be just as well to interest certain groups in my project. I didn't. I can't imagine belonging to a group, a Theatre Guild for instance—cooperation, the decision of the majority, the lowest common denominator. . . . I like monarchies, tyrants, prima donnas, the insane. I even like Mussolini—at least *he* is having fun, though Rome is a terrible place today.

So I refused any suggestion of group action. I would consent only to the Floyd Dell soirées. At these we discussed names. But no one could think of a good name. I've forgotten what Floyd offered. Arthur Davison Ficke wanted it called the *March Review* since it was to begin in March. He seemed to feel that this was a charming kind of joke. Finally, in desperation I wanted to call it the *Seagull* (soaring and all that kind of thing). Then I suspected that this was a bit fancy and decided that a simple name like the *Little Review* would be better, the little theatre movement being at the moment in violent vogue. All that group effort resulted in nothing—not even a name.

We decided to honor Clara Laughlin by taking her to tea and telling her all about it. This turned out to be no privilege at all. Clara was more articulate than anyone had yet been about the impossibility of a little review.

Poor innocent, she said, you can't do such a thing. Look at the *Yellow Book*. It had the backing of John Lane and had everyone on its staff, even Henry James. And it couldn't keep alive a year.

Well, yes, I said, look at the *Yellow Book*. You can look at it on the library shelves of almost any book lover, richly bound, and rated among his more precious possessions.

Clara continued to discourage us. Fortunately I am never depressed by that kind of argument. If a doctor told me I had a cancer I couldn't manage to believe it with any amount of effort. Somehow I wouldn't feel it to be appropriate. I knew Clara Laughlin was wrong—that she could measure neither my passion, my brain, nor my resistance.

Dick may have thought she was right. But it would have taken a far stronger man to have communicated such a thought to me. Instead he suggested that I go to New York and Boston to get advertisements for the first number. This seemed to me more than good sense.

*　　*　　*

I don't remember ever having explained to anyone that the *Little Review* couldn't pay for contributions. It was quite taken for granted that since there was no money there would be no talk of remuneration. No one ever asked me why I didn't pay, no one ever urged me to pay, no one ever made me feel that I was robbing the poor artist. It was nine years later in Paris that Gertrude Stein told me I couldn't hope to do such a thing in Europe. Her tone was almost reproachful, although she had always offered her manuscripts to the *Little Review* with the same high disregard of payment that characterized all our contributors. She merely didn't consider it good principle. Well, neither do I consider it good principle for the artist to remain unpaid—it's a little better than for him to remain unprinted, that's all.

Practically everything the *Little Review* published during its first years was material that would have been accepted by no other magazine in the world at the moment. Later all the art magazines wanted to print our contributors and, besides, pay them. The contributors took the same stand as Sherwood Anderson. If they had something we especially wanted they gave it to us before the *Dial* was permitted to see it—and pay. The best European writers and painters did the same. I can't help feeling that Gertrude Stein is wrong. I believe that a little review can exist in any country, at any time—not only "before the war." I believe that an analogous thing exists always, somewhere; exists in any epoch of an upheaval in the arts and exists by the same dispensations.[56]

32.

Eunice Tietjens

The *Little Review*

During those early years there were two other centers of artistic activity in Chicago which shared my interest, in a lesser degree, with *Poetry*.

One was the Chicago Little Theatre, Maurice Browne and his wife Ellen Van Volkenburg's fine challenge to the commercialism of the regular theatre. It occupied a tiny auditorium of ninety-eight seats in the old Fine Arts Building on Michigan Avenue, and it held its plume of courage and foresight high, though some of those conducting it were half starved physically. Time has proven its wisdom, for the little theatre movement which caught fire from Browne's torch has now spread over the whole country and has contributed greatly towards what is finest in the American theatre. But in those days it also suffered the fate of all beginnings, was laughed at by the regulars, condescendingly patronized from time to time by the society women, and finally left to die, an orphan on the doorstep of our commercial civilization. . . .

But the *Little Review*! Seldom in this all too practical world has there been an adventure like the early days of the *Little Review*. It was the perfect flower of adolescence, the triumph of wide-eyed and high-hearted ineptitude. It was a blaze of courage and a mine of foolishness. It was delicious.

I had the good luck to be in at the take-off. One day Margery Currey, whose parties are classic in the memory of all who knew them, announced that a big dinner was to be given at her studio to launch a new magazine. We attended eagerly, thirty or forty of us. People were there whom I did not know: a young round-faced man named DeWitt Wing, who was pointed out as the financial backer; George Soule, later of the New York literary world; Alexander Kaun, a dreamy, lovable young Russian who now teaches in a western university; Llewellyn Jones, afterwards for years literary editor of the *Chicago Evening Post*, Ben Hecht, and others. But when after the dinner a young woman named Margaret Anderson got up to speak, we all knew that she was the burning core of the matter. And burn she did.

She was as beautiful as Rupert Brooke and as flaming as Inez Milholland. In her severe black suit and little black hat, under which her blond hair swept like a shining bird's wing, she stood pouring out such a flood of high-hearted enthusiasm that we were all swept after her into some dream of a magazine where Art with a capital A and Beauty with a still bigger B were to reign supreme, where "Life Itself" was to blossom into some fantastic shape of incredible warmth and vitality. Many of us knew that such a thing was impossible, but in those days the person who could resist Margaret Anderson was granite and cold steel. The most hard-boiled advertising managers gave her ads, and printers were wax in her hands. So we all went up in smoke together and promised our help.

Margaret took a little office, and the fun began. We held rosy meetings in little groups where the forthcoming masterpiece assumed proportions which not the *Atlantic Monthly*, the *Masses*, and the *Seven Arts*—our favorites then—could have touched if all their good points had been combined. I was rallied a good bit on my coldness. After all I was a few years older than many of them, and I knew something of what it takes to publish a magazine. But as I look back on it now, I know that I was only a degree or two cooler than they were.

At last the first number appeared. It had a severe outside, like Margaret's tailored suit, and the inside was the usual tentative array of ill-assorted things which might have been expected. But Margaret's editorial blazed with hope only less brightly than she did herself.

It was not, however, till I held this first number in my hand that I began to see the amazing person who was Margaret Anderson, the incredible mixture of adolescent dreams and vitality, of colossal blindness, and of a kind of savage scorn of everything she did not understand. The magazine, when it appeared, was the worst-printed screed I ever saw. When I taxed Margaret with it she told me with gay insouciance and a kind of irritation that she had made it up directly from the first printer's galleys—and he must have been a very bad printer at that. "It simply never occurred to me that one had to proofread things that come from the printers!" she said.

Somehow the magazine continued. For a month or two DeWitt Wing continued to pay the bills and the office rent; then he quarreled with Margaret and fell out. After that it appeared through a monthly miracle. Person after person, caught in the blaze of Margaret's enthusiasm, came forward with money. Only recently I discovered that my brother-in-law Hi Simons—who later became the well-known conscientious objector and spent two years in Leavenworth prison where he led the folded-arm strike—reading the magazine somewhere in the North, had been inspired to send her money to bring out a number, money which he had painfully saved for quite another purpose. And I know that I pawned, and was never able to redeem, the diamond engagement ring which was all that then remained of my marriage to Paul Tietjens. How many more of us there were could probably be found by counting the issues.

The queer thing was that even as we did these things we knew how inept the result was, how brainlessly joyous and savage and scrambled each number appeared. There were a few good poems and articles, but they added up to nothing. Margaret could never think, never distinguish one thing from another. She could only feel in a glorious haze. And the emotion back of the adventure caught at us in spite of our minds.

Margaret herself was the adventure. She was so unbelievably beautiful, so vital, and so absurd! She was also terribly poor, always being put out of one place after another, at first with her furniture, afterwards without. Her wardrobe consisted literally of two garments, her black tailored suit with a white blouse which was always spotlessly clean because she washed it every night—she wore her clothes as a queen might wear them—and a lovely blue satin dressing gown. She had nothing else. The place where she happened to be living was always a jumble of people. Her sister Lois Peters presently came with her two small babies, sturdy little chaps, to live with Margaret, and a girl named Harriet Dean, and usually one or two others, sometimes amorphous young men, almost anybody who had no place to go or was fired by her enthusiasm. The food was casual beyond anything I had ever seen. Sometimes dinner would consist of bread and dill pickles, and sometimes, when a check had come from some mysterious source, breakfast would have ham, eggs, potatoes, hot cakes, and whatnot. The babies, I believe, were always reasonably fed, but mere food was beneath the serious consideration of the rest of them.

Once I remember spending the night at Margaret's with my own little daughter, Janet, then four or thereabouts. Margaret was then living in a large and imposing apartment overhanging the lake somewhere about Rogers Park. It had great rooms with imposing mirrors and high ceilings, but for furniture it contained nothing at all but a number of narrow iron cots, a kitchen table, and three or four chairs. The living room was quite innocent of everything except a few prints pinned on the walls and a cushion or two on the polished floor. But that troubled no one among us. We dined on pickles and frankfurters. When it came time for bed Janet and I were given a single narrow cot. Towards morning I fell asleep, only to be awakened at dawn to see Margaret standing over me.

Her blue satin dressing gown was like a shining skin upon her. The light of the rising sun shimmered on it and on her upraised arms, stretched high above her head, and her smooth gold hair. Aphrodite could hardly have been more lovely.

"Oh, Eunice!" she cried, her voice vibrant with a clear joy of living. "It is a new day, and I am alive! Come out quickly and swim before the sun is really up!"

She was so like some antique goddess of dawn that I could only unlimber myself stiffly and follow her out into the cold water of the lake, where she splashed and swam happily and so gayly that presently a sleepy head was stuck out of a near-by window and a gruff voice bade us, "For God's sake, shut up!" That is the trouble with goddesses in a workaday world. They are seldom appreciated.

Presently that apartment too was lost, and after a while they were living thirty miles or so north of Chicago in Lake Bluff. Here things were even more chaotic than before. There seemed to be more people and less food. Finally, again dispossessed, they moved to a sort of summer-house on the beach belonging to Harry Bunting. He let them have it rent-free, I believe. It was bitter cold on the lakefront in winter, but they survived somehow. When Christmas came Margaret had no money for a tree; but little things of this sort never disturbed her. She went forth with a hatchet, found a beautiful blue spruce, perfectly formed, and chopped it down. I believed her, knowing her, when she told me later that it "simply never occurred" to her that the tree was part of a carefully landscaped ravine belonging to Harry Bunting and had been put there at considerable expense. But Bunting felt— and I can understand that too—that she should be taught a lesson. So he had her arrested. I don't suppose the case reads in the records "Dawn Goddess versus Law and Order," but it should. Margaret was scolded, but let off. Bunting had accomplished all he wanted. But Margaret was unrepentant. "It is perfectly absurd!" was her final comment.[57]

33.

Ben Hecht

from *A Child of the Century*

The *Little Review* was a deceptively thin and modest-looking magazine published from a cubbyhole in the Fine Arts Building on Michigan Avenue. Its innocuous title and its wrenlike tan covers have remained in my mind for thirty years as a piece of the True Cross, glimpsed by a pilgrim in his youth. It was Art. I have met many things in my life that were Art, but they were always Art plus something else—Art plus fame, money, vanity, success, politics, complexes, etc. The *Little Review* was, nakedly and innocently, *Art*.

There were, and still are, scores of art periodicals in our Republic, but Miss Anderson's publication was like none of them. Unlike the *Dial*, the *New Masses*, the *New Republic*, *Poetry*, *Others*, the *Mercury*, the *Bookman*, the *Little Review* never found an audience. It found only writers. Its continued emergence off the press seemed always a miracle, and I used to hold my breath from month to month in fear that it would vanish, genie fashion, from the earth.

It paid no money for contributions. Its lovely pilot spent half her time charming printers and paper salesmen into sheathing their claws and swallowing their bills. Occasionally its staff was unable to find money for food or lodging. They fled the city, then, and pitched three tents on the beach near Lake Forest. Here, apparently, the ravens fed them, and inside the leaky canvas shelters

Art was served and the Land of the Philistines laid low.

To this harum-scarum, bankruptcy-haunted and unsalable publication, manuscripts poured in from all the geniuses of the world. So it seemed to me then; so it still seems when I remember its electric pages. James Joyce's *Ulysses* ran as a serial in them. Ezra Pound, still blond and sane, flooded them with his bright parrotings of ancient Greeks and Chinese. In them appeared the first trumpet calls of Wyndham Lewis, T. S. Eliot, Carl Sandburg, Jules Romains, Jean Cocteau, Sherwood Anderson, André Gide, Carlos Williams, Djuna Barnes, Edgar Lee Masters, Amy Lowell, and platoons of similar moon-shooters.

None of them received a dime for his work and, as often as not, had his manuscript returned with a disdainful line from Miss Anderson, "I don't like this," or "I couldn't read this." Nevertheless, Miss Anderson's desk (or tent) was always heaped with copy signed by names a-gallop to fame.

It was youth that spoke in the *Little Review*, sometimes even juvenilia. Between its covers flared an arrogance now gone out of the world. Each issue was full of the only battle bulletins to be read in that day—triumphant communiqués from all the advancing fronts.

Why a magazine with so many geniuses writing so brilliantly in it should fail to attract any attention to speak of was never a mystery to me, as a contributor, or to Miss Anderson, or to most of the new Byrons and Dostoyevskys who panted to get into its unread pages. We would all have regarded the success of the *Little Review* as a blow to our prestige. We were dedicated to rescuing the art of writing from the latrines of popularity. We considered the approval of either the crowd or critics a mark of final failure. To fascinate "the mob"—as we dubbed the distraught and troubled millions of our neighbors in that day—was proof of having fallen to its canned-soup level. Art was not a thing to sell or to offer for applause. It was the individual's lonely response to the mysteries of man and nature. It was to be enjoyed chiefly by the artist making it, and by a handful of other artists who might weary for an hour of admiring themselves.

This love affair between oneself and one's mind was endangered by any public. It ran the risk of becoming a love affair between oneself and such a public, and we all knew where this led—to fame, fortune, and the respect of one's fellows. I am not being facetious. What I write is true. We held Art to be, like Virtue, its own riches.

A ringing line was its own reward. And having written it and had it printed without pay in a magazine nobody read was the finest triumph in the world. We left the Fine Arts Building with fresh copies of the *Little Review* under our arms—we who were lucky enough to be in it—and felt big in the street, anointed but unknown, which was the Shekinah of the True Artist.[58]

34.

from the *Little Review*

Ben Hecht

The Mob-God

The seats creak expectantly. The white whirr of the movie machine takes on a special significance. In the murky gloom of the theater you can watch row on row of backs becoming suddenly enthusiastic, necks growing suddenly alive, heads rising to a fresh angle. Turning around you can see the stupid masks falling, vacant eyes lighting up, lips parting and waiting the smile, mouths opening waiting to laugh. A miracle is transpiring. A sodden mass inclined toward protoplasmic atavism, a smear of dead nerves, dead skin, fiberless flesh, is beginning to quiver with an emotion. Laughter is about to be born. The lights dance on the screen in front. Letters appear in two short words and a gasp sweeps from mouth to mouth.

The name of a Mob-God flashes before the eyes. Suddenly the screen in front vanishes. In its place appears a road. stretching away to the sky and lined with trees. The sky is clear. The scene is cool and healthy. The leaves of the trees flutter familiarly. The road smiles like an old friend. And far in the distance a speck appears and moves slowly and jerkily. Wide open mouths and freshened eyes watch the speck grow larger. It takes the form of a man, a little man with a thin cane. At last his baggy trousers and his slovenly shoes are visible. His thick curly hair under the battered derby becomes clear. He walks along carelessly, quietly, with an infinite philosophy. He walks with an indescribable step, kicking up one of his feet, shuffling along.

Laughter is born. The vapid faces respond magically to His presence. Pure, childish delight sounds. The faces are bathed in a human light. A noisy, wholesome din fills the theater. And the little man comes down the road with his calm and solemn face, his sad eyes, his impossible mustache, his ridiculous trousers, and his nervous, spasmodic gait amid the roars and wild elation of idiots, prostitutes, crass, common churls, and empty souls converted suddenly into a natural and mutual simplicity. The stuffy, maddening "bathos" that clings to the mob like a stink is dispelled, wiped out of the air. Laughter, laughter, shrieks and peals, chuckles and smiles, the broad permeating warmth of the simplest, deepest joy is everywhere.

Charlie Chaplin is before them, Charles Chaplin with the wit of a vulgar buffoon and the soul of a world artist. He walks, he stumbles, he dances, he falls. His inimitable gyrations release torrents of mirth clean as spring freshets. He is cruel. He is absurd; unmanly; tawdry; cheap; artificial. And yet behind his crudities, his obscenities, his inartistic and outrageous contortions, his "divinity" shines. He is the Mob-God. He is a child and a clown. He is a gutter snipe and an artist. He is the incarnation of the latent, imperfect, and childlike genius that lies buried under the fiberless flesh of his worshippers. They have created Him in their image. He is the Mob on two legs. They love him and laugh.

"Fruits to Om."

"Glory to Zeus."

"Mercy, Jesus."

"Praised be Allah."

"Hats off to Charlie Chaplin."[59]

35.

Mark Turbyfill

from *Whistling in the Windy City*

Late in the summer, with my parents, I left Cedar Street and moved into an apartment much farther north, on Racine Avenue, near Wilson. Wilson Avenue, lively with its smartly dressed people, colorful clothing shops, music stores, photographers' studios, ice cream parlors, new movie and vaudeville theatres, seemed to me an attractive thoroughfare, and it was somehow flattering to hear that it had been referred to by an imaginative observer as having a bit of the charm of Paris.

Lake View High School, boasting a prouder history and superior academic rating than any other Chicago high school, was located several blocks south and west, within reasonable walking distance of the flat on Racine. In the fall of 1912, I became a freshman at Lake View. . . .

There was a bookstore on Wilson Avenue, near the new, architecturally attractive DeLuxe movie theatre, where my classmate, Royall Snow, and I enjoyed going to see the weekly installments of *The Perils of Pauline* and *The Diamond from the Sky*. . . .

[One] day I had the fortune to discover among the current magazines one that was to play a leading role in both my near, and relatively distant, future. My discovery was the *Little Review*, so unusual looking in its dress, with its name on a gummed label, and its bird-brown cover telling the world it was "a magazine of the arts making no compromise with the public taste."

Holding the strange little magazine in hand was as exciting as holding a small, throbbing bird. It seemed ready to get away at once, yet also to promise a satisfying, half-secret, shock. The pages fluttered open to reveal more, but never quite all.

It was the poems that especially interested me. They brought to mind the poems I had read in the "scandal sheet" of a Sunday newspaper—poems from a book called *Tender Buttons* by a woman named Gertrude Stein. They were as strange as the strangest picture I had ever seen. That was the picture they showed in 1913 at the Chicago Art Institute, the one called *Nude Descending a Staircase*. If there was really a nude in the picture, she was so subtly hidden that you had to slant your mind and your eyes in a strange, unheard-of way to uncover and see her. But there was something about the painting that made you want to keep on looking.

That was the way I felt about the poems in the *Little Review*. There was something moving in them below the surface that impelled me to read them again and again.

Surprises sprang from every page of the issue I had just found. Margaret Anderson, the editor, was making an announcement so urgent that it was hard to realize she meant what she was saying. Unless people who cared came and saved it, the *Little Review* was going to die! But she was offering a plan that she fervently hoped would work. Readers were beseeched to buy books of all publishers and order them through the *Little Review*. If she could earn enough commissions through such friendly sales her magazine of the Arts could go on living. Margaret Anderson emphasized that the purchase of even one book, if you ordered it from her, would help save the *Little Review*. . . .

If I needed further reason for calling on Miss Anderson, I had it. I wanted to own a copy of Maeterlinck's *Wisdom and Destiny;* and without a doubt, Miss Anderson was the person from whom to buy it.

On the ninth floor of the Fine Arts Building, on exhilarating Michigan Avenue, I found the office of the *Little Review*. The door was slightly ajar. I gave a little tap of warning, and walked in.

For an instant it appeared a tiny place, about to burst with all the wonder expanding there. What seemed four walls, closing in, could have been no more substantial than a mirage—a concession to pedestrian eyes. For here was something else than the tiny room the walls were simulating. It was more. It was Space!

A great, Dark Being floated toward the center with uplifted, arousing wing, dispelling an old belief that a piano could be corporeal. The golden light that swam everywhere at once like a diaphanous fish in infinite sunset—or was it dawn?—could hardly be emanating from what appeared simply as an electric bulb wrapped in an amber-colored scarf.

That shape must have been but a glimmering reflection come to steady a tyro suddenly finding himself in the presence of essential radiance. Our need to bestow names is deep and ever-present. And so I felt the need to name those transparencies for the loveliness of the young woman at whom I was staring; and silently I called them auburn hair, beautiful mouth, wide blue eyes.

Facing her radiance, I confessed that I had come only to buy a book. I felt remiss in saying it was only one book, *Wisdom and Destiny*, that I had come to order. But Margaret Anderson's gracious appreciation relieved embarrassment. I wished it were possible to order an extensive library, the better to help save the *Little Review*. Suddenly I felt that time was running out, and could think of no excuse to linger longer. Turning to go, I was thrilled to hear Miss Anderson inviting me to call again.[60]

36.

Harriet Monroe

from *A Poet's Life*

As the stage for the poet's drama, the scene and center of all controversial action in the art, the old *Poetry* office in Cass Street began to develop "atmosphere." I had never been the actual mistress of any home which had sheltered me, but this little kingdom was mine, and I rather enjoyed dispensing its fleeting hospitalities. Not quite mine alone, however, for a succession of clever associate editors shared my work and its rewards, and most inconsiderately their agile minds kept me scrambling for precedence.

I have mentioned the first of these, Alice Corbin, the poet—Alice Henderson, the wife and mother and critic—who enlivened our office for three and a half years. Her round face with its smiling Cupid mouth, blue eyes, and impertinent little nose, set in a pretty tangle of curly blond hair, looked blandly innocent, never preparing one for the sharp wit which would flash out like a sword. She was a pitiless reader of manuscripts; nothing stodgy or imitative would get by her finely sifting intelligence, and we had many a secret laugh over the confessional "hot stuff" or the boggy word weeds which tender-minded authors apparently mistook for poetry. We had long sessions over the poems which she, as first reader, had found perhaps worth printing, discussing their qualities with searching frankness. In her province was the registration of successful contributors, she sent back rejections and typed a few letters, though most of the correspondence fell to my share. I made the final decisions and wrote the letters to poets recording acceptance, these being usually in uncopied longhand, for I have never learned to run a typewriter, or to dictate with any style. Alice and I made a strong team, and our arguments never quite brought us to blows or bloodshed.

When in the early spring of 1916, the doctors found that tuberculosis was the cause of Alice's waning strength, and exiled her to Santa Fe for a strict regimen of rest and quiet in a less rigorous climate, I felt her banishment not only as a personal grief but also as a very serious loss to the magazine. By way of grateful acknowledgment of her service I kept her name, for seven years more, on the staff list which we publish in every volume, though her work for *Poetry* ceased absolutely when she left us. This honorary listing was a mistaken policy as it has led to misapprehension, certain critics assuming that she actually worked for the magazine throughout its first decade. . . .

During those first years Alice Corbin was not only a well-nigh indispensable member of *Poetry*'s staff, but also one of the gayest and most brilliant slingers of repartee in the groups which soon began to gather in the *Poetry* office. For amid all the exciting controversy we enjoyed the chief reward of editorial labors when some of the new poets opened our office door. . . .

One of the first of these visitors was Rabindranath Tagore, the serenely noble Laureate of Bengal. We had assumed, in printing his "Gitanjali" in our third number, that the distinguished Bengali poet was in London or India; but when the poems had made their first appearance in the English tongue, and the *Chicago Tribune* had welcomed them in an editorial, we received a letter from young Tagore, a student of chemistry in the University of Illinois, informing us that his father was his guest in Urbana and would like a few copies of the magazine containing his poems. . . .

Tagore was a patriarchal figure in his gray Bengali robe, with a long gray beard fringing his skin. . . . "India has been conquered more than once," he would say, "but when the conquest was over life would go on much as before. But this conquest is different; it is like a great hammer, crushing persistently the spirit of the people."[61]

37.

from *Poetry: A Magazine of Verse*

Rabindranath Tagore

The Tryst

Upagupta, the disciple of Buddha, lay asleep on the dust by the wall of Mathura. Lamps were all out, doors were all shut in the town, and stars were hidden in clouds in the murky sky of August.

Whose feet were those tinkling with anklets, touching his breast of a sudden? He woke up starting, and the rude light from the woman's lamp struck his forgiving eyes.

It was the dancing girl drunk with the wine of youth, starred with jewels and clouded with a pale blue mantle.

She lowered her lamp and saw the young face, where mercy shone in the eyes and purity beamed from the forehead.

"Forgive me, young ascetic," said the woman; "graciously come to my home. This hard dusty earth is not a fit bed for you."

The ascetic answered, "Go on your way, fair woman. When the time is ripe, I will come and see you."

Suddenly the dark black night showed its teeth in a flash of lightning. The storm-fiend growled in the sky and the woman trembled in fear.

*   *   *

The New Year had not yet begun. It was an evening of

March. The wind was wild. The branches of the wayside trees were aching with blossoms.

Gay notes of the flute came floating in the warm spring air from afar. The citizens had gone to the woods, to the festival of flowers. From the mid-sky smiled the full moon on the empty and silent town.

The young ascetic was walking alone in the lonely city road. The moon-beam checkered with shadows fell on his path and sleepless koels sang from the flowering mango branches.

He passed through the city gates and stood at the base of the rampart.

What woman was it lying on the earth in the shadow of the wall at his feet?

She was struck with the black pestilence; her body was spotted with sores. She was driven from the town with haste for the fear of her fatal touch.

The ascetic sat by her side, gently took her head on his knees, moistened her lips with water and smeared her body with balm.

"Who art thou, kind angel of mercy?" asked the woman.

"The time, at last, has arrived for me to visit you, and I have come," replied the young ascetic.[62]

38.

Harriet Monroe

from *A Poet's Life*

In those days there was an Italian restaurant around the corner, which served *vin ordinaire*, red or white, with its *table d'hôte* luncheon. Here we had parties when there were enough poets around to make an excuse for it, and our discussion would thrash out fine points of the art's province and technique. Lindsay used to say that he learned more in those talks than a whole college course or years of solitary study could have taught him—sparks flashed from the sharp encounter of sympathetic or opposing minds. And after lingering past luncheon most of us would adjourn to the *Poetry* office to carry on the arguments.

John Gould Fletcher, fresh from his English sojourn, was an early visitor, pausing for a few months in Chicago on his way to his native Arkansas, and telling us, in the falling cadences of his precisely rounded English, about his literary affiliations with Ezra's and Hueffer's groups in London, and his enthusiasm for Japan and Japanese prints.[63]

Another new acquaintance in those days was a stalwart slow-stepping Swede named Carl Sandburg, the son of illiterate sturdy immigrants who had reared their family on an Illinois farm. Alice had handed over to me a group of strange poems in very individual free verse, beginning with "Chicago" as the "hog-butcher of the world." This line was a shock at first, and was laughed at scornfully by critics and columnists when we gave it the lead in

March, 1914. Carl was a typical peasant of proletarian sympathies in those days, with a massive frame and a face cut out of stone. He had earned his living at rough jobs ever since fourteen, had volunteered for the Spanish War, and during a lazy station in Puerto Rico had saved his pay to be used later for a few terms at Knox College; and at this time he was reporting for that early Chicago tabloid, the *Day Book*. His delicate-featured very American wife told me that ours was the first acceptance of Carl's poems, although for two years she had been collecting rejection slips from a steady campaign against editors. Carl would come in often to sit in our "poet's chair," and talk of life and poetry with whoever might be there, weighing his words before risking utterance in his rich, low-pitched, quiet voice.[64]

*   *   *

"I was to hear this voice for many years," said Ben Hecht later—"in the streets during long walks, in the *Daily News* office at the desk beside mine. To this day I remember it as the finest voice I ever heard, reading or talking, better even than the remarkable voices of Paul Muni, Jack Barrymore, and Helen Hayes. In Sandburg's voice lived all his poetry. It was a voice of pauses and undercurrents, with a hint of anger always in it and a lift of defiance in its quiet tones. It was a voice that made words sound fresh, and clothed the simplest of sentences with mysteries."[65]

39.

Margaret Anderson

from *My Thirty Years' War*

I was having a marvelous time being an editor. I was born to be an editor. I always edit everything. I edit my room at least once a week. Hotels are made for me. I can change a hotel room so thoroughly that even its proprietor doesn't recognize it. I select or reject every house seen from train windows and install myself in all the chosen ones, changing their defects, of course. Life becomes confusing. . . . Where haven't I lived?

I edit people's clothes, dressing them infallibly in the right lines. I am capable of becoming so obsessed by the lines of a well-cut coat that its owner thinks I am flirting with him before I've realized he is in the coat. I change everyone's coiffure—except those that please me—and these I gaze at with such satisfaction that I become suspect. I edit people's tones of voice, their laughter, their words. I change their gestures, their photographs. I change the books I read, the music I hear. In a passing glance I know a man's sartorial perfections or crimes—collar, cravat, handkerchief, socks, cut of shoulders, lapels, trousers, placement of waistline, buttons, pockets, quality of material, shoes, walk, manner of carrying stick, angle of hat, contour of hair. It is this incessant, unavoidable observation, this need to distinguish and impose, that has made me an editor. I can't make things. I can only revise what has been made. And it is this eternal revising that has given me my nervous face.

Someone sent in a poem with a line I still remember without references to the back files (which I haven't anyway)—"moon paint on a colorless house." I sent for the poet who turned out to be Maxwell Bodenheim. He smoked a long white malodorous pipe. Sometimes he decorated it with a large knot of baby blue ribbon—toward what end I have never discovered. His eyes were the same blue. It may have been that.

Everybody came to the studio. Ben Hecht with his "pale green face," his genius for adjectives, his tender cynicism for my enthusiasm.

You stole my metaphor. I was just going to compare the piano to the Winged Victory myself. It's a shame, because you can't write. I'll teach you to write if you like.

I don't like. I'm not a writer. I will never be one. I'm merely an inspiration to writers—I tell them what they should be. Ben Hecht for instance should be a decadent rather than a socialist.

Carl Sandburg was intensely socialist and was publishing a working-man's daily. Then he suddenly began to write poems and chants which he intoned in such a deep voice that the studio furniture shook under its vibrations. He lived a domestic suburban life but tramped the Chicago streets composing his working-man's saga.

Edgar Lee Masters was the funny man of the literati. His eyes twinkled (it's the only verb) and he indulged with obvious pleasure in the lowest slap-stick humor. He looked like Thackeray. His *Spoon River Anthology* had just been published in *Poetry*, Harriet Monroe's magazine of verse which bore the ill-advised slogan of Whitman's: "To have great poets we must have great audiences too." Not true, however you look at it. Great poets create great audiences, just as great people create their experiences instead of being created by them.[66]

40.

Harriet Monroe

from *A Poet's Life*

Poetry was for poets, and even the "business manager" had to be a poet to be worthy of her job. Eunice Tietjens was one of the first of these. After her return to a Chicago suburb from family life in Germany, a few of her poems had appeared in 1912, under the pseudonym "Eloise Briton," in Ferdinand Earle's *Lyric Year*, so, being a poet, she naturally drifted toward our office and joyfully gave up her kindergarten work for our small unlucrative post, later rising directly to associate editorship when ill health banished Alice Henderson to a softer climate in the spring of 1916. Eunice was as tall and dark as Alice was blond and little, and her olive skin and midnight eyes were emphasized by a heavy mass of dark brown hair. She was a clever talker in three or four languages, and she loved the new contacts, personal and correspondence, with writers more or less provocative. She was less ruthless than Alice, more tender toward the hapless aspirants whose touching letters and worthless verses might move us to tears of sorrow or mirth, but never to acceptance.

Helen Hoyt also began as a mere recorder, a "subscription slavey." Her much-quoted poem "Ellis Park" arrived in 1913 from some South Side office where she was employed, and when she came over in response to our acceptance we found her a singularly free-spirit who had escaped from a too narrow New England environment to lead her own life in the more spacious West. Soon she resigned her clerkship in favor of our ill-paid half-time job, managing to eke out her small salary with the aid of other work. The high spirits of these two young women, their undaunted sincerity which nothing could shake or frighten, were a tonic not only to the editors but to unrecognized poets—good, bad, and indifferent—who would stray into the office for entertainment and consolation.

We women of the "staff" and our visitors used to have lively discussions during those first years, and each new letter from Ezra Pound sharpened the edge of them. Poetic technique was an open forum, in which everyone's theories differed from everyone else's, and the poems we accepted and published were a battleground for widely varying opinions. . . . I remember one night, after a dinner I had given for Robert Frost, when he and I argued about poetic rhythms till three in the morning, against a background of cheers and jeers from three or four other poets who lingered as umpires, until at last Mrs. [Vaughn] Moody called up my apartment and asked me to remind my guest of honor (her house guest) that she was waiting up for him. . . .

More ideas came to me for editorials than I had time to use; suggestions from many sources—from chance words by poets and others, from incidents, from items in newspapers and magazines. People were in a hopeful mood everywhere, unaware of the impending World War.[67]

41.

Eunice Tietjens

from *The World at My Shoulder*

Never shall I forget the feeling of awe with which I first set foot in the little office on Cass Street which was the physical seat of so much vitality. It had once been the old-time "front parlor" of a private residence, now become an office building, and the white marble fireplace, doubtless once the center of social formality, had by the alchemy of change now become the very opposite, giving a mood of informality and humanity to the place which set it apart at once from other offices. But even without it *Poetry* could never have seemed entirely commercial. It has never attained to the sort of frozen and deliberate informality which the offices of the large commercial magazines and publishers in the East have developed, where authors feel at once subtly flattered by so much magnificence and properly subdued to their status as mere feeders of the printing press. *Poetry* has always been a homelike place, cluttered with books in every available spot—since there has never been space enough or time enough among the short-handed staff to cope with the endless stream of them—crowded with desks and filing cases and at times actually littered with stray poets. I remember Floyd Dell saying once that he had to brush a poet off his desk every day at the old *Chicago Evening Post* before he could begin work. On Poetry we were in a far more delightful state even than this.

* * *

I had at first most to do with my immediate superior, the associate editor, Alice Corbin Henderson. Alice was small, crisp, and incisive, full of an enduring energy in spite of a frail physique, and a thorough-going modern with an unfailing ear for the cadence of a new voice. Much of the attitude of the magazine towards the experimentation in new technique which was then beginning is due to her. She plugged wittily and indefatigably for the new, the untried. She was more susceptible even than Harriet herself to the possibilities of the future. She was the first of us who truly grasped the quality of the Imagists, then beginning in London, and of the elliptical school of which T. S. Eliot became the most noted protagonist. As for me I loved the Imagists at once, but the elliptical school was for a considerable time beyond me. "But, Alice," I remember expostulating on one occasion, "I don't understand in the least what this poem means, what it is trying to say." Alice grinned up at me her impish smile. "Do you need to?" she asked. "Neither do I exactly; but it's beautiful, and it opens doors in my head. That's enough for me."

* * *

I have spoken of Alice first because, as I say, she was my immediate superior and in the beginning I saw far more of her than of the somewhat austere Miss Monroe who sat behind the supreme editorial desk. It took time for me to realize how deeply human and warm-hearted Harriet Monroe was, beneath her often prickly exterior. She grew less austere, less prickly with time, but even to the end there were moments when she froze the blood of the unknowing. I have seen her look up over her glasses at some timid young thing who had with inward quaking offered a distilled essence of soul for her editorial consideration, and blast him, or her, with a caustic criticism so devastating that visibly the edges of his soul seared and curled, like the edges of an egg frying in too hot a pan. It has been one of my tasks all the years of my connection with the magazine to soften and tone down in the visiting poets these unexpected attacks of severity that sometimes seized her.

*　　*　　*

Alice Henderson said something to me too, soon after I arrived. "Working with Harriet is like swimming in a sea which has warm and cold currents. One never knows where one is. Sometimes the current is all warm, and then in a single moment it is all cold and one does not know how it happened." And that was true too, except that whenever one really needed the warm current and cried for it, it was always there.

Harriet all those years was the Mother in Israel to hundreds of young poets. She encouraged them, helped them with their work, published them when nobody else would, fed them when they were hungry, and loaned or gave them money which she could ill spare herself. I used at times to be furious with the way they imposed on her generosity. Three of them at least to my own knowledge came to her and told her they were about to commit suicide if she did not give them considerable sums of money. And of course she did. If they had known what her salary then was, perhaps they would not have done it. Only one of these was of the slightest real importance as a poet, and that infuriated me still more. One would gladly starve oneself to feed Keats, but why preserve the poetasters at the expense of Harriet Monroe? Especially when I knew very well that they would not really kill themselves. But Harriet could not see it my way, and I know that later, when I had made myself clear on the subject, she took them away from the office to give them money so I would not know it.

She was, however, strictly impersonal in her judgment of anyone's work. No amount of personal affection would make her take a poem she didn't think good enough. And on the other hand I have seen her making up the magazine, giving the coveted place of honor, the lead, to a certain poet, and seen her look up from correcting proof to say, "Ugh! How I hate that man!" without desisting from honoring him.

*　　*　　*

It would be quite wrong, however, to conclude that Harriet was one who lay down under provocation. Quite the reverse. She was a born fighter, as many a man discovered to his discomfort, a little dynamo of determination. Her crisp incisive prose attacks on careless or prejudiced thinking with regard to the poets, who were always her darlings, have done much for the cause of the art in America. And during the early years she had great need for this determination. It is hard even for me to remember, in this day when if a poet chooses he may write without complete sentences, without capitals or punctuation, even without recognizable sense, and no voice raised even to mention the fact—it is hard to realize how savage was the attack on *Poetry* when we first printed the crystalline jade-hard poems of the Imagists, those little bits many of which might have come from the Greek anthologies or from the Japanese. We were mocked in every conceivable fashion. Pieces of prose from the *Congressional Record* and like sources were chopped up into little bits and printed derisively as Imagist poems. The poems themselves were printed backward, even printed upside down in mockery. And a storm of criticism arose which used up many gallant forest trees in paper pulp. Harriet enjoyed it all, like the almost extinct war-horse. She answered many of the critics with a pen of vitriol; she lectured, she scolded and defended. And in the end she won out. The Imagists flourished and had their day, and if the fashion has gone past them now it is because they have been absorbed, not beaten down.

*   *   *

Looking back at it now, I can see that Harriet's peculiar combination of trust in her own judgment, fighting spirit, thrift, and patience made Poetry possible and pulled it through many years of life and influence. This and her warm understanding heart. All the rival poetry magazines have come and gone, and it is safe to predict that most of those which have not yet gone will soon do so. But *Poetry* has remained, a stable refuge for beauty in a fluid mechanistic universe. A month before her death she told me that it had already been published for a longer period than any other publication devoted to the art of poetry in the history of English literature. That is a fine record, and the credit for it belongs exclusively and solely to Harriet Monroe.[68]

42.

Floyd Dell

from *Homecoming*

Those who associate with artists come to envy them the spaciousness and simplicity of their studio homes. . . . The regular studios were too expensive; but there was in Chicago, besides such studio buildings, a place where artists lived, down on the South Side, by Jackson Park. There, on Stony Island Avenue fronting the Park, and on both sides of Fifty-Seventh Street, were what had once been rows of small shops, in temporary structures built at the time of the World's Fair, only one story high, without basements, and with broad plate-glass windows on each side of the door; these had never been torn down, and were now mostly inhabited by artists. The rents were very cheap; and when that summer two of them fell vacant, around the corner from each other, we left our Rogers Park apartment and moved in; Margery's place was on Stony Island Avenue, and mine on Fifty-Seventh Street, with the back doors adjoining. These places each consisted of one very large room, which could be separated into two by a temporary partition. Hers had the luxury of a bathtub, but in mine the bathing arrangements were more primitive—one stood up in an iron sink and squeezed water over oneself with a sponge. We were delighted with this bohemian simplicity; and, with so many good restaurants, there would be no occasion to do any cooking except when there was a party. In my studio there had been left by the previous occupant a huge round wooden model stand, like a turntable in the railroad switch-yards, which could be set up on a small table and made to accommodate a remarkable number of dinner guests.

*   *   *

All of us were going to write novels.[69]

43.

Eunice Tietjens

from *The World at My Shoulder*

It is not my intention, indeed it is not my place, to give here anything like a consecutive story of the magazine, nor of the history of the art which was made there. . . . Instead I shall give here certain stories of the poets as I knew them in the old days when we were all younger, and living seemed to have a core of fire.

The first shall be Carl Sandburg. Carl was in those days a tall, somewhat gawky Scandinavian, always badly dressed, always fomenting in spirit. But there was in him a passion of sympathy for anything downtrodden or hurt, and a vitality of the spirit which made everyone love him. He was working then on the *Day Book*, a small Socialist newspaper where his salary, if I remember right, was fifteen dollars a week. This was hard going for him and his quiet charming wife and his little girl, but such was Carl's loyalty to the cause that I believe he would have gone on working for it indefinitely if it had not folded up and ceased, thereby releasing to the world the undoubted genius which burned behind his blue eyes.

Floyd Dell had showed me some of his early poems, loosely woven bits of free verse, not up to his later standard, but interesting. None of them had yet been published. But I was not prepared for the sweep and vitality of the *Chicago Poems* which he brought into the office the first day I met him. They quite took us all off our feet and it was with much pride that we introduced this new star in the firmament. The poems created a great stir. There was no denying their impact, yet they roused a veritable storm of protest over what was then called their brutality. Many Chicagoans were furious at seeing the city presented in this, to them, unflattering light, and Harriet received many complaints. But we adopted Carl at once and loved him. He used to drop over often after work, and we would go out and eat pork chops—Carl always liked sustaining food—and have much fine ranging conversation on the universe in general and the injustice of man in particular. He had a deep sympathetic sense of humor which always kept him from being the usual thumping radical.

*   *   *

Sandburg showed a continuing vitality and variety in his later work, including such different successes as the life of Lincoln and *The American Songbag*, which made him for a long time the outstanding member of the group as it was then. But in those days, though his *Chicago Poems* made a great stir, it did not equal in intensity the real explosion of interest which greeted Edgar Lee Masters' *Spoon River*. Indeed I do not remember any book of poems in my day which has had the *éclat* that this book of stark condensed portraits in free verse produced. The critics throughout the country were carried away by it in a wave that almost amounted to hysteria. They kotowed in rows, bumping their heads on the ground and groveling. No words in the language were spared in praise. Masters was a second Shakespeare, a giant of almost legendary proportions. And this I believe was unfortunate for him later. For when the hysteria had passed, the critics, as is the way of human beings, bethought them that they had been somewhat undignified in their protestations. They rose, dusted themselves off, and found it necessary, in order to preserve their self-respect, to assume a condescending attitude towards Masters' later work which was quite unjust. . . .

Masters was not a young man when he wrote *Spoon River*, being then over forty. The story of his sudden finding of himself is one of the most amazing in the history of the poets and will bear repeating. He was a lawyer, had been at one time partner of

Clarence Darrow. Also he wrote poetry and plays in verse. But they were privately printed and utterly negligible, all of them. He afterwards gave me copies of them, and I searched dazedly for any spark of the great fire that burned in him when I first met him. Quite without success. They were Shelley seven times removed, pale ruminations on stars and mountains and ships of fancy, or windy historical tragedies in pedestrian blank verse. Masters has always been a prodigious worker, pouring out stuff as steadily as Old Faithful Geyser pours out water. But he has been blest with little or no literary judgment. He seems not to recognize what is good and what downright bad among his productions.

The way of his release was this. I give it here because he told it to me while it was still burning in him. He was an old friend of William Marion Reedy, then publishing the *St. Louis Mirror*, and he kept trying to persuade Reedy to publish some of his poems. But Reedy, a man of fine literary perceptions, would have none of them. And he rallied Masters.

"Why," he asked him in substance, "do you keep on writing these foolish watery lyrics and these remote fulminations? You know life. You have seen more of it than anyone I know. Why don't you write about life as you know it? Why not write something with guts in it?"

And something answered in Masters one day, some burst of creative energy engendered by rage, which swept away his complexes, his ideas of what poetry should be like, as a flood sweeps away dykes. "You want life?" he answered. "Very well, you shall have life, and by God you shall have it raw!"

So he went home, "took off his coat" metaphorically speaking, and began *Spoon River*, not thinking of the sketches as poetry, thinking of them as a means of refuting Reedy. But this astute editor recognized them for what they were and published them at once. And he called steadily for more. By the time a score of them had been published those critics with an ear to the ground were already acclaiming them. In our own office Alice Henderson picked them up and showed them about. And she wrote in the magazine the first review of them. I followed suit with a review in the *Chicago Evening Post* while they were still appearing in the *Mirror*, and others throughout the country did likewise. Thus even before the book appeared the landslide had begun. By the time it had been on the market a week the slide had become an avalanche.[70]

44.

Harriet Monroe

from *A Poet's Life*

In those days we were seeing a lot of the author of *The Spoon River Anthology*: this middle-aged dark-haired stocky Chicago lawyer was one of the most dynamic of our visitors. Edgar Lee Masters, until that first success, had had a disappointing literary history. He had brought out, since the later '90s, three or four small books of academic verse which no one had paid any attention to, using various pseudonyms to conceal his literary weakness from his clients. One morning in August, 1914, Alice, looking over our exchanges, paused with *Reedy's Mirror*, our most progressive contemporary, and I heard little exclamations of delight as she read a serial fragment of *The Spoon River Anthology*, by an unknown named "Webster Ford." She wrote up her find for our October number, quoting some of the spirit monologues of which the anthology was composed, and her selections delighted even Ezra by return mail. It was not long before the true author was revealed, not only to us but to all the world . . . which led publishers to his door and brought him immediate and enduring fame.

From that time he came often to the office of *Poetry*, and for ten years or so was a close friend of its editors. A man of the world who had gone through many excesses of experience and emotion, he had become a passionately cynical and incurably humorous observer of life. More than any human being I have ever met, he was capable of ecstasy and agony; indeed, he lived in extremes and passed from one mood to another fitfully and without warning....

A paragraph in one of Masters' letters sums up his philosophy: "I am an optimist in this sense—that there is no evil that in any wise interferes with the cosmic scheme and beauty; and though I be destroyed and cast aside, the great stream is undisturbed."[71]

45.

Eunice Tietjens

from *The World at My Shoulder*

[Masters] and I grew to be great friends and were much together. His conversation had—and still has—the greatest range of any I know. He had read everything, history, literature, law, science, and he remembered it all. His thoughts were continually grappling with the major problems of man's existence, with the place of religion, with historical perspective, with social adjustments. At times it was like listening to a major prophet. I used to hold my breath in order not to disturb him. He suffered too very greatly from the only real case of world-sorrow I have ever met. The sight of the people in the street from his office window, with their pale unhappy faces and their petty preoccupations, used at times to hurt him so greatly that he could hardly bear it. It was an impersonal sorrow, but a very real one. As Sara Teasdale said to me once, "Edgar Lee can be forgiven much, for he suffers much."

He had too at this time a tremendous hunger to know all about people, all about everyone whom he met. I have seen him throw casual people into a real panic with his direct lawyer's questions. Where did they come from? What were their parents like? What education had they had? What religion did they believe in? Why were they alive? One had the feeling that he had gone through one's personality as one of those factory knives goes through a fruit, and had extracted all that mattered in a few moments. It was a disconcerting experience and many did not appreciate it! But

Masters seemed to be quite unaware of the fact.

At times too his conversation would come suddenly down to earth. He often talked then of the *Spoon River* people as though they were real. A few of them were. He would break off some cosmic thought in the middle and begin to tell an earthy tale about old Bill Hopkins and a tailless cat—never troubling to tell me who old Bill might have been—or he would go into a huge Rabelaisian streak of pornography which was terribly startling at first. His vulgarity, in the best sense—meaning that closeness to earth and the things of the earth which is an undoubted part of every really inclusive genius—was as huge as the rest of him. I have a collection of Masters' pornography which could probably only be surpassed in the crypt of the museum at Weimar where Goethe's pornography is carefully preserved. He offended many people, among them his wife, by this streak in him, but it is an essential part of him.

When his fame was in full bloom, his exhaustless energy— his mind was like a great engine that whirled night and day, never resting, never giving him any respite—caused him to invent several imaginary personages, among whom his favorite was Dr. Elmer Chubb, LL.D., Ph.D. Dr. Chubb used to send to the periodicals eloquent vituperations, in the best style of William Jennings Bryan, whom Lee detested, against Masters and all that he stood for, bolstering them up with quotations from the Scriptures. And Masters would sometimes reply in his own person. It was a great lark, and Lee took infinite pleasure in it. He even had a handbill printed telling of a forthcoming debate, which of course could never take place, between Chubb and Masters on some forensic subject. Indeed he was rather fond of having things printed for his own amusement. I still have too a large placard with which he one day walked into the office, carrying it under his arm for me. He had been rereading *Don Quixote* and had come upon a sentence which seemed to him a fitting answer to all the bunk and welter of our civilization of which he was so acutely conscious. The card carries only this sentence: " 'All this is most important,' said Don Quixote, 'only it happens not to be so.' "

An afternoon or an evening with Masters was physically exhausting. There are persons whose mental vitality is such that ordinary people cannot follow them without strain. They seem to take the life from their listeners. Amy Lowell was such a person, but never so much so to me as Masters. I well remember that once, after I had married again and was large with child, Lee came to spend a day and a night with us where we were living in Lake Forest in Mary Aldis' "Playhouse." In the morning my husband went to work in the city, leaving Lee and me to talk the day through on the lawn, among the apple blossoms and the robins. I enjoyed it immensely, but I was so completely exhausted, not being in the best of health, that after he had gone I took to my bed for three days.[72]

46.

Edgar Lee Masters

from *Across Spoon River*

In a word, it was the really glorious year of 1914 that was making all America happy. After the Tory days of Taft, after the puerile imperialism of McKinley and Roosevelt, after a long domination by the trusts, after twenty years of Republican rule Woodrow Wilson was president and laws for the realization of the New Freedom were coming from a Congress that did not adjourn, but kept steadily at the task of reclaiming the country. The ideas of Ibsen, of Shaw, of the Irish Theatre, of advancing science, of a re-arisen liberty were blossoming everywhere, and nowhere more than in Chicago, where vitality and youth, almost abandoned in its assertion of freedom and delight, streamed along Michigan Avenue carrying the new books under their arms, or congregated at bohemian restaurants to talk poetry and the drama. All this came to my eyes as though I had been confined in darkness and had suddenly come into the sunlight. . . .

I saw that there had come into being a Chicago of which I had had but faint intimations. The town had studios where there were painters and sculptors, it had the precursors of the flappers, and here and there men and women were living together in freedom, just as they did in Paris. This year of 1914 was miraculous, not only in Chicago but over America. But right through history one can see that these joyous periods come into being only to be quickly wiped out, and generally by war.[73]

Interlude:
Ford Madox Ford & Ezra Pound in London

London was adorable then at four in the morning after a good dance. You walked along the south side of the park in the lovely pearl-gray coolness of the dawn. A sparrow would chirp with a great volume of distinct sound in the silence. Another sparrow, another—a dozen, a hundred, ten thousand. They would be like the violins of an orchestra. Then the blackbirds awakened, then the thrushes, then the chaffinches. It became the sound of an immense choir with the fuller notes of the merle family making obligatos over the chattering counterpoint of the sparrows. Then, as like as not, you turned into the house of someone who had gone before you from the dance to grill sausages and make coffee. Then you breakfasted—usually on the lead roof above a smoking room, giving on to a deep garden. There would be birds there too. Those who cannot remember London then do not know what life holds.

—Ford Madox Ford[74]

I would rather talk about poetry with Ford Madox Ford than with any man in London.

—Ezra Pound[75]

47.

Ford Madox Ford

Les Jeunes and *Des Imagistes*

I

Well, here they are, my young friends, with their lovelocks flowing from the seas beyond. . . . Let us examine the volume that they have put forth: *Des Imagistes: An Anthology.*[76]

Well, one end of this volume is Hellenic, the other extremity Sinetic, if that be the proper term for things which show a Chinese influence. The middle regions contain the very beautiful poems of Mr. Flint, which are upon the whole most what I want, since they are about this city. Indeed the most memorable of this very beautiful little collection is Mr. Flint's poem about a swan—and that is also the truest piece of Imagisme, at any rate in this volume. This poem however by Mr. Ezra Pound is more valuable as an example of what Imagisme really is (Mr. Flint's I will save for the end).

Liu Ch'e

The rustling of the silk is discontinued,
Dust drifts over the courtyard,
There is no sound of footfalls and the leaves
Scurry into heaps and lie still,
And she the rejoicer of the heart is beneath them:

A wet leaf that clings to the threshold.

That seems to me a very perfect poem of a school that I have always·
desired to see. (I should like to make it plain before going any
farther that I am not now attempting to appraise the relative
values of the poets here represented. . . .) And these verses seem
to me also extremely beautiful. They are by H. D.

> . . . The boughs of the trees
> Are twisted
> By many bafflings;
> Twisted are
> The small-leafed boughs.
> But the shadow of them
> is not the shadow of the masthead
> Nor of torn sails
>
> Hermes, Hermes,
> The great sea foamed,
> Gnashed its teeth about me;
> But you have waited
> Where sea-grass tangles with
> Shore-grass.

And here again is a poem by Mr. Richard Aldington that would
come almost exactly into the canons of my school, if I had founded
a school:

Aux Vieux Jardins

> I have sat here happy in the gardens,
> Watching the still pool and the reeds
> And the dark clouds
> Which the winds of the upper air
> Tore like the green leafy boughs
> Of the divers-hued trees of late summer;
> But though I greatly delight
> In these and the water-lilies,
> That which sets me nighest to weeping

Is the rose and white color of the smooth
  flag-stones,
And the pale yellow grasses
Among them.

These then are the poems that I most like in this anthology. Stop,
though. This [by Amy Lowell] also is very beautiful:

And I wished for night and you.
I wanted to see you in the swimming pool,
White and shining in the silver-flecked water.
While the moon rode over the garden,
High in the arch of night,
And the scent of the lilacs was heavy with stillness.

Night and the water, and you in your whiteness,
  bathing!

. . . [These poems] are almost invariably short. The effect
then of their unrhymedness is to give to swallow-flights an appre-
ciable weight, a certain dignity, a certain length. I do not know
quite about the meters. Or rather I know quite well what is my private opinion about them; but it probably differs from any explanation that would be given by the Imagistes themselves. They
would probably tell you—if you could understand what they say,
which is more than I mostly can—that rhyme and meter are shackles. And so indeed they are. Reasoning the matter out with myself,
I seem to find that the justification for vers libre is this: It allows a
freer play for self-expression than even narrative prose; at the same
time it calls for an even greater precision in that self-expression.

It is the perpetual torment, it is the *ignis-fatuus* of the artist,
in whatever medium, to seek for new forms. I do not know how
much of my time has not been spent in discussing the possibility
of finding a new form for the novel. One discusses it hopelessly,
as if it were floating in the air above the mist in which we live; one
discusses it irritatedly, as if it were a word that is forever on the tip
of the tongue and yet will never come forth. But in *vers libre* as it is

practiced today I really think that a new form has been found, if not for the novel, then for the narrative of emotion. Mr. Pound's poem that I have quoted is in reality a tiny novel, and as such it is doubly interesting to me who am only a dabbler in verse. But at any rate the immediate interest of *vers libre* is that, whatever its form, it is in its unit an expression of the author's brain-wave. The unit of formal poetry is the verse of so many lines, or the line itself. The unit of cadenced prose is the paragraph. But the unit of vers libre is really the conversational sentence of the author. As such it is the most intimate of means of expression. . . .

Let me say that this tiny anthology of the Imagistes contains an infinite amount of pure beauty—of abstract beauty. That is my simple opinion. It is the beauty of music—that is to say, of music without much meaning, but of very great power to stir the emotions. And that is the sole real province of all the arts.

Here is Mr. Flint's poem:

The Swan

Under the lily-shadow
and the gold
and the blue and mauve
that the white and the lilac
pour down on the water
the fishes quiver.

Over the green cold leaves
and the rippled silver
and the tarnished copper
of its neck and beak,
toward the deep black water
beneath the arches
the swan floats slowly.

Into the dark of the arch the swan floats
and into the black depth of my sorrow
it bears a white rose of flame.[77]

The fact is that any very clear and defined rendering of any material object has power to convey to the beholder or to the reader a sort of quivering of very definite emotions. In its very clearness and in its very hardness it seems to point to the moral of the impermanence of matter, of human life, or, if you will, of the flight of birds. You can get indeed more emotion out of the exact rendering of the light reflected in the bonnet of an automobile than out of the lamentation of fifty thousand preachers. The point is, I suppose, that just as very vivid and perfectly disproportionate emotions are aroused in you by meeting certain persons, so equally vivid emotions will be aroused if you come in contact with their manifestations, with their records, with their art. And the justification of any method of art, the measure of its success, will be just the measure of its suitability for rendering the personality of the artist.

I am thinking of course of the *vers libre* of my Imagiste friends as a vehicle for the expression of personality. Last week, if you will remember, I said that the unit of verse of the poems in this particular volume appeared to be the conversational sentences of the poet. You must, I think, be aware that whenever you frame a conversational sentence with any care you try to get into it a certain cadence. If you are merely asserting to your fishmonger your reasons for considering the prices he charges for red mullet to be exorbitant, if you are asserting it carefully, you must be aware that, whilst you are listening to his reply to your last sentence, you will be preparing in your mind, you are balancing, you are stressing the sentence with which you will reply to him. You may open your conversation with a long sentence to which he may reply as best suits his temperament. You will then utter a sentence which he may interrupt; you will probably take up your sentence and finish it, partly because you wish to convey certain facts to that fishmonger, but almost certainly very much more because your ear does not wish to be cheated of its cadence, of its stresses, of its balance. And those sentences will be extraordinarily characteristic of you. They will be more characteristic than your hands, than your eyes, than the set of your shoulders, or than the way you lift your feet when you walk. And, if any really observant friend wished to render you to an admiring or to a perturbed world, he would render you more exactly by catching the cadence of your sort of typical sentence than by almost any other means. (I do not mean to say that this is the only form characterization takes, but I certainly think it is the most subtle and the most intimate.)

And the more formal your conversation may be the more characteristic will your cadences become—the more characteristic, that is to say, of your mood at the time. If you are at a stiff and frigid tea-party you will arrange them so as to conceal emotion, but they will be nonetheless you. Or if you have ever had occasion to plead for a long time for something that you very much wanted, with a rather silent person, you will, if you take the trouble to remember—not the context of what you said, but the sound, the rhythm of your utterances—you will remember an effect like that of a sea with certain wave-lengths going on and on and on. They may be long rollers, or they may be a short and choppy sea with every seventh sentence a large wave.

And that seems to me to be the importance of the *vers libre* of this volume. It seems to me to be important not so much because of the context of the poetry as because it is a definite progress towards the intimate rendering of the writers' personalities. The vers libre that we have had up to this date has been, as far as its cadence is concerned, more or less derivative. Whitman, for instance, is nearly always blank verse, arbitrarily distributed, and as much might be said of Henley. They wrote, that is to say, rather to satisfy an existent meter, a meter evolved by ages of convention, than to satisfy the personal needs of their ears. And that is true of all other verse forms, whether the line be octosyllabic, or deca- or endecasyllabic, or spondaic, or what you will. I am not of course decrying all other forms of meter and I am not throwing rhyme to the dogs. All that I am trying to say is that verse which is cut to a pattern must sacrifice a certain amount—not necessarily very much, but still a certain amount—of the personality of the writer. And inasmuch as the personality of the writer is still the chief thing in a work of art, any form that will lead to the more perfect expression of personality is a form of the utmost value.

I suppose that what I have been aiming at all my life is a literary form that will produce the effect of a quiet voice going on talking and talking, without much ejaculation, without the employment of any verbal strangeness—just quietly saying things. Of course I do not lay that down as a canon for the whole world. The universe is very large and in it there is room for an infinite number of gods. There is room even for Mr. Marinetti's declamations of his battle-pieces. But one is very tired; writing is a hopeless sort of job, words are very hard to find, and one frequently wishes that one were dead, and so on. It is at such times that one welcomes the quiet voice that will just go on talking to one about nothing in particular, just to keep one from thinking.[78]

48.

Ezra Pound

Extract from a Letter

Poetry must be *as well written as prose*. Its language must be a fine language, departing in no way from speech save by a heightened intensity (i.e., simplicity). There must be no book words, no periphrases, no inversions. It must be as simple as De Maupassant's best prose, and as hard as Stendhal's.

There must be no interjections. No words flying off to nothing. Granted one can't get perfection every shot, this must be one's INTENTION.

Rhythm MUST have a meaning. It can't be merely a careless dash off, with no grip and no real hold to the words and sense, a tumty tum tumty tum tum ta.

There must be no clichés, set phrases, stereotyped journalese. The only escape from such is by precision, a result of concentrated attention to what one is writing. The test of a writer is his ability for such concentration AND for his power to stay concentrated till he gets to the end of his poem, whether it is two lines or two hundred.

Objectivity and again objectivity, and expression: no hind-side-beforeness, no straddled adjectives (as, "addled mosses dank"), no Tennysonianness of speech; nothing—nothing that you couldn't in some circumstance, in the stress of some emotion, actually say. Every literaryism, every book word, fritters away a scrap of the reader's patience, a scrap of his sense of your sincerity.

When one really feels and thinks, one stammers with simple speech; it is only in the flurry, the shallow frothy excitement of writing, or the inebriety of a meter, that one falls into the easy, easy—oh, how easy!—speech of books and poems that one has read.

Language is made out of concrete things. General expressions in non-concrete terms are a laziness; they are talk, not art, not creation. They are the reaction of things on the writer, not a creative act by the writer. . . . The only adjective that is worth using is the adjective that is essential to the sense of the passage, not the decorative frill adjective.[79]

✳   ✳   ✳

In Harriet Monroe's memoir, A Poet's Life, *there is a footnote to this letter, added by Ezra Pound himself*: "It should be realized that Ford Madox Ford had been hammering this point of view into me from the time I first met him (1908 or 1909) and that I owe him anything I don't owe myself for having saved me from the academic influences then raging in London."[80]

To my way of thinking, it's unfortunate that Pound didn't extend his admonition about simplicity to the way in which poets treat their subject matter. His Cantos, *for example, seem to me at times merely an exercise in obscurantism. As Pound said elsewhere about the use of symbols,* "I believe that the proper and perfect symbol is the natural object, that if a man use 'symbols' he must so use them that their symbolic function does not obtrude; so that a sense, and the poetic quality of the passage, is not lost to those who do not understand the symbol as such, to whom, for instance, a hawk is a hawk."[81] *Speaking for myself, at any rate, I would rather not have to read the* Cantos *with a scholarly exegesis by my side.*

49.

Ford Madox Ford

Those Were the Days

And indeed they were.

For you have no idea how nearly a band of filibusters, largely American, captured the citadel of Anglo-Saxon thought. So that but for mightier thunders and invasions who knows what London might not have been today—a more extended Paris? a Greenwich Village with a uniform of green billiard-cloth trousers, red side-whiskers and sombreros? . . .

I like to think that my ceaseless hammerings upon the note, that the word, written or spoken, has energies that transgress the limits of the fetters that cage or the sounds that *cabine* it. . . . I like to think that my hammerings on that note and also on the other notes—that emotions have their own peculiar cadences and that poetic ideas are best expressed by the rendering of concrete objects—had their effect on the promoters of this slender and lovely little Movement. . . .

I considered that in this group of young people were writers perfectly calculated to carry on the work that I had, not so much begun, as tried to foster in others. I desired to see English become at once more colloquial and more exact, verse more fluid and more exacting of its practitioners . . . and above all, as I have said, that it should be realized that poetry, as it were dynamically, is a matter of rendering, not comment. You must not say: "I am so happy"; you must behave as if you were happy. . . . And perhaps above all I was anxious that Anglo-Saxondom should realize that all creative prose, like all imaginative verse, is Poetry.

Well, in these young people I saw a body that appeared to be acting along the lines of my unceasing preachments. Their work had exactitude; their words came from vocabularies more actual than those of the academic writers who have made of London the city of Chinese mental stagnation that it was and is. They had beauties and actualities of ideas which they rendered rather than stated; they had a fine command of a great range of cadences— and they had a great love for the art of letters.[82]

50.

Douglas Goldring

Portrait of Ezra Pound

The transformation of [Violet Hunt's] South Lodge from a rather stuffy and conventional Campden Hill villa, into a stamping ground for *les jeunes* was brought about far more by Ezra Pound than by Ford. Ezra's irreverence towards Eminent Literary Figures was a much needed corrective to Ford's excessive veneration for those of them he elected to admire. From his room in a lodging house in the little paved court behind St. Mary Abbot's, Kensington, Ezra sallied forth in his sombrero with all the arrogance of a young, revolutionary poet who had complete confidence in his own genius. He not only subjugated Ford by his American exuberance, but quickly established himself at South Lodge as a kind of social master of ceremonies.

Opposite the house there was a communal garden containing tennis courts, which the Hunts and other local residents were accustomed to hire for their annual garden parties. Ezra immediately grasped its possibilities and having a liking for tennis which, with his long reach and lithe, wiry figure, he played excellently, insisted that the tennis courts should be made available. Ford and Violet, both of whom adored every form of entertaining and loved to be surrounded by crowds of friends, were delighted. The garden was taken over and every afternoon a motley collection of people, in the oddest costumes, invaded it at Ezra's instigation, and afterwards repaired to South Lodge—or to 84 Holland Park Avenue [the editorial office of the *English Review*]—to discuss *vers libre*, the prosody of Arnaut Daniel and, as Ford records, "the villainy of contributors to the front page of the *Times Literary Supplement*."

Of Ezra, in those days, Ford remarks: "His Philadelphian accent was comprehensible if disconcerting; his beard and flowing locks were auburn and luxuriant; he was astonishingly meager and agile. He threw himself alarmingly into frail chairs, devoured enormous quantities of your pastry, fixed his pince-nez firmly on his nose, drew out a manuscript from his pocket, threw his head back, closed his eyes to the point of invisibility and, looking down his nose would chuckle like Mephistopheles and read you a translation from Arnaut Daniel. The only part of that *albade* that you would understand would be the refrain: 'Ah me, the darn, the darn it comes toe sune.'"

I was a bit suspicious of Ezra at first, and, though I am rather ashamed to admit it, perhaps a trifle jealous of him. He struck me as a bit of a charlatan, and I disliked the showy blue glass buttons on his coat; indeed, his whole operatic outfit of "stage poet," stemming from Murger and Puccini. As I was a great admirer of [James Elroy] Flecker's poetry—and still am: it wears remarkably well—I failed to appreciate Ezra's cosmopolitan Yankee Muse, and thought much of his verse pretentious. But one day I happened to see round Ezra's pince-nez, and noticed that he had curiously kind, affectionate eyes. This chance discovery altered my whole conception of him. Perhaps it reveals part of the secret of his hold over Ford. Ezra could be a friend, and not merely a fair-weather one.

By his insistence that poets should stick together, help one another, and present a united front to the Philistine world, Ezra taught literary London a lesson which, unfortunately, it refused to learn. He was intensely proud of his calling, and on passports and other official documents always described himself as "poet," *tout court*. He was not only fundamentally genial—except, of course, to the objects of his professional scorn such as *Times* reviewers and English university professors who mocked at his claims to be regarded as an expert on Romance languages—but took a genuine pleasure in advancing the cause of other poets including those, like his compatriot T. S. Eliot, whom he might have looked on as dangerous rivals. He was as free from petty jealousy as from the least trace of servility to the Established and, like Ford, he had a wholly disinterested love of good writing.

One of his greatest triumphs in London was the way in which he stormed 18 Woburn Buildings, the Celtic stronghold of W. B. Yeats, took charge of his famous "Mondays," precisely as he took charge of the South Lodge tennis-parties, and succeeded in reducing him from master to disciple. The "later Yeats," which is now so universally admired, was unmistakably influenced by Pound. I shall never forget my surprise, when Ezra took me for the first time to one of Yeats's "Mondays," at the way in which he dominated the room, distributed Yeats's cigarettes and Chianti, and laid down the law about poetry.[83]

51.

Ford Madox Ford

Portrait of Ezra Pound

I have had a try at most things, and there was a time when I aspired to be the *arbiter elegantiarum* of the British metropolis. So, of a morning I would set out on my constitutional, arrayed in the most shining of top hats, the highest of Gladstone collars, the most ample of black-satin stock ties, the longest tailed of morning coats, the whitest of spats, the most lavender of trousers. Swinging a malacca cane with a gold knob and followed by a gray Great Dane I used to set forth on a May morning to walk in the park among all of rank and all of fashion that London had to show.

Now, to the right of me lived a most beautiful lady. She was so beautiful that Mr. Bernard Shaw broke up the City Socialist Club by drinking champagne out of her shoe. But when she was not wearing shoes she wore sandals on bare feet, draped herself in a tiger's hide, and walked bareheaded and slung with amber beads. Of a morning, being a faithful housekeeper, she also carried a string bag, which usually contained red onions, visible through the netting.

Well, almost as soon as I stood on my doorstep Fate would send that Beautiful Lady bearing down on me. At the same moment from the left Ezra would bear down. Ezra had a forked red beard, luxuriant chestnut hair, an aggressive lank figure; one long blue single stone earring dangled on his jawbone. He wore a purple hat, a green shirt, a black velvet coat, vermillion socks, open-work, brilliant tanned sandals . . . and trousers of green brilliant cloth, in addition to an immense flowing tie that had been hand-painted by a Japanese Futurist poet.

So, with the Beautiful Lady on my left and Ezra on my right, Ezra scowling at the world and making at it fencer's passes with his cane, we would proceed up Holland Park Avenue. The Beautiful Lady in the most sonorous of voices would utter platitudes from Fabian Tracts on my left, Ezra would mutter Vorticist truths half inaudibly in a singularly incomprehensible Philadelphia dialect into my right ear. *And I had to carry the string bag.* . . .

If only he would have consented to carry it, it would have been all right. I have never objected to being seen in the company of great poets and beautiful ladies, however eccentrically dressed. As it was, few of the damned can have suffered more.[84]

52.

Ezra Pound

The Legacy of Ford Madox Ford

For the ten years before I got to England there would seem to have been no one but Ford who held that French clarity and simplicity in the writing of English verse and prose were of immense importance, as in contrast to the use of a stilted traditional dialect, a "language of verse" unused in the actual talk of the people, even of "the best people," for the expression of reality and emotion. . . .

The justification or program of such writing was finally (about 1913) set down in one of the best essays (preface) that Ford ever wrote.

It advocated the prose value of verse-writing, and it, along with his verse, had more in it for my generation than all the groping (most worthily) after "quantity" (i.e., quantitative metric) of the late Laureate Robert Bridges, or the useful, but monotonous, in their day unduly neglected, as more recently unduly touted, metrical labors of G. Manley Hopkins. . . .

That Ford was almost an *halluciné* few of his intimates can doubt. He felt until it paralyzed his efficient action, he saw quite distinctly the Venus immortal crossing the tram tracks. He inveighed against Yeats' lack of emotion as, for him, proved by Yeats' so great competence in making literary use of emotion.

And he felt the errors of contemporary style to the point of rolling (physically, and if you look at it as mere superficial snob, ridiculously) on the floor of his temporary quarters in Giessen when my third volume displayed me trapped, fly-papered, gummed and strapped down in a jejeune provincial effort to learn, *mehercule*, the stilted language that then passed for "good English" in the critical circles, Newbolt, the backwash of Lionel Johnson, Fred Manning, the Quarterlies and the rest of 'em.

And that roll saved me at least two years, perhaps more. It sent me back to my own proper effort, namely, toward using the living tongue (with younger men after me), though none of us has found a more natural language than Ford did.

This is a dimension of poetry. It is, *magari*, an Homeric dimension, for of Homer there are at least two dimensions apart from the surge and thunder. Apart from narrative sense and the main construction, there is this to be said of Homer, that never can you read half a page without finding melodic invention, still fresh, and that you can hear the actual voices, as of the old men speaking in the course of the phrases.

It is for this latter quality that Ford's poetry is of high importance, both in itself and for its effect on all the best subsequent work of his time. Let no young snob forget this.[8]

Part Two: And the War Came to Europe

All July we waited. We moved as if paralyzed among our neighbors who were sure that everything would "blow over" and that it was all "hot air." Our friends teased my father when he refused to go abroad for our usual summer holiday. . . . "I cannot understand why the Germans want to fight," my father said while we were watering the garden together, "they will have world trade securely in their hands in another few years without firing a shot. . . . You must realize, Miggy," my father said as we went on tying up the tomato plants, "nothing will ever be the same."

—Bryher[86]

The German has in a strongly developed form a race-hatred for the Jew, and it was for the German for many years a source of humiliation to think that the entire banking system of Germany was in the hands of houses like those of Rothschild and Oppenheimer. The statement that was frequently made to Germans that Germany could never go to war because the Rothschilds would not allow them was apt, possibly with some reason, to cause Germans to feel not only humiliation, but deep rage and a determination to change the system.

And if I have heard once I have heard fifty times during the years 1910–11–12 expressions of the deepest satisfaction that immense joint-stock banks in the hands of Christians had largely ousted the Jews from the control of the German money-markets.

—Ford Madox Ford[87]

For generations, English sporting shotguns had been regarded all over the world as the best. Forty years ago, the sportsmen who came together to compete for the great pigeon-shooting prizes at Monte Carlo were all equipped with English weapons. About twenty years later, however, it became known that barrels of Krupp steel were superior to English barrels. First one sportsman and then another bowed to German superiority. Now, in the catalogues of British firms, you find the announcement: "Barrels of Krupp steel can be supplied for £10 extra."

—Frank Harris[88]

What the Orderly Dog Saw

A Winter Landscape
To Mrs. Percy Jackson

The seven white peacocks against the castle wall
In the high trees and the dusk are like tapestry;
The sky being orange, the high wall a purple barrier,
The canal dead silver in the dusk:
And you are far away.

Yet I see infinite miles of mountains,
Little lights shining in rows in the dark of them—
Infinite miles of marshes;
Thin wisps of mist, shimmering like blue webs
Over the dusk of them.

Great curves and horns of sea,
And dusk and dusk, and the little village;
And you, sitting in the firelight.

II

Around me are the two hundred and forty men of B
          Company,
Mud-colored;
Going about their avocations,
Resting between their practice of the art
Of killing men;
As I too rest between my practice
Of the art of killing men.
Their pipes glow over the mud and their mud-color,
          moving like fireflies beneath the trees—
I too being mud-colored—
Beneath the trees and the peacocks.
When they come up to me in the dusk

189

They start, stiffen and salute, almost invisibly.
And the forty-two prisoners from the battalion
       guard-room
Crouch over the tea-cans in the shadow of the wall.
And the bread hunks glimmer, beneath the peacocks—
And you are far away.

Presently I shall go in.
I shall write down the names of the forty-two
Prisoners in the battalion guard-room
On fair white foolscap:
Their names, rank and regimental numbers;
Corps, Companies, Punishments and Offences,
Remarks, and By whom confined.
Yet in spite of all I shall see only
The infinite miles of dark mountain,
The infinite miles of dark marshland,
Great curves and horns of sea,
The little village;
And you,
Sitting in the firelight.

—Ford Madox Ford[89]

53.

Ray Stannard Baker

from *Seen in Germany*

A stranger in Germany soon makes the acquaintance of the police, little as he may desire it. A German socialist once said: "It takes half of all the Germans to control the other half," and one who sees Germany's immense army, her cloud of officials, great and small, and her omniscient policeman, is inclined to believe that the socialist was right. You have been in Germany a week, more or less, when the policeman calls. At first you cannot believe that he is really after you, and then your mind runs back guiltily over your past. He takes out his little book, one of a small library of little books which he carries in his blouse, and inquires your age, your nationality, and how long you intend to stay. You learn subsequently that a record of every person in the empire is carefully kept, with full details as to his occupation, material wealth, and social standing. If you move into a new house, you must notify the police; if you move out, you must notify the police; if you hire a servant girl, you must purchase a yellow blank and report the fact, the girl also making a report. When she leaves, you must send in a green blank stating why she is dismissed, where she is going, and so on. If you fail in any one of these multitudinous requirements of the government—and I have mentioned only a few of them—there is a fine to pay, each fine graduated to the enormity of the offense. There are offenses graded as low as two cents.

This paternal system of watchfulness and supervision by

the police has made every German neighborhood a sort of whispering gallery. Within a few days after you move into new apartments, you find that nearly everyone in the block, from the milkman up, knows who you are, what your business is and how long you expect to remain, and your place in the social scale fixed once for all with mathematical precision. And directly you begin to pay taxes, for the police have learned, in some mysterious manner, just how much money you have in the bank, and where it comes from; if you are earning a salary they also hear about that, and all these facts speedily reach your neighbors.

* * *

War anywhere in the world mounts like strong wine to [Kaiser] William's head. He hears afar the sounds of strife, and he longs to be there to see. And sometimes he grows so excited that, like a small boy at a fire, he can't help shouting, and then the world wonders over his curious cablegrams of sympathy or encouragement. There was no more fascinated observer of our war with Spain than William of Germany; he watched every phase, he studied every maneuver, and later he used this information well in persuading his obdurate legislators that Germany must at least have a navy equal to that of the United States.

More recently he has been interested in submarine boats, and when the English pounded the old *Belle Isle* to pieces he was one of the most eager of inquirers as to the exact effect of the shells on the sides of the old hulk and in her hold. Indeed, as soon as the bare report of the tests had been telegraphed to Berlin, William was discussing them eagerly with the foreign military attachés. . . .

The German navy and the advance of German shipping are without doubt the Kaiser's strongest interests at present. Connected with this hobby, and growing out of it, is his deep enthusiasm for what is now the most striking feature of German development—commercial and industrial expansion. No monarch in Europe takes such keen interest in the industrial affairs and in the extension of the export business of his domain as William. . . .

The Kaiser is a shrewd and far-sighted man, and he sees

clearly that the great coming struggle among the nations is a struggle for commerce. Virgin continents and islands have now all been occupied; the United States has at last supplied her own vast necessities, and is preparing to enter the foreign market with huge surpluses of manufactured goods; and that nation will prosper most which secures and holds the best markets. Hence the scramble for China; hence the Kaiser's eagerness for more territory, no matter where located.

* * *

To the old "inevitables," death and taxes, the German adds a third, military service. From the time he is old enough to go to school, he looks forward and plans for it. It is said that the first great event in the life of a German boy is his confirmation, and the second his first week as a soldier. A huge red placard appears one day on the bill-posting tower so familiar to German towns. It contains a list of the names of all the young men in the district who have reached military age, and his is among them. He has been expecting it, and he knows that the authorities never forget.[90]

54.

John Maynard Keynes

Europe before the War

What an extraordinary episode in the economic progress of man that age was which came to an end in August, 1914! ... The inhabitant of London could order by telephone, sipping his morning tea in bed, the various products of the whole earth, in such quantity as he might see fit, and reasonably expect their early delivery upon his doorstep; he could at the same moment and by the same means adventure his wealth in the natural resources and new enterprises of any quarter of the world, and share, without exertion or even trouble, in their prospective fruits and advantages; or he could decide to couple the security of his fortunes with the good faith of the townspeople of any substantial municipality in any continent that fancy or information might recommend.

He could secure forthwith, if he wished it, cheap and comfortable means of transit to any country or climate without passport or other formality . . . and could then proceed abroad to foreign quarters, without knowledge of their religion, language, or customs, bearing coined wealth upon his person, and would consider himself greatly aggrieved and much surprised at the least interference.

But, most important of all, he regarded this state of affairs as normal, certain, and permanent, except in the direction of further improvement, and any deviation from it as aberrant, scandalous, and avoidable. The projects and politics of militarism and imperialism, of racial and cultural rivalries, of monopolies, restrictions, and exclusion, which were to play the serpent to this paradise, were little more than the amusements of his daily newspaper, and appeared to exercise almost no influence at all on the ordinary course of social and economic life.[91]

55.

Stefan Zweig

from *The World of Yesterday*

It may perhaps be difficult to describe to the generation of today, which has grown up amidst catastrophes, collapses, and crises, to which war has been a constant possibility and even a daily expectation, that optimism, that trustfulness in the world which had animated us young people since the turn of the century. Forty years of peace had strengthened the economic organism of the nations, technical science had given wings to the rhythm of life, and scientific discoveries had made the spirit of that generation proud; there was a sudden upsurge which could be felt in almost identical measure in all the countries of Europe. The cities grew more beautiful and more populous from year to year. The Berlin of 1905 no longer resembled the city that I had known in 1901; the capital had grown into a metropolis and, in turn, had been magnificently overtaken by the Berlin of 1910. Vienna, Milan, Paris, London, and Amsterdam on each fresh visit evoked new astonishment and pleasure.

The streets became broader and more showy, the public buildings more impressive, the shops more luxurious and tasteful. Everything manifested the increase and spread of wealth. Even we writers experienced it in the editions of our works which, within some ten years, had increased three-, five- and ten-fold. New theaters, libraries, and museums sprang up everywhere; comforts such as bathrooms and telephones, formerly the privilege of the few, became the possession of the more modestly placed, and the proletariat emerged, now that working hours had been shortened, to participate in at least the small joys and comforts of life. There was progress everywhere. Whoever ventured, won.

Whoever bought a house, a rare book, or a painting saw it increase in value; the more daring and the larger the scale on which an enterprise was founded, the more certain a profit. A wondrous unconcernedness had thus spread over the world, for what could interrupt this rapid ascent, restrict the *élan*, which constantly drew new force from its own soaring? Never had Europe been stronger, richer, more beautiful, or more confident of an even better future. None but a few shriveled graybeards bemoaned, in the ancient manner, the "good old days."

Not only the cities, the people too looked handsomer and healthier because of sports, better nutrition, shorter working hours, and a closer tie with Nature. Winter, formerly a dreary time which men spent in ill-humor at cards in the cafés, or bored in over-heated rooms, had been rediscovered on the mountain-tops as a fount of filtered sunshine, as nectar for the lungs, as delight for the flushed and ruddy skin. . . . On Sundays thousands and tens of thousands in gaudy sport coats raced down the snowbanks on skis and toboggans; sport-palaces and swimming pools appeared everywhere, and it was just in the pools that the transformation was most noticeable; whereas in my youth a really well-built man attracted attention among the thick necks, the fat bellies, and the sunken chests, now persons athletic, lithe, browned by the sun and steeled through sport vied with one another in gay competition as in the days of antiquity. None but the very poorest remained at home on Sundays, and all of youth hiked, climbed, and gamboled, schooled in every type of sport. . . . The world began to take itself more youthfully and, in contrast to the world of my parents, was proud of being young. Suddenly beards began to disappear among the young, then the elders followed lest they appear old. . . . The women threw off the corsets which had confined their breasts, and abjured parasols and veils since they no longer feared air and sunshine. They shortened their skirts so that they could use their legs freely at tennis, and were no longer bashful about displaying them if they were pretty ones.... The world had become not only more beautiful, but more free.

This health and self-confidence of the generation that succeeded mine won for itself freedom in modes and manners as well. For the first time girls were seen without governesses on excursions with their young friends, or participating in sports in frank, self-assured comradeship; they were no longer timid or prudish, they knew what they wanted and what they did not want. Freed from the anxious control of their parents, earning their own livelihood as secretaries or office workers, they seized the right to live their own lives. ... More freedom, more frankness, more spontaneity had been regained in these ten years than in the previous hundred years.

For a different rhythm prevailed in the world. None could foretell all that might happen in a single year! One discovery, one invention, followed another, and instantly was directed to the universal good; for the first time the nations sensed in common that which concerned the commonweal. On the day that the Zeppelin made its first flight I happened to be in Strasbourg on my way to Belgium when, amidst the jubilant roaring of the crowd, it circled the cathedral as if to pay homage to the thousand-year-old edifice. ... In Vienna we shouted with joy when Blériot flew over the Channel as if he had been our own hero; because of our pride in the successive triumphs of our technics, our science, a European community spirit, a European national consciousness was coming into being. How useless, we said to ourselves, are frontiers when any plane can fly over them with ease, how provincial and artificial are customs-duties, guards, and border patrols, how incongruous in the spirit of these times which visibly seeks unity and world brotherhood! This soaring of our feelings was no less wonderful than that of the planes, and I pity those who were not young during those last years of confidence in Europe.[92]

56.

Harold Stearns

from *The Street I Know*

To people a generation younger than I am it may seem incredible, the easy-come, easy-go fashion in which people went abroad in those mythical pre-war days. No red-blooded American citizen ever bothered with such nonsense as a passport; that was for diplomats and big-wigs. Your face—and your pocket-book—were what constituted sufficient passport in any country. And usually, too, you didn't decide on what boat you were going—very often, indeed, where you were going—until the last minute. It was considered quite "chic," if you had a few hundred dollars in your pocket, or had a checkbook that really warranted that amount, to step into a taxicab in front of the bar where you had been garnering Dutch courage, and say to the driver, "Pier So-and-So," and to your admiring friends, "See you in Paris next month."

* * *

Stearns arrives in England in July of 1914.

On a chance—for it was Saturday, and I thought everybody in London went out of town for the weekend in the summer—I rang up Somerset Maugham. To my surprise, he answered himself, and said, "Where are you staying?" I replied that I didn't know, as I had just got in that morning. "Well then," he said, "get your bags and come up here. I may be out when you come, and I may have to stay out for dinner, but the servant will attend to you. The address is so-and-so, Chesterfield Street, Mayfair West. In any event, I'll see you in the morning for breakfast." . . .

The Ulster and Irish situation, like everything else that summer, was very bad. Everybody was nervous about the Sarajevo business, and Maugham said that day, I recall, that the outlook was very black. After lunch we took a trip out to Windsor in the car; it was a lovely summer day, and he kept repeating that a general European war was "unthinkable." I know now—and I somewhat dimly understood and felt even at the time—that he was saying that because he *wanted* it to be unthinkable. But he was afraid of it. It was an obsession with him—as, indeed, it was with every intelligent man in Europe during those first few weeks of July, 1914. I think now that everybody in their heart of hearts knew there was going to be war—how great, how calamitous, how terrific, no; but war of some kind, and probably a general European war—just because that was what everybody *didn't* want. It is not easy for me to convey my exact feeling about this now, years after the fact, especially as I was an American—and such a thing as our ever getting into it seemed then as preposterous as a new Civil War. In fact, even the idea of a general European war seemed more like an H. G. Wells fantasy than a sober possibility. But everybody was talking about it.

*   *   *

And Stearns goes to Paris.

My conversational French was poor and halting—it was the conventional High School and year-of-college French of my day, which enabled one to read the language easily enough but was of very little help to me in speaking—and I made no attempt to enter into conversation with anybody. Besides, I wanted to read the newspapers, and I bought several, including of course *Le Temps*. Was there, after all, to be war? I couldn't understand many of the editorial arguments pro and con, but I was shocked at the tone of the comments—not at their violence, I mean to say, but at their gravity. It was obvious every editorial writer regarded war as inevitable —and the accent was ominous. But a European war! No, no, that was like one of the H. G. Wellsian fantasies of the future, which I had just been reading. "In our civilized era of 1914 a general European war is unthinkable." I kept saying that over and over to myself—and yet, somehow (perhaps it was a sort of telepathic nervousness in the air about me), I didn't believe what I was saying either. I didn't know what to believe; I felt jumpy—and alien. Almost I wished I hadn't come to Europe at all. Yet that was not true, either; it really was wonderful to be in Paris of all places at such a time. Yet . . .

After reading the newspapers I wandered around a bit more, still curious, still eager to see. Finally I went inside a restaurant, which had the usual sidewalk tables spread out on this hot night, and started to order my first meal in France. The waiter had just taken my order, when everybody was startled by a sharp, ominous crack, like a whip—yet not like a whip. I think everybody knew what it was instinctively. There was an immediate uproar, suddenly the street was crowded, and the police seemed to be everywhere. I had only seen a man topple over a table, then everything was confusion. Somebody had been murdered, I knew that. I wondered if it had anything to do with the war. I walked on for almost an hour, found a quiet little café, and sat down and had a delayed meal. But even then I noticed the quality of some of the dishes, which years later were to become as familiar to me as my own native codfish and baked beans. I should have noticed that quality even more critically, had my mind not been on that dramatic episode.

The newspapers seemed to be on the street everywhere at once. The shouts came from all sides—"*Jaurès est assassiné!*" And my heart stood still for a moment; I knew that was the spark which might kindle the whole arsenal of rebellion in Europe. Would the murder of such a man make it possible for the Socialists of the world to unite? Only they could stop the war. I knew that then instinctively. Would they do it?

I do know, no matter what the history books may tell you,

that for a few hours in Paris that night it looked almost like an even-money bet. I walked down the Boulevards, arm in arm with people I had never seen and whose language then I knew but slightly, singing with them—and my heart was in it, too—of all songs in the world to sing on the streets of Paris in the summer of 1914, the great "Internationale." As long as I live the swing and pathos of those first words will be with me: "C'est la lutte finale." . . .

Saturday morning my nervousness increased. I thought I would go out to Saint-Cloud, though not to see the races—at that time I didn't know there were races at Saint-Cloud, and even had I known it, it would have meant nothing to me. I went out by street car, and took a walk in the park near the famous Sèvres pottery works. It was still hot—abnormally, terribly hot. So, after my walk, I came back by one of the little riverboats. I got off at the Concorde landing, and walked up the Rue Royale. It was about quarter past four in the afternoon.

I noticed a crowd gathered round what looked like a bulletin-board of a post-office. Everybody was reading it—quietly, intensely, tragically. It was the order for "General Mobilization of the Forces of the Land, the Sea, and the Air."

It was war!—Everybody knew it. I knew it. It was then I heard all about me the French expression, so difficult to translate, though meaning, more or less, it has happened at last: "ça y'est!"[93]

57.

John Cournos

1914

I do not remember a more perfect Spring. The days were sunny and brisk, with that touch of softness in the air which never lapsed into sultry warmth nor relapsed into biting cold. The bright red pillar-boxes, the bright red buses and the bright red uniforms of the guards had never seemed so cheerful nor so appropriate. London could be like a dream, and during that April of 1914 it was like a dream.

The papers were repeating fragments of nightmares: woman suffrage agitation, labor difficulties, and other such things inherent in our cogwheel world. But of a war one never dreamt. Happy young couples walked arm in arm in the parks, or in the evening without reserve lay embraced in each other's arms on the grass, often mouth to mouth, for the most part utterly still, as only the English can be, little dreaming of battlefields with countless bodies embraced by death.

✳ ✳ ✳

The beginning of August. The orators were busy in Hyde Park and Trafalgar Square. They were talking against war. They were heckled by those who wanted war. The living equestrian figure of that noble-looking man, Cunningham-Graham, stood on the steps of the Nelson Column and exhorted the crowd to oppose war. A silent crowd listened to him, neither heckling nor cheering. And Jaurès had already been shot in France by a fierce patriot.

If there had been the least little doubt in anyone's mind, the invasion of Belgium resolved it. After that, it needed no diplomatic exertion on England's part, if there had been any such intention, to bring England into the war. The rape of Belgium fired English people as nothing else could have done. Germany, which believed in the *kolossal*, had committed a colossal stupidity. All you had to do was to go out into the streets among the crowds to realize it. Anti-war orators, who still dared to raise their voices, were distinctly out of luck. Yesterday they were still listened to; today they were jeered. Who will say that the people, the common people, were not moved by an honest impulse? A few days before they had had no thought of war, and no desire for war. Then, presto—as it were, in a single instant—the whole mood was changed to one of indignation, of fierce anger.

* * *

Passing a barracks, I saw men in the yard embracing one another and dancing in twos and threes—madly and wildly.[94]

58.

Julius Koettgen

from *A German Deserter's War Experience*

The following narrative first appeared in German in the columns of the New Yorker Volkszeitung, *the principal organ of the German speaking Socialists in the United States. Its author, who escaped from Germany and military service after fourteen months of fighting in France, is an intelligent young miner. He does not wish to have his name made public, fearing that those who will be offended by his frankness might vent their wrath on his relatives. . . .*

The translator hopes that he has succeeded in reproducing faithfully the substance and the spirit of the story, and that this little book will contribute in combating one of the forces that make for war—popular ignorance of war's realities. Let each individual fully grasp and understand the misery, degradation, and destruction that await him in war, and the barbarous ordeal by carnage will quickly become the most unpopular institution on earth.

At the end of July our garrison at Koblenz was feverishly agitated. Part of our men were seized by an indescribable enthusiasm, others became subject to a feeling of great depression. The declaration of war was in the air. I belonged to those who were depressed. For I was doing my second year of military service and was to leave the barracks in six weeks' time. Instead of the long wished-for return home war was facing me.

Also during my military service I had remained the antimilitarist I had been before. I could not imagine what interest I could have in the mass murder, and I also pointed out to my comrades that under all circumstances war was the greatest misfortune that could happen to humanity.

Our sapper battalion, No. 30, had been in feverish activity five days before the mobilization; work was being pushed on day and night so that we were fully prepared for war already on the 23rd of July, and on the 30th of July there was no person in our barracks who doubted that war would break out. Moreover, there was the suspicious amiability of the officers and sergeants, which excluded any doubt that anyone might still have had. Officers who had never before replied to the salute of a private soldier now did so with the utmost attention. Cigars and beer were distributed in those days by the officers with great, uncommon liberality, so that it was not surprising that many soldiers were scarcely ever sober and did not realize the seriousness of the situation. But there were also others. There were soldiers who also in those times of good-humor and the grinning comradeship of officer and soldier could not forget that in military service they had often been degraded to the level of brutes, and who now thought with bitter feelings that an opportunity might perhaps be offered in order to settle accounts.

The order of mobilization became known on the 1st of August, and the following day was decided upon as the real day of mobilization. But without awaiting the arrival of the reserves we left our garrison town on August 1st. Who was to be our "enemy" we did not know; Russia was for the present the only country against which war had been declared.

We marched through the streets of the town to the station between crowds of people numbering many thousands. Flowers were thrown at us from every window; everybody wanted to shake hands with the departing soldiers. All the people, even soldiers, were weeping. Many marched arm in arm with their wife or sweetheart. The music played songs of leave-taking. People cried and sang at the same time. Entire strangers, men and women, embraced and kissed each other; men embraced men and kissed each other. It was a real witches' sabbath of emotion; like a wild torrent, that emotion carried away the whole assembled humanity. Nobody, not even the strongest and most determined spirit, could resist that ebullition of feeling.

But all that was surpassed by the leave-taking at the station, which we reached after a short march. Here final adieus had to be said, here the separation had to take place. I shall never forget that leave-taking, however old I may grow to be. Desperately many women clung to their men; some had to be removed by force. Just as if they had suddenly had a vision of the fate of their beloved ones, as if they were beholding the silent graves in foreign lands in which those poor nameless ones were to be buried, they sought to cling fast to their possession, to retain what already no longer belonged to them.

Finally that, too, was over. We had entered a train that had been kept ready, and had made ourselves comfortable in our cattle-trucks. Darkness had come, and we had no light in our comfortable sixth-class carriages.

The train moved slowly down the Rhine, it went along without any great shaking, and some of us were seized by a worn-out feeling after those days of great excitement. Most of the soldiers lay with their heads on their knapsacks and slept. Others again tried to pierce the darkness as if attempting to look into the future; still others drew stealthily a photo out of their breast-pocket, and only a very small number of us spent the time by debating our point of destination. Where are we going to? Well, where? Nobody knew it. At last, after long, infinitely long hours the train came to a stop. After a night of quiet, slow riding we were at Aix-la-Chapelle! At Aix-la-Chapelle! What were we doing at Aix-la-Chapelle? We did not know, and the officers only shrugged their shoulders when we asked them.

After a short interval the journey proceeded, and on the evening of the 2nd of August we reached a farm in the neighborhood of the German and Belgian frontier, near Herbesthal. Here our company was quartered in a barn. Nobody knew what our business was at the Belgian frontier. In the afternoon of the 3rd of August reservists arrived, and our company was brought to its war strength. We had still no idea concerning the purpose of our being sent to the Belgian frontier, and that evening we lay down on our bed of straw with a forced tranquility of mind. Something was sure to happen soon, to deliver us from that oppressive uncertainty. How few of us thought that for many it would be the last night to spend on German soil![95]

59.

Henry N. Brailsford

On the Invasion of Belgium

No honest man defends the German invasion of Belgium. The German Chancellor himself could only avow, with a certain brutal frankness, that he was doing wrong under the pressure of some supposed necessity. The German Social Democrats have, in the Reichstag, unanimously and officially condemned this violation of public law. There is, in the terrible spectacle of the wrong done to an innocent little people by a great and highly-civilized Power, a summons to an attitude more intelligent than anger. How shall we explain it? How shall we provide against its repetition? Why was it that we in [England] could only set out to avenge what we were unable to prevent? These questions lie far beyond the scope of this pamphlet. To answer them, we need only recall the divisions which for a generation had made Europe an armed camp of rival allies. For at least ten years this universal war had been in the making, and the war that came over Serbia is the war we just escaped over Morocco, and Bosnia, and Albania. . . .

The motive which led the German Government into this crime against Belgium is not obscure. Austria had a legitimate grievance against Serbia, and Russia had intervened as the protector of the Serbs, who had been for some years the tools of Russian policy in the prosecution of Pan-Slavist ambitions, which aimed at the dismemberment of Austria. Germany intervened as the ally of Austria; France, though she had no direct concern in the quarrel, was bound by treaty to fight as Russia's ally. So far the dispute had been one of contending Imperial ambitions ... of one militarism against another, with nothing at issue save the mastery of the Near East. It was because France had allied herself with Russia, that the perils and horrors of this conflict were brought into the West.

The German staff had for twenty years been studying the strategy which it would have to follow in such a war—that is the business of general staffs, and a consequence of the armed peace and our system of alliances. It came to the conclusion that since Russia can gather her forces only very slowly, whereas France mobilizes as rapidly as Germany, the proper course to follow, when war should break out, would be to make a rapid attack with nearly all its forces on France, to beat her to her knees, and then to turn at leisure to the East to deal with Russia. Only by this plan could it hope to meet the enormous numerical superiority which France and Russia possess in combination. But a rapid attack on France would not be an easy task. France had steadily perfected the defenses of her Eastern frontier, and the German soldiers calculated that if they tried to invade through the line of barrier forts that stretches from Verdun to Belfort, they would be exposed to an attack from Russia in the rear, long before France had succumbed to their invasion. That is why they decided to invade France by way of her undefended northern frontier, in spite of Belgian neutrality.[96]

60.

Harriet Monroe

from *A Poet's Life*

When the storm broke in Europe, my feeling was of blank amazement and bitter rebellion. It was a sudden shattering of hope, a brutal denial of progress, a bloody anachronism in a civilization of peaceful industry built up slowly and painfully through many centuries. . . .

From the first we began to receive comments on the war from poets in England. D. H. Lawrence wrote from Buckinghamshire October 1, 1914: "In this god-forsaken little hole I sit like a wise rabbit with my pen behind my ear, and listen to distant noises. I am not in the war zone." When he had to be examined later for military service, of course his frail health exempted him. . . .

A year later he wrote: "How is poetry going in America? There is none in England: the muse has gone, like a swallow in winter."[97]

61.

PROTESTING WOMEN MARCH IN MOURNING

Muffled Drums Beat as the Somber Parade
Moves Down Fifth Avenue.

HATS RAISED TO PEACE FLAG

Only 1,500 Are in Line, but Crowds along Thoroughfare
Show Sympathy by Silence.

With muffled drums, a small army of women robed in black marched down Fifth Avenue from Fifty-Eighth Street to Union Square yesterday afternoon as a protest against the war. It was not a large parade, for there were no more than 1,500 marchers, but it was impressive, and the crowd that lined Fifth Avenue from the beginning to the end of the march received it almost in silence.

Here and there a woman would leap forward from the crowd of spectators and clap vigorously. In another place a man would do the same, and once two or three persons applauded at the same time, but the general silence of the great gathering was considered the best evidence of understanding. At different places men stood with raised hats as the peace flag passed.

The crowd which saw the parade was immense. It began at Fifty-Eighth Street, and from there down the avenue the people stood three deep on both sides, while children sat on the curbstones at their feet. The crowd massed on the steps of St. Patrick's

Cathedral, with its drapery of mourning for the Pope, and was greatest at the Public Library.

The parade started at 4:40, and at 5:45 it was disbanding at Union Square.

—*New York Times*, August 29, 1914

62.

Woodrow Wilson

On Neutrality

August 19, 1914.

I suppose that every thoughtful man in America has asked himself, during these last troubled weeks, what influence the European war may exert upon the United States, and I take the liberty of addressing a few words to you in order to point out that it is entirely within our own choice what its effects upon us will be and to urge very earnestly upon you the sort of speech and conduct which will best safeguard the Nation against distress and disaster. . . .

The United States must be neutral in fact as well as in name during these days that are to try men's souls. We must be impartial in thought as well as in action, must put a curb upon our sentiments as well as upon every transaction that might be construed as a preference of one party to the struggle before another.

My thought is of America. I am speaking, I feel sure, the earnest wish and purpose of every thoughtful American that this great country of ours, which is, of course, the first in our thoughts and in our hearts, should show herself in this time of peculiar trial a Nation fit beyond others to exhibit the fine poise of undisturbed judgment, the dignity of self-control, the efficiency of dispassionate action; a Nation that neither sits in judgment upon others nor is disturbed in her own counsels and which keeps herself fit and free to do what is honest and disinterested and truly serviceable for the peace of the world.[98]

* * *

December 8, 1914.

We are at peace with all the world. No one who speaks counsel based on fact or drawn from a just and candid interpretation of realities can say that there is reason to fear that from any quarter our independence or the integrity of our territory is threatened. Dread of the power of any other nation we are incapable of. We are not jealous of rivalry in the fields of commerce or of any other peaceful achievement. We mean to live our own lives as we will; but we mean also to let live. We are, indeed, a true friend to all the nations of the world, because we threaten none, covet the possessions of none, desire the overthrow of none. Our friendship can be accepted and is accepted without reservation, because it is offered in a spirit and for a purpose which no one need ever question or suspect. Therein lies our greatness. We are the champions of peace and of concord. . . .

From the first we have had a clear and settled policy with regard to military establishments. We never have had, and while we retain our present principles and ideals we never shall have, a large standing army. If asked, Are you ready to defend yourselves? we reply, Most assuredly, to the utmost; and yet we shall not turn America into a military camp. We will not ask our young men to spend the best years of their lives making soldiers of themselves. There is another sort of energy in us. It will know how to declare itself and make itself effective should occasion arise. And especially when half the world is on fire we shall be careful to make our moral insurance against the spread of the conflagration very definite and certain and adequate indeed.[99]

* * *

May 10, 1915.

The example of America must be a special example. The example of America must be the example not merely of peace because it will not fight, but of peace because peace is the healing and elevating influence of the world and strife is not. There is such a thing as a man being too proud to fight. There is such a thing as a nation being so right that it does not need to convince others by force that it is right.[100]

63.

Henry N. Brailsford

The Origins of the Great War

For Englishmen this war is primarily a struggle between Germany and France. For the Germans it is emphatically a Russo-German war. . . . To the diplomatists and the statesmen the issue was from the first not merely whether Austria or Russia should exert a hegemony in the Balkans, but also whether Russia, using Serbia as her vanguard, should succeed in breaking up the Austrian Empire.

It is not merely a tie of sentiment or kinship which unites Germany to Austria. Austria is the flying buttress of her own Imperial fabric. Cut the buttress and the fabric itself will fall. To the masses of the German people the fate of Serbia and even of Bosnia was a matter of profound indifference. A month before the war broke out, three Germans in four would probably have said that not all the Serbs in Christendom were worth the bones of one Pomeranian grenadier.[101] But the Russian mobilization and the outbreak of war made even for the German masses a supreme and only too intelligible issue.[102] There is rooted deep in the memory of the German people a recollection of the exploits of the Cossacks during the Seven Years' War. The simplest peasant of the Eastern marches has his traditions of devastated fields, and ruined villages. He knows, moreover, that the intervening generations which have transformed the West have left the Russian steppes still barbarous. Even for the Social Democrat the repugnant thought that he was marching out to shoot down his French and Belgian comrades was overborne by the imperious necessity of arming to defend his soil against the millions which the Russian Tsar had mobilized.[103]

So Russia mobilized to support her ally Serbia against the Austrians—who were seeking, after the assassination of the Archduke Ferdinand and his wife, to subdue once and for all the troublesome Balkans. France, in turn, had since the end of the nineteenth century fostered a strategic alliance with Russia, as both countries feared the increasing power and population of Germany. Perceiving a menace on both eastern and western borders, the German General Staff had developed a strategic plan to attack France first—because Russia's size made mobilization a slow process—and to overwhelm the French army in what would later be called a Blitzkrieg. *Then the Kaiser could turn his armies against the Russian hordes.*

Because of the robust French defenses along the Franco-German border, the von Schlieffen plan, as it was called, necessitated a German invasion through Belgium into northern France, with the westernmost German soldier "to brush the English Channel with his sleeve." But when the British sent their Expeditionary Force to France, stiffening the left flank of the French army, their combined forces proved too much for the German attackers, whose lines grew ever more extended and exhausted as they approached Paris, and after horrific casualties on both sides the Entente Allies turned back the German tide at the Battle of the Marne in September, 1914. Four years of bloody trench warfare ensued on the Western Front, and continuing battles in the East also resulted in enormous numbers of casualties.[104]

By the time the guns fell silent in 1918, somewhere in the neighborhood of ten million soldiers had met their deaths in Europe—and this does not include the wounded and traumatized, nor the deaths and other casualties among the civilian population. In the decade which began in August 1914, war, famine, and disease killed somewhere around one hundred million people across the globe (a conservative estimate if we take into account the influenza pandemic of 1918–1920), making the period one of the deadliest in human history. And more than a century later we are still living with its consequences—in the tumultuous Middle East, for example.

64.

Frederic C. Howe

from *Why War*

The real cause of the war is to be found far back of the summer of 1914; it is to be found in the new economic and financial forces set in motion in the closing years of the last century.

The present war and the wars of the past ten years are the result of endless conflicts and suspicions, of balked ambitions and fears, of diplomatic overreachings and injured dignity, of a thousand irritations that do not appear in the diplomatic correspondence. Present-day wars are primarily the result of the conflict of powerful economic interests radiating out from the capitals of Europe, which, with the foreign office behind them, have laid the whole world with explosives which only needed a spark to set all Europe aflame. Surplus wealth seeking privileges in foreign lands is the proximate cause of the war, just as wealth seeking monopoly profits is the cause of the civil conflicts that have involved our cities and states. It is the struggle of high finance bent on the exploitation of weaker peoples that has turned Europe into a human slaughter-house and arrayed four hundred million peaceful people against one another in a death struggle.

When the story of the war comes to be written the origin will be found hidden in the diplomatic victories and resentments over Morocco and Turkey rather than in the murder of the Archduke Ferdinand; it will be found in the aggressions of British, French, and German financiers and concession seekers rather than in the ambitions of the Czar or Kaiser; it will be found in the struggle for the exploitation of weaker peoples, of whom no less than 140 million together with ten million square miles of territory have fallen under the dominion of Great Britain, France, and Germany during the last thirty years.

These conflicts have been on a titanic scale. . . . They have created a thousand rumors, suspicions, and hatreds, a great increase in armaments for the protection of private investments; they have given birth to diplomatic intrigues and demonstrations of force that have changed a conflict of private groups into a conflict of peoples. [105]

65.

John Reed

The Traders' War

The Austro-Serbian conflict is a mere bagatelle—as if Hoboken should declare war on Coney Island—but all the Civilization of Europe is drawn in.

The real War, of which this sudden outburst of death and destruction is only an incident, began long ago. It has been raging for tens of years, but its battles have been so little advertised that they have been hardly noted. It is a clash of Traders.

It is well to remember that the German empire began as a business agreement. Bismarck's first victory was the "*Zollverein*," a tariff agreement between a score of petty German principalities. This Commercial League was solidified into a powerful state by military victories. It is small wonder that German business men believe that their trade development depends on force.

"*Ohne Armee, kein Deutschland*" ["Without an Army, no Germany"] is not only the motto of the Kaiser and the military caste. The success of the Militarist propaganda of the Navy League and other such jingo organizations depends on the fact that nine Germans out of ten read history that way. There never was any Germany worth talking about except when, under the Great Elector, Frederick the Great, and Bismarck, the Army was strong.

It is this belief, that the power and prosperity of Germany depends on its Army, which explains the surprising fact that one of the most progressive, cultured and intellectually free nations on earth allows the Kaiser to kaise.

The progressive burghers of Germany would have put an end to "personal government" and military domination long ago if they had not believed that they were threatened by their neighbors, that their very existence hinged on the strength of their Army. They have grumbled under their grievous taxes, but in the end they have paid, because they believed they were menaced.

And they *were* menaced.

After the Franco-Prussian war of 1870 came the "*grunderzeit*"—the "foundation period." Everything German leaped forward in a stupendous impulse of growth.

The withdrawal of the German mercantile marine from the sea has reminded us of the worldwide importance of their transportation services. All these great German fleets of ocean liners and merchantmen have sprung into being since 1870. In steel manufacture, in textile work, in mining and trading, in every branch of modern industrial and commercial life, and also in population, German development has been equally amazing.

But geographically all fields for development were closed. In the days when there had been no army and no united Germany, the English and French had grabbed all the earth and the fullness thereof.

No colonial markets—on which her rivals subsist—were left open to Germany. . . .

England and France met German development with distrust and false sentiments of Peace. "We do not intend to grab any more territory. The Peace of Europe demands the maintenance of the Status Quo."

With these words scarcely cold on her lips, Great Britain took South Africa. And pretended to endless surprise and grief that the Germans did not applaud this closing of another market. In 1909, King Edward—a great friend of Peace—after long secret conferences, announced the *Entente Cordiale* whereby France promised to back up England in absorbing Egypt, and England pledged to support France in her Morocco adventure.

The news of this underhand "gentleman's agreement" caused a storm. The Kaiser, in wild indignation, shouted that

"Nothing can happen in Europe without my consent."

The Peace-lovers of London and Paris agreed that this threat of war was very rude. But they were getting what they wanted without dirtying their hands in blood, so they consented to a Diplomatic Conference at Algeciras. France solemnly promised not to annex Morocco, and above all pledged herself to maintain "the Open Door." Everyone was to have an equal commercial chance. The storm blew over.

The unbiased observer must admit that the Kaiser had made a rude noise. But after all, why should anything happen in Europe without Germany being consulted? There are half a hundred million Teutons in Central Europe. They certainly have a stake in the fate of the Continent.

It was bad form for the War Lord to let off bombastic epigrams and to "rattle his sword." But it was *bad faith* for pretended advocates of Peace to conspire in secret conclave to back each other up in repudiating their engagements to preserve the Status Quo. . . .

For a couple of decades the Germans have felt that their normal industrial development was being checked on every hand—not by the forces of nature, nor their own shortcomings, but by willful, hostile, organized opposition.

Perhaps the most exasperating thing of all has been the row over the Baghdad Railroad. A group of German capitalists secured a franchise for a railroad to open up Asia Minor by way of Baghdad and the Persian Gulf. It was an undeveloped country which offered just the kind of commercial outlet they needed. The scheme was blocked by England on the pretext that such a railroad might be used by the Kaiser to send his army half-way round the world to steal India.

But the Germans understood very well that the English merchants and ship owners did not want to have their monopoly of Indian trade threatened.

Even when they scored this big commercial victory—the blocking of the Baghdad Railroad—the English diplomats protested their love of Peace and their pure-hearted desire to preserve the Status Quo. It was at this juncture that a Deputy in the Reichstag said, "The Status Quo is an aggression."

The situation in short is this. German Capitalists want more profits. English and French Capitalists want it all. This War of Commerce has gone on for years, and Germany has felt herself worsted. Every year she has suffered some new setback. The commercial "smothering" of Germany is a fact of current history.

This effort to crowd out Germany is frankly admitted by the economic and financial writers of England and France. It comes out in a petty and childish way in the popular attempts to boycott things "Made in Germany." On a larger scale it is embodied in "ententes" and secret treaties. . . .

"Every year of peace," another leader of German public opinion exclaimed, "is for us a defeat!" And every German business man believed him. And every German workingman, who thinks that his own welfare depends on the prosperity of his employer, believed it, too. . . .

No one can have a more utter abhorrence of Militarism than I. No one can wish more heartily that the shame of it may be erased from our century. . . .

But worse than the "personal government" of the Kaiser, worse even than the brutalizing ideals he boasts of standing for, is the raw hypocrisy of his armed foes, who shout for a Peace which their greed has rendered impossible.

More nauseating than the crack-brained bombast of the Kaiser is the editorial chorus in America which pretends to believe—would have us believe—that the White and Spotless Knight of Modern Democracy is marching against the Unspeakably Vile Monster of Medieval Militarism.

What has democracy to do in an alliance with Nicholas, the Tsar? Is it Liberalism which is marching from the Petersburg of Father Gapon, from the Odessa of Pogroms? Are our editors naive enough to believe this?

No. There is a falling out among commercial rivals. One side has observed the polite forms of Diplomacy and has talked of "Peace"—relying the while on the eminently pacific Navy of Great Britain and the Army of France and on the millions of semi-serfs whom they have bribed the Tsar of All the Russias (and The Hague)

to scourge forward against the Germans. On the other side there has been rudeness—and the hideous Gospel of Blood and Iron. . . .
This is not our War.[106]

66.

Scott Nearing

When the Guns Began to Shoot

Chautauqua Institution ran a summer hotel. Many faculty members who were in Chautauqua without their families stayed in the hotel and ate their meals at a big round table in the main dining room. Psychologists, musicians, historians, economists, visiting celebrities made up the membership of the select round-table company. On July 31, 1914, the usual group gathered around the faculty table for lunch. A late arrival, brandishing a newspaper, hurried into the room and sat down with the announcement: "War has broken out in Europe!"

The whole table was aghast. It fell silent, then murmuring comments began. "Surely there is some mistake." "Newspapers need headlines to sell copies. This headline is startling enough in all conscience, but it will be contradicted in a later edition." "War among the big powers of Europe? Impossible! A minor upset in the Balkans, perhaps, but not a general war." "The peoples of Europe want peace. For peace, the balance of power must be preserved. They can't do this." "A general war is unthinkable. Europe is too civilized." "If a general war actually began, every European power would be bankrupt within six weeks."

Chautauqua's highly selected, intellectual, and supposedly well-informed faculty of academic notables was unanimous in rejecting the report of a general European war. It was either an error or a fabrication. The last general war in Europe had ended in 1815 with a carefully constructed balance of power that made a general war improbable or impossible. Besides, the people of Europe did not want a general war: again and again, in one country after another, they had been organizing hundreds of thousands in mass demonstrations against war. Why should millions of Europeans tolerate something they abominated?

Socialists in the United States who had cast nearly a million votes for Eugene V. Debs, their candidate in the 1912 presidential election, had been predicting war as a logical outcome of the dog-eat-dog struggle for wealth and power and the current arms race between the big European rivals. But members of our University of Pennsylvania History Department, where I had taken undergraduate and graduate courses, had agreed that western civilization had progressed too far to permit another war such as that which had devastated Europe between 1793 and 1815. Reputable academicians in the social science field took the same position.

An American socialist, George Kirkpatrick, had written a book, *War, What For?* He explained that the frenzied struggle between British, German, and other business interests to get and keep markets for their wares and raw materials for their industries had been pushed beyond economic competition onto the field of battle. . . .

Before the war broke out in 1914, Germany was Britain's best customer in Europe. Britain was Germany's best customer. But these two countries became leaders of the two rival warring groups, fighting for markets and world power.

War in Europe gave a wonderful lift to United States business. Its economy, perched uneasily on the brink of depression, took heart and cheered up in anticipation of the war orders from both sides in the European conflict. Fears of depression lessened. Business boomed. Manufacturers, transporters, bankers were soon being flooded with orders.

This was only the beginning.[107]

67.

from the *Little Review*

Margaret Anderson

Armageddon

The greatest war of history flames away all other human concerns. Upon the reaction of humanity to this gigantic thing depends the future. No one can foresee what will happen to the cultures and the peoples which already crackle in its vortex.

*   *   *

A great newspaper has published a cartoon picturing Uncle Sam on a harvesting machine, calmly saying "Giddap" to his horses, while a neglected sheet with the inscription "European war" blows to one side. As long as devastation and horror do not exist on his own piece of land, Uncle Sam doesn't care—while he can harvest his wheat and sell it at a good high price to starving people. Even the dramatic aspect of the tremendous conflict does not impinge on his provincial consciousness. Can this contemptible attitude represent that of any great number of our people? . . .

A more creditable reaction is anger. With such titanic wrath blazing in Europe, any sensitive person must reflect a little of it. Anger at what? We don't know precisely until we stop to think. The emotion comes before the intellectual objective. Anger perhaps at the terrific human waste. Twenty-odd million men flying at each other's throats and destroying the bitterly won triumphs of years of peace, without any good reason. We hear phrases like "balance of power," "dynastic supremacy," "the life of our country," "patriotism," "racial prejudice," "difference of religion." Each individual nation is praying to God with profound sincerity for its own success.

Well, the brutal fact stands out like a giant against the sky, that if such motives can produce such a result, they are working only for their own destruction. Not a single nation, whether conqueror or victim, can come out of the struggle as strong or as great as it went in. All alike must be swept into destitution of all the things civilization has taught us to value. And this is the result of civilization![108]

68.

Brand Whitlock

from *Belgium: A Personal Narrative*

And then standing by the window, suddenly we had our first view of the German troops. Without music or fife, or drums or flag, a company of infantry came down the boulevard; they were all in gray—a sinister, lurid-greenish gray—even to the helmet-covers they wore, and they were in heavy marching order. They swung along somewhat wearily close to the Allée des Piétons at the corner where they were to turn down into the Boulevard du Jardin Botanique. Two of the men fell out of line, took their post at the corner, and lowered their rifles. One of them rested his foot in the sling of his rifle; the other drew a box of cigarettes from his tunic, proffered it to his comrade, fumbled for a match, then asked a light from a Belgian standing near. The Belgian gave it to him with Belgian kindness. A little knot of men stared at them. And that was all. It did not seem so bad.

"Poor fellows," sighed the Countess.

I assumed that the poor fellows had fallen out to mark the way for those who were to follow, though the route was already marked by arrows painted on boards that had been fixed to the trees. We waited, but no more came. . . .

We drove then to Ste.-Gudule and, at Villalobar's insistence, out onto the terrace of the old church itself, overlooking the little Place du Parvis. And there, between the hedges of the silent crowds packed along the sidewalks, slowly descending the Rue

Ste.-Gudule from the Treurenberg and turning into the Rue de la Montagne, which twisted away to our left, riding in column of twos, in the same gray uniforms, their black-and-white pennants fluttering from their lances, was a squadron of German hussars. And as they rode they chanted in rude chorus: "*Heil Dir im Siegerkranz.*"

It was very still; the crowds sullen and silent, there in the glitter of the sunlight—the horses' hoofs clattering on the stones of the uneven pavement, the lances swaying, the pennants fluttering, and that deep-throated chant, to the tune that we know as "America" and the British as "God Save the King"—and over us the gray façades of the stately old church. The scene had the aspect of medievalism; something terrible too, that almost savage chant and those gray horsemen pouring down out of the Middle Ages into modern civilization.

Villalobar turned and looked at me. "We'll remember this scene," he said.

"And think where we are!" said Bottaro-Costa, glancing up at the two lofty towers of Ste.-Gudule behind us, looking down, as calmly as they had looked for seven centuries, on a scene that was not, after all, new to them. They had seen Frenchmen and Austrians and Spaniards riding thus, singing their song of conquest.

The columns halted, the chanting ceased; the last two troopers promptly turned their horses around. No rear attacks! Then after a moment they moved again, taking up their savage hymn, and, still singing in those hoarse gutturals, wound down and away and out of sight behind the walls, the tiles and the chimney-pots, where the Rue Ste.-Gudule turns into the Rue de la Montagne, and so to the Grand Place. We thought we had seen it all, and turned away and drove back to the Italian Legation.

And as we turned into the Boulevard Bischoffsheim there was the German army. All that we had seen was but an advance guard, mere videttes, for there up and down the boulevard under the spreading branches of the trees, as far as we could see, were undulating, glinting fields of bayonets and a mighty gray, grim horde, a thing of steel, that came thundering on with shrill fifes and throbbing drums and clanging cymbals, nervous horses and lumbering guns and wild songs.

And this was Germany! Not the stolid, good-natured, smiling German of the glass of beer and tasseled pipe, whiling away a Sunday afternoon in his peaceful beer-garden, while a band played Strauss waltzes, not the sentimentality of the blue flowers and moonlight on the castled Rhine, not the poetry of Goethe and Schiller, not the insipid sweet strains of Mendelssohn nor the profound harmonies of Wagner, nor the philosophy of Immanuel Kant; but this dread thing, this monstrous anachronism, modern science yoked to the chariot of autocracy and driven by the cruel will of the pagan world.

We sat there in the motor [car] and stared at it. No one spoke for a long time. Then, as under scrutiny masses disintegrate into their component elements, we began to note individual details: the heavy guns that lurched by, their vicious mouths of steel lowered toward the ground; officers erect on their superb horses, some of them thin, of the Prussian type with cruel faces, scarred by dueling, wearing monocles and carrying English riding crops; some of the heavier type, with rolls of fat, the mark of the beast, as Emerson says, at the back of the neck, and red, heavy, brutal faces, smoking cigarettes, looking about over the heads of the silent, awed, saddened crowd with arrogant, insolent, contemptuous glances. Their equipment, of course, was perfect; sabers, revolvers in holsters, field-glasses, maps in a leather case, with isinglass to protect them, small electric lamps slung about their necks—not a detail had been overlooked in those provisions of forty-four years.

The infantry marched in column of fours with heavy methodical German precision—squat Germans for the most part, their trousers untidily thrust in their heavy boots, that drummed with iron-shod heels heavily on the pavement; an extra pair of boots dangled from each knapsack.

There were Germans of all the familiar German types: thick necks and flattened occiputs, low foreheads and yellow hair shaved closely, like convicts; stolid, indifferent faces, with no ray of mirth or humor, but now and then eyes of the pale blue of porcelain gazing through spectacles—the familiar student type. Their low spiked helmets were covered with cloth of that same greenish-gray of the uniform; every bit of metal on the uniform, indeed, was covered, and in most instances the numbers on their shoulders were similarly concealed. They were all young men, strong, with long backs and short stout legs, hard thews and sinews, and all individuality, all initiative, had been drilled out of them; they plodded on with the dumb docility of fatalism, and their officers, across the vast gulf that militarism places between officers and men, were as contemptuous of them as they were of the awed crowds along the sidewalks.[109]

69.

Julius Koettgen

from *A German Deserter's War Experience*

About ten minutes we might have lain in the grass when we suddenly heard rifle shots in front of us. Electrified, all of us jumped up and hastened to our rifles. Then the firing of rifles that was going on at a distance of about a mile or a mile and a half began steadily to increase in volume. We set in motion immediately.

The expression and the behavior of the soldiers betrayed that something was agitating their mind, that an emotion had taken possession of them which they could not master and had never experienced before. On myself I could observe a great restlessness. Fear and curiosity threw my thoughts into a wild jumble; my head was swimming, and everything seemed to press upon my heart. But I wished to conceal my fears from my comrades. I know I tried to with a will, but whether I succeeded better than my comrades, whose uneasiness I could read in their faces, I doubt very much.

Though I was aware that we should be in the firing line within half an hour, I endeavored to convince myself that our participation in the fight would no longer be necessary. I clung obstinately, nay, almost convulsively to every idea that could strengthen that hope or give me consolation. That not every bullet finds its billet; that, as we had been told, most wounds in modern wars were afflicted by grazing shots which caused light flesh-wounds; those were some of the reiterated self-deceptions indulged in against my better knowledge. And they proved effective. It was not only that they made me in fact feel more easy; deeply engaged in those thoughts I had scarcely observed that we were already quite near the firing line.

The bicycles at the side of the road revealed to us that the cyclist corps were engaged by the enemy. We did not know, of course, the strength of our opponents as we approached the firing line in leaps. In leaping forward every one bent down instinctively, whilst to our right and left and behind us the enemy's bullets could be heard striking; yet we reached the firing line without any casualties and were heartily welcomed by our hard-pressed friends. The cyclists, too, had not yet suffered any losses; some, it is true, had already been slightly wounded, but they could continue to participate in the fight.

We were lying flat on the ground, and fired in the direction indicated to us as fast as our rifles would allow. So far we had not seen our opponents. That, it seemed, was too little interesting to some of our soldiers; so they rose partly, and fired in a kneeling position. Two men of my company had to pay for their curiosity with their lives. Almost at one and the same time they were shot through the head. The first victim of our group fell down forward without uttering a sound; the second threw up his arms and fell on his back. Both of them were dead instantly.

Who could describe the feelings that overcome a man in the first real hail of bullets he is in? When we were leaping forward to reach the firing line I felt no longer any fear and seemed only to try to reach the line as quickly as possible. But when looking at the first dead man I was seized by a terrible horror. For minutes I was perfectly stupefied, had completely lost command over myself and was absolutely incapable to think or act. I pressed my face and hands firmly against the ground, and then suddenly I was seized by an irrepressible excitement, took hold of my gun, and began to fire away blindly. Little after little I quieted down again somewhat, nay, I became almost quite confident as if everything was normal. Suddenly I found myself content with myself and my surroundings, and when a little later the whole line was commanded, "Leap forward! March, march!" I ran forward demented like the others, as if things could not be other than what they were. The order, "Position!" followed, and we flopped down like wet bags. Firing had begun again.[110]

70.

May Sinclair

from *A Journal of Impressions in Belgium*

Except for sentries and straggling troops and the long trains of refugees, the country is as peaceful between Ghent and Saint Nicolas as it was last week between Ostend and Ghent. It is the same adorable Flemish country, the same flat fields, the same paved causeway and the same tall, slender avenues of trees. But if anything could make the desolation of Belgium more desolate it is this intolerable beauty of slender trees and infinite flat land, the beauty of a country formed for the very expression of peace. In the vivid gold and green of its autumn it has become a stage dressed with ironic splendor for the spectacle of a people in flight. Half the population of Antwerp and the country round it is pouring into Ghent.[III] First the automobiles, Belgian officers in uniform packed tight between women and children and their bundles, convoying the train. Then the carriages secured by the bourgeois (they are very few); then men and boys on bicycles; then the carts, and with the coming on of the carts the spectacle grows incredible, fantastic. You see a thing advancing like a house on wheels. It is a tall hay-wagon—the tallest wagon you have ever seen in your life—piled with household furniture and mattresses on the top of the furniture, and on top of the mattresses, on the roof, as it were, a family of women and children and young girls. Some of them seem conscious of the stupendous absurdity of this appearance; they smile at you or laugh as the structure goes towering and toppling by.

Next, low on the ground, enormous and grotesque bundles, endowed with movement and with legs. Only when you come up to them do you see that they are borne on the bowed backs of men and women and children. The children—when there are no bundles to be borne these carry a bird in a cage, or a dog, a dog that sits in their arms like a baby and is pressed tight to their breasts. Here and there men and women driving their cattle before them, driving them gently, without haste, with a great dignity and patience.

These, for all the panic and ruin in their bearing, might be pilgrims or suppliants, or the servants of some religious rite, bringing the votive offerings and the sacrificial beasts. The infinite land and the avenues of slender trees persuade you that it is so.

And wherever the ambulance cars go they meet endless processions of refugees; endless, for the straight, flat Flemish roads are endless, and as far as your eye can see the stream of people is unbroken; endless, because the misery of Belgium is endless; the mind cannot grasp it or take it in. You cannot meet it with grief, hardly with conscious pity; you have no tears for it; it is a sorrow that transcends everything you have known of sorrow. These people have been left "only their eyes to weep with." But they do not weep any more than you do. They have no tears for themselves or for each other.[112] This is the terrible thing, this and the manner of their flight. It is not flight, it is the vast, unhasting and unending movement of a people crushed down by grief and weariness, pushed on by its own weight, by the ceaseless impact of its ruin.[113]

71.

Irvin S. Cobb

from *Paths of Glory*

Now, too, we became aware of something else—aware of a procession that advanced toward us. It was the head of a two-mile long line of refugees, fleeing from destroyed or threatened districts on beyond. At first, in scattered, straggling groups, and then in solid columns, they passed us unendingly, we going one way, they going the other. Mainly they were afoot, though now and then a farm wagon would bulk above the weaving ranks; and it would be loaded with bedding and furniture and packed to overflowing with old women and babies. One wagon lacked horses to draw it, and six men pulled in front while two men pushed at the back to propel it. Some of the fleeing multitude looked like townspeople, but the majority plainly were peasants. And of these latter at least half wore wooden shoes so that the sound of their feet on the cobbled roadbed made a clattering chorus that at times almost drowned out the hiccupping voices of the guns behind them.

Occasionally there would be a man shoving a barrow, with a baby and possibly a muddle of bedclothing in the barrow together. Every woman carried a burden of some sort, which might be a pack tied in a cloth or a cheap valise stuffed to bursting, or a baby—though generally it was a baby; and nearly every man, in addition to his load of belongings, had an umbrella under his arm. In this rainy land the carrying of umbrellas is a habit not easily shaken off; and, besides, most of these people had slept out at least one night and would probably sleep out another, and an umbrella makes a sort of shelter if you have no better.[114]

72.

from the *Little Review*

Amy Lowell

A Letter from London

August 28, 1914.

As I sit here, I can see out of my window the Red Cross flag flying over Devonshire House. Only one short month ago I sat at this same window and looked at Devonshire House, glistening with lights, and all its doors wide open, for the duke and duchess were giving an evening party. Powdered footmen stood under the porte-cochère, and the yard was filled with motors; it was all extremely well-ordered and gay.

I watched the people arriving and leaving, for a long time. It was a very late party, and it was not only broad daylight, but brilliant sunshine, before they went home. They did have such a good time, those boys and girls, and they ended by coming out on the balcony and shouting and hurrahing for fully ten minutes. How many of those young men were among the "two thousand casualties" at the Battle of Charleroi, of which we have just got news?

Devonshire House is as busy this afternoon, but it is no longer gay. In the yard is a long wooden shed, with a corrugated iron roof; there are two doors on opposite sides, like barn doors, and black against the light of the farther door I can see men sitting at a table, and boy scouts running upon errands. The yard is filled with motors again, and there is a buzz of coming and going. Yesterday a man brought a sort of double-decked portable stretcher, with a place above and below, and a group stood round it and talked about it for a long time. For this is the headquarters of the Red Cross Society. So, in one short month, has life changed, here in London.

A month ago I toiled up the narrow stairs of a little out-house behind the Poetry Bookshop, and in an atmosphere of over-whelming sentimentality, listened to Mr. Rupert Brooke whispering his poems. To himself, it seemed, as nobody else could hear him. It was all artificial and precious. One longed to shout, to chuck up one's hat in the street when one got outside; anything, to show that one was not quite a mummy, yet.

Now, I could weep for those poor, silly people. After all they were happy; the world they lived in was secure. Today this horrible thing has fallen upon them, and not for fifty years, say those who know, can Europe recover herself and continue her development. Was the world too "precious," did it need these violent realities to keep its vitality alive? History may have something to say about that; we who are here can only see the pity and waste of it.

So little expectation of war was there, so academic the "conversations" between the powers seemed, that on the Friday preceding the declaration of war, we went down to Dorchester and Bath for a weekend outing. It was rather a shock to find the marketplace at Salisbury filled with cannon, and the town echoing with soldiers. The waiter at the inn, however, assured us that it was only maneuvers. But the next day our chauffeur, who had been fraternizing with the soldiers, told us that it was not maneuvers; they had started for maneuvers, but had been turned round, and were now on their way back to their barracks.

As we came back from Bath, on Monday, we were told that gasoline was over five shillings a can. That was practically saying that England had gone to war. But she had not, nor did she, until twelve o'clock that night. When we reached our hotel we found a state bordering on panic. There was no money to be got, and all day long, for two days, people (Americans) had been arriving from the Continent. Without their trunks, naturally. There was no one to handle trunks at the stations in Paris. These refugees were all somewhat hysterical; perhaps they exaggerated when they spoke of disorder in Paris; later arrivals seemed to think so. But we are untried in war—war round the corner. It is a terrifying nightmare which we cannot take for reality. Or could not. For it is now three weeks since the war burst over us, and already we accustom ourselves to the new condition. That is perhaps the most horrible part of it.

But that first night in London I shall never forget. A great crowd of people with flags marched down Piccadilly, shouting: "We want war! We want war!" They sang the Marseillaise, and it sounded savage, abominable. The blood-lust was coming back, which we had hoped was gone forever from civilized races.

But the Londoners are a wonderful people. Or perhaps they have no imagination. London goes on, and goes on just as it did before, as far as I can see. I understand that the American papers, possibly taking their cue from the German papers, say that London is like a military camp, that soldiers swarm in the streets, and that its usual activities are all stopped. It is not true. "Business as usual" has become a sort of motto. And it is as usual—perhaps a bit too much so. The mass of the people cannot be brought to realize the possibility of an invasion. In vain the papers warn them, they believe the navy to be invincible. And Heaven grant that it is!

When, that first week of the war, bank holiday was extended to four days instead of one; when the moratorium was declared, which exempted the banks from paying on travelers cheques and letters-of-credit; and when, to add to that, so many boats were taken off, and there were no sailings to be got for love or money, something closely approaching a panic broke out among the Americans. And what wonder! They felt caught like rats in a trap, with the impassable sea on one side and the advancing Germans on the other. For Americans have not been brought up with the tradition of England's invincibility at sea. They have heard of John Paul Jones and the *Bonhomme Richard*. And they have imagination. I was told that one woman had killed herself in an excess of fear, and I have heard of another who has had to be put in an asylum, her mind given way under the strain. Many of these people had no money, and they could not get any; they came from the Continent and had to find lodgings, and they could offer neither money nor credit. The Embassy had no way of meeting the strain flung upon it. The Ambassador is not a rich man, and the calls for money were endless. Finally some public-spirited American gentlemen started a Committee, with offices at the Hotel Savoy, to help stranded Americans. And the work they have done has been so admirable that it is hard to find words to describe it. The Committee cashes cheques, gets steamship bookings, suggests hotels and lodgings, provides clothes, meets trains. I cannot write the half it does, but it makes one exceedingly proud. I do not believe that there is an American in London who has not helped the Committee with time or money, or been helped by it.

Perhaps the panicky ones have all been cared for and gone home, or perhaps man is a very adaptable animal. But we who are still in London have settled down and accepted things. The town is not like a camp, but still regiments of soldiers in khaki pass along fairly often. And during the few days when it was my duty to meet trains at Victoria Station, no train from the South Coast either arrived or left without its quota of soldiers. We motored down to Portsmouth last Sunday, and we were stopped at the entrance to the town and asked to prove that we were not Germans. It was not a very difficult task. Portsmouth *is* swarming with soldiers, but until we reached it, the only evidence of changed conditions was the strange absence of cyclists and motorcyclists on the roads.

The other day I was waiting on a street corner. I was going to cross over and buy a paper. (The papers bring out new editions all day long, and in taxis, on buses, walking along the street, everyone is reading a paper.) Suddenly I heard someone shout my name, and there were Richard Aldington and F. S. Flint. They were in excellent spirits; Richard Aldington had just been down to put his name on the roster of those willing to enlist. Flint cannot enlist; he is already serving his country in the Post Office, and sits all day long in the most important and most dangerous building in the world next to the Bank of England. It is guarded by soldiers and surrounded by bomb-nets, but London is full of spies! I thought of the exquisite and delicate work of these two men in the anthology *Des Imagistes*, and it seemed barbarous that war should touch them—as cruel and useless as the shattering of a Greek vase by a cannon ball. I remembered the letters of Henri Regnault I had read, long ago. I remembered how he gave up his studio in Algiers and came back to fight for France, and died in the trenches. We read of these things, but when we find ourselves standing on a street corner talking to two young poets who are preparing to face the same experiences—Well! It is different!

This is one side. There is, unhappily, another. Something that one feared, and is not glad to see. There is not that realization that there should be of the danger England is in, nor that rush to defend her that one associates with the English temper. They are not enlisting as they should, and that is the bare truth of the matter. [115]And there is a certain hysteria beginning to show, which is terribly un-English, as "English" has hitherto been. The appeal to men to enlist has become almost a scream of terror. The papers are full of it, in editorials, in letters from private persons. And still the Government delays to declare general mobilization. Instead, it adopts measures which seem positively childish. Lord Kitchener asks the taxi-cabs to carry placards urging enlistment, and when some of the union cab-drivers refuse, the papers solemnly urge a patriotic public to boycott the placardless cabs. And all England is supposed to be under martial law! Could anything be more miserably humorous? It is hard to imagine Wellington asking favors of cabmen, and, when he was refused, begging the populace to punish the offenders. The following advertisement in this morning's *Times* illustrates the enthusiasm and the apathy which are rife at the same time:

> Doctor's wife, middle-aged, will undertake to perform the work of any tramway conductor, coachman, shop-assistant, or other married worker with children, provided that worker will undertake to enlist and fight for his country in our hour of need. All wages earned will be paid over to the wife and family.—Apply Mrs. Lowry, 1, Priory-terrace, Kew Green, S.W.

Perhaps one of the saddest evidences of a changed England is Mr. H. G. Wells's letter to Americans in the *Chronicle* of August 24th. For an Englishman to *implore* a foreign country to do or not to do anything, is new. Englishmen have not been used to beg weakly, with tears in their eyes.

Whatever one may think of Mr. Wells's contention in this letter, the tone in which it is written is a lamentable evidence of panic. Panic has never been an English trait, and neither has whining servility. And the Americans are the last people in the world to be moved by it. We are a just people, and we admire valor. I think Mr. Wells need not have *stooped* to ask us for justice or sympathy.

After all, it purports little to point out the spots on the sun. England is still the mother-country of most Americans, even if that was a good while ago. And we love her. She has given us not only our blood, but our civilization. Since this war broke out she has harbored us and kept her ships running for us. In Paris, one must get a permit from the police to stay or leave. In England, one is free and unmolested. England has always been the refuge of oppressed peoples. Does she need to ask our sympathy now that she is, herself, oppressed? Neutral we must be, and neutral we shall be, but we are not a military nation, and despotism can never attract us.

Every American would rather a bungling democracy than the wisest despot who ever breathed.[116]

73.

Margaret Anderson

from *My Thirty Years' War*

Harriet Monroe appeared at the door of 917 one morning with a visitor—a large and important visitor whom I have always considered among the most charming people I have known. Physically she was of such vastness that she entered the door with difficulty. She came from Brookline, Massachusetts, and her name was Amy Lowell. On my last trip to New York she had telephoned me from Brookline and I had visualized her, from her high rapid telephone voice, as a slender and imperious blond. She had wanted me to rush to Brookline and tell her about the *Little Review*. But I hadn't gone, being pressed for time. We had corresponded since that time and she had sent me poems for the magazine.

She was dressed that morning in the mode of *Godey's Lady's Book*. Culture and good taste were stamped upon her. She was brunette, her voice was contralto, her nose like a Roman emperor's and her manner somewhat more masterful. But I learned later she wept on the slightest provocation and had more feminine whims and humors than any ten women.

Her first words were congenial to me.

I've had a fight with Ezra Pound. When I was in London last fall (spring, summer?) I offered to join his group and put the Imagists on the map. Ezra refused. All right, my dear chap, I said, we'll see who's who in this business. I'll go back to America and advertise myself so extensively that you'll wish you had come in with me.

I gathered that she wanted to subsidize modern poetry and push it ahead faster than it could go by its own impetus. A little review would be a helpful organ for such a purpose.

I love the *Little Review*, she went on, and I have money. You haven't. Take me in with you. I'll pay you one hundred and fifty dollars a month, you'll remain in full control, I'll merely direct your poetry department. You can count on me never to dictate.

No clairvoyance was needed to know that Amy Lowell would dictate, uniquely and majestically, any adventure in which she had a part. I should have preferred being in the clutches of a dozen groups. So I didn't hesitate. I was barely polite.

It's charming of you but I couldn't think of it.

Your reasons?

I have only one. I can't function in "association."

Amy was furious. She concealed it. She argued, implored. I could see that she had set her mind on the idea. But she had a redeeming trait—when she was finally convinced that I meant what I said she dropped the subject and never reverted to it.

Come and lunch with me tomorrow at the Annex. . . .

When I went in she was sitting in a huge armchair, enveloped in a huge lounging robe, smoking a huge cigar.

Have a cigarette. *I* smoke cigars.

She had taken a suite, brought a friend, a secretary, and a staff of servants with her. Her meals were served in her apartment. She was sensitive about her size and never appeared in public. After lunch she dressed in her severe clothes and hat and told a servant to call a taxi.

Come with me. I'm going to Eugene Hutchinson in the Fine Arts Building to have my picture taken.

You won't need a taxi, I said. The Fine Arts Building is next door.

I always ride.

And so we stepped into the taxi . . . and stepped out again.

Amy Lowell couldn't have liked to write letters. Her conversation was often prose of quality, but the prose of her letters was oftener that of a business man.[117]

74.

from the *Little Review*

Florence Kiper Frank

The Moving-Picture Show

We sat at a moving-picture show. Over a little bridge streamed the Belgian refugees, women, children, boys, dogs, horses, carts, household goods—an incongruous procession. The faces were stolid, the feet plodded on—plodded on.

"See!" said my friend, "sometimes a woman turns to look at a bursting shell."

I murmured, "How interesting!"

And my soul shuddered. It shuddered at sophistication.

The man who had taken the pictures told us about them. He had been not more than three weeks ago in Belgium.

"Huzza!" sang my ancestor of five thousand years back. He led a band of marauders into an enemy's village. They ripped things up and tore about the place singing and looting. There was nothing much left to that village by the time they got through with it.

But the people many miles away did not behold his exploits. Alas, there were no moving-picture shows in those days.[118]

75.

Albert J. Beveridge

On the Doorstep of War

For forty-eight hours before walking down the gangplank from the ship and setting foot on Dutch soil at Rotterdam, signs and omens of the approach of danger and tragedy are plain and vivid. From the moment English shores are sighted until the gun of salute booms out upon entering the Maas, the river that leads to Rotterdam, one cannot escape the advertisements that one is entering and, indeed, is within the zone of peril.

The English search-lights glow from the far-off Lizard. On nearer approach to Dover they flash and circle and search. Just beyond this British harbor nearest to France, and at the point where the Channel is narrowest, your neutral ship is halted by a British vessel of war. Down comes your ship's wireless apparatus and down it stays, not only until your vessel is released, but almost until her prow is thrust into the waters of the North Sea. A British naval officer comes aboard and scrutinizes with the eye of a Sherlock Holmes the cargo manifest, the separate bills of lading, and anything else that may throw light on the contents of the ship's hold.

"Your passenger list, please," requests, or rather orders, this uniformed watchman at England's gates; and no biologist with a microscope ever examined more carefully his specimens than does this keen-eyed officer the names and descriptions of those who have sailed from America for this domain of turmoil and strife. Nobody may pass who might turn out to be a fighting man on Germany's side.

Two Luxembourg youths are called to the captain's cabin. The British officers (by now the examining officer has gone and two of higher rank are aboard) are decidedly suspicious. May these not be German reservists? Luckily for the young Luxembourgers, Doctor Henry van Dyke, American Minister to the Netherlands, is aboard. It is that admirable diplomatist and cultured gentleman who examines the suspected boys, for he represents America in Luxembourg as well as Holland. Also he knows intimately every foot of that tiny and charming country.

"Where do you live? How is the land on this or that side of the town? What is its location with reference to the forest? Where does the river flow?" Promptly, correctly, the test inquiries are answered. The Englishmen are convinced and the trembling young fellows sent to their quarters.

In the cargo is found copper wire. For hours the ship is detained; but, plainly, copper wire is not the cause, for it is consigned to the Dutch government. Nobody knows the reason except the British authorities, but probably someone on board is suspected of bearing communications or something else which the British do not wish to reach Germany.

When, finally, the ban is lifted and the captain told that he may go ahead, the anchor is not hauled up, for the Channel is heavily mined, and only a narrow passage between the minefield and the shore is safe, while only three or four hours beyond is the North Sea, sown with explosives. So, while it is quite safe by daylight, no chances are taken in the dark.

"Your place will be in boat No. 2, starboard." Lists of passengers, grouped and assigned to the life-boats, are posted up. Morning reveals every boat on the ship swung over the side, provisioned and ready for lowering away. Yes, surely, war is in the air! There is really very little danger, of course; but no infinitesimal precaution is neglected, for a few of the hundreds of mines have broken from their moorings and are afloat. Most of these are supposed to lose their destructive power after a few hours awash; but it is not always so.

And the life-boats! If, by the millionth chance, one of these marine bombs should strike the prow of a modern liner, she would not go down. Even if the explosion came amidships, fifteen minutes at the very least would pass before the vessel could sink; and in ten minutes at the outside, as this ship is managed, every passenger and every member of the crew could be off in those waiting life-boats, swinging so confidently from their davits over the sides. The boat goes slowly, very, very slowly through the danger zone—the Dutch captain takes no chances, runs no risks.

So, with every preparation made for every possible happening, nothing, of course, happens—so well marked is the passageway through the mine fields to the ports of neutral Holland. Whether nervous with apprehension or eagerly curious to look upon a visible cause of all this ado, everybody is secretly or openly disappointed that a mine is not at least sighted. And here comes a wireless from a sister ship, only four miles distant, that she has just passed two mines, one only a few hundred yards away and the other directly alongside. Alas!

Yet on the still and peaceful waters something is floating. It is not too far away to be seen plainly. But it is not a mine. It is not a plank or spar—it is just part of the flotsam and jetsam of war. The body of a man drifts upon the indifferent waters. Face downward it is, swimming the course of death, the dead eyes peering into the depths for the eternal mysteries. A sailor he had been, English or German, one of those who had fought in the North Sea battle a few weeks before. Thus he lingered upon the element where he had lived and worked until red combat put a period to it all.

So once again before the peaceful Netherlands shores were sighted came this reminder that the nations are in arms.[119]

76.

Edith Wharton

from *Fighting France*

We had been shown, impressively, what it was to live through a mobilization; now we were to learn that mobilization is only one of the concomitants of martial law, and that martial law is not comfortable to live under—at least till one gets used to it.

At first its main purpose, to the neutral civilian, seemed certainly to be the wayward pleasure of complicating his life; and in that line it excelled in the last refinements of ingenuity. Instructions began to shower on us after the lull of the first days: instructions as to what to do, and what not to do, in order to make our presence tolerable and our persons secure. In the first place, foreigners could not remain in France without satisfying the authorities as to their nationality and antecedents; and to do this necessitated repeated ineffective visits to chanceries, consulates, and police stations, each too densely thronged with flustered applicants to permit the entrance of one more. Between these vain pilgrimages, the traveler impatient to leave had to toil on foot to distant railway stations, from which he returned baffled by vague answers and disheartened by the declaration that tickets, when achievable, must also be *visés* by the police. There was a moment when it seemed that one's inmost thoughts had to have that unobtainable visa—to obtain which, more fruitless hours must be lived on grimy stairways between perspiring layers of fellow-aliens. Meanwhile one's money was probably running short, and one must cable or telegraph for more. Ah—but cables and telegrams must be *visés* too—and even when they were, one got no guarantee that they would be sent! Then one could not use code addresses, and the ridiculous number of words contained in a New York address seemed to multiply as the francs in one's pockets diminished. And when the cable was finally dispatched it was either lost on the way, or reached its destination only to call forth, after anxious days, the disheartening response: "Impossible at present. Making every effort." It is fair to add that, tedious and even irritating as many of these transactions were, they were greatly eased by the sudden uniform good-nature of the French functionary, who, for the first time, probably, in the long tradition of his line, broke through its fundamental rule and was kind.

Luckily, too, these incessant comings and goings involved much walking of the beautiful idle summer streets, which grew idler and more beautiful each day. Never had such blue-gray softness of afternoon brooded over Paris, such sunsets turned the heights of the Trocadéro into Dido's Carthage; never, above all, so rich a moon ripened through such perfect evenings. The Seine itself had no small share in this mysterious increase of the city's beauty. Released from all traffic, its hurried ripples smoothed themselves into long silken reaches in which quays and monuments at last saw their unbroken images. At night the fire-fly lights of the boats had vanished, and the reflections of the street lamps were lengthened into streamers of red and gold and purple that slept on the calm current like fluted water-weeds. Then the moon rose and took possession of the city, purifying it of all accidents, calming and enlarging it and giving it back its ideal lines of strength and repose. There was something strangely moving in this new Paris of the August evenings, so exposed yet so serene, as though her very beauty shielded her.

So, gradually, we fell into the habit of living under martial law. After the first days of flustered adjustment the personal inconveniences were so few that one felt almost ashamed of their not being more, of not being called on to contribute some greater sacrifice of comfort to the Cause. Within the first week over two thirds of the shops had closed—the greater number bearing on their shuttered windows the notice "Pour cause de mobilisation," which showed that the "patron" and staff were at the front. But enough remained open to satisfy every ordinary want, and the closing of the others served to prove how much one could do without. Provisions were as cheap and plentiful as ever, though for a while it was easier to buy food than to have it cooked. The restaurants were closing rapidly, and one often had to wander a long way for a meal, and wait a longer time to get it. A few hotels still carried on a halting life, galvanized by an occasional inrush of travel from Belgium and Germany; but most of them had closed or were being hastily transformed into hospitals.

The signs over these hotel doors first disturbed the dreaming harmony of Paris. In a night, as it seemed, the whole city was hung with Red Crosses. Every other building showed the red and white band across its front, with "Ouvroir" or "Hôpital" beneath; there was something sinister in these preparations for horrors in which one could not yet believe, in the making of bandages for limbs yet sound and whole, the spreading of pillows for heads yet carried high. But insist as they would on the woe to come, these warning signs did not deeply stir the trance of Paris. The first days of the war were full of a kind of unrealizing confidence, not boastful or fatuous, yet as different as possible from the clear-headed tenacity of purpose that the experience of the next few months was to develop. It is hard to evoke, without seeming to exaggerate it, that mood of early August: the assurance, the balance, the kind of smiling fatalism with which Paris moved to her task. It is not impossible that the beauty of the season and the silence of the city may have helped to produce this mood. War, the shrieking fury, had announced herself by a great wave of stillness. Never was desert hush more complete: the silence of a street is always so much deeper than the silence of wood or field.

The heaviness of the August air intensified this impression of suspended life. The days were dumb enough; but at night the hush became acute. In the quarter I inhabit, always deserted in summer, the shuttered streets were mute as catacombs, and the faintest pin-prick of noise seemed to tear a rent in a black pall of silence. I could hear the tired tap of a lame hoof half a mile away, and the tread of the policeman guarding the Embassy across the street beat against the pavement like a series of detonations. Even the variegated noises of the city's waking-up had ceased. If any sweepers, scavengers, or rag-pickers still plied their trades they did it as secretly as ghosts. I remember one morning being roused out of a deep sleep by a sudden explosion of noise in my room. I sat up with a start, and found I had been waked by a low-voiced exchange of "Bonjours" in the street. . . .

Another fact that kept the reality of war from Paris was the curious absence of troops in the streets. After the first rush of conscripts hurrying to their military bases it might have been imagined that the reign of peace had set in. While smaller cities were swarming with soldiers no glitter of arms was reflected in the empty avenues of the capital, no military music sounded through them. Paris scorned all show of war, and fed the patriotism of her children on the mere sight of her beauty. It was enough.[120]

77.

Richard Harding Davis

The Burning of Louvain

At seven o'clock in the evening we arrived at what for six hundred years had been the city of Louvain. The Germans were burning it and to hide their work kept us locked in the railroad carriages. But the story was written against the sky, was told to us by German soldiers incoherent with excesses; and we could read it in the faces of women and children being led to concentration camps and of citizens on their way to be shot.

The day before, the Germans had sentenced Louvain to become a wilderness, and with German system and love of thoroughness they left Louvain an empty, blackened shell. The reason for this appeal to the torch and the execution of non-combatants, as given to Mr. Whitlock and myself on the morning I left Brussels by General von Lutwitz, the military governor, was this: The day before, while the German military commander of the troops in Louvain was at the Hôtel de Ville talking to the burgomaster, a son of the burgomaster, with an automatic pistol, shot the chief of staff and German staff surgeons.

Lutwitz claimed this was the signal for the Civil Guard, in civilian clothes on the roofs, to fire upon the German soldiers in the open square below. He said also the Belgians had quick-firing guns, brought from Antwerp. As for a week the Germans had occupied Louvain and closely guarded all approaches, the story that there was any gun-running is absurd.

"Fifty Germans were killed and wounded," said Lutwitz, "and for that Louvain must be wiped out—so!" In pantomime with his fist he swept the papers across his table.

"The Hôtel de Ville," he added, "was a beautiful building; it is a pity it must be destroyed."

Were he telling us his soldiers had destroyed a kitchen-garden, his tone could not have expressed less regret.

Ten days before I had been in Louvain, when it was occupied by Belgian troops and King Albert and his staff. The city dates from the eleventh century, and the population was forty-two thousand. The citizens were brewers, lace-makers, and manufacturers of ornaments for churches. The university once was the most celebrated in European cities and was the headquarters of the Jesuits. In the Louvain college many priests now in America have been educated, and ten days before, over the great yellow walls of the college, I had seen hanging two American flags. I had found the city clean, sleepy, and pretty, with narrow, twisting streets and smart shops and cafés. Set in flower gardens were the houses, with red roofs, green shutters, and white walls.

Over those that faced south had been trained pear-trees, their branches, heavy with fruit, spread out against the walls like branches of candelabra. The town hall was an example of Gothic architecture, in detail and design more celebrated even than the town hall of Bruges or Brussels. It was five hundred years old, and lately had been repaired with taste and at great cost.

Opposite was the Church of St. Pierre, dating from the fifteenth century, a very noble building, with many chapels filled with carvings of the time of the Renaissance in wood, stone, and iron. In the university were one hundred and fifty thousand volumes.

Near it was the bronze statue of Father Damien, priest of the leper colony in the South Pacific, of whom Robert Louis Stevenson wrote.

On the night of the 27th these buildings were empty,, exploded cartridges. Statues, pictures, carvings, parchments, archives—all these were gone.

No one defends the sniper. But because ignorant Mexicans, when their city was invaded, fired upon our sailors, we did not destroy Vera Cruz. Even had we bombarded Vera Cruz, money could have restored that city. Money can never restore Louvain. Great architects and artists, dead these six hundred years, made it beautiful, and their handiwork belonged to the world. With torch and dynamite the Germans turned those masterpieces into ashes, and all the Kaiser's horses and all his men cannot bring them back again.

When our troop train reached Louvain, the entire heart of the city was destroyed, and the fire had reached the Boulevard Tirlemont, which faces the railroad station. The night was windless, and the sparks rose in steady, leisurely pillars, falling back into the furnace from which they sprang. In their work the soldiers were moving from the heart of the city to the outskirts, street by street, from house to house.

In each building they began at the first floor and, when that was burning steadily, passed to the one next. There were no exceptions—whether it was a store, chapel, or private residence, it was destroyed. The occupants had been warned to go, and in each deserted shop or house the furniture was piled, the torch was stuck under it, and into the air went the savings of years, souvenirs of children, of parents, heirlooms that had passed from generation to generation.

The people had time only to fill a pillow-case and fly. Some were not so fortunate, and by thousands, like flocks of sheep, they were rounded up and marched through the night to concentration camps. We were not allowed to speak to any citizen of Louvain, but the Germans crowded the windows of the train, boastful, gloating, eager to interpret.

In the two hours during which the train circled the burning city war was before us in its most hateful aspect.

In other wars I have watched men on one hilltop, without haste, without heat, fire at men on another hill, and in consequence on both sides good men were wasted. But in those fights there were no women or children, and the shells struck only vacant stretches of veldt or uninhabited mountain sides.

At Louvain it was war upon the defenseless, war upon

churches, colleges, shops of milliners and lace-makers; war brought to the bedside and the fireside; against women harvesting in the fields, against children in wooden shoes at play in the streets.

At Louvain that night the Germans were like men after an orgy.

There were fifty English prisoners, erect and soldierly. In the ocean of gray the little patch of khaki looked pitifully lonely, but they regarded the men who had outnumbered but not defeated them with calm, uncurious eyes. In one way I was glad to see them there. Later they will bear witness. They will tell how the enemy makes a wilderness and calls it war.

It was a most weird picture. On the high ground rose the broken spires of the Church of St. Pierre and the Hôtel de Ville, and descending like steps were row beneath row of houses, roofless, with windows like blind eyes. The fire had reached the last row of houses, those on the Boulevard de Jodoigne. Some of these were already cold, but others sent up steady, straight columns of flame. In others at the third and fourth stories the window curtains still hung, flowers still filled the window-boxes, while on the first floor the torch had just passed and the flames were leaping. Fire had destroyed the electric plant, but at times the flames made the station so light that you could see the second-hand of your watch, and again all was darkness, lit only by candles.

You could tell when an officer passed by, the electric torch he carried strapped to his chest. In the darkness the gray uniforms filled the station with an army of ghosts. You distinguished men only when pipes hanging from their teeth glowed red or their bayonets flashed.

Outside the station in the public square the people of Louvain passed in an unending procession, women bareheaded, weeping, men carrying the children asleep on their shoulders, all hemmed in by the shadowy army of gray wolves. Once they were halted, and among them were marched a line of men. These were on their way to be shot. And, better to point the moral, an officer halted both processions and, climbing to a cart, explained why the men were to die. He warned others not to bring down upon themselves a like vengeance.

As those being led to spend the night in the fields looked across to those marked for death they saw old friends, neighbors of long standing, men of their own household. The officer bellowing at them from the cart was illuminated by the headlights of an automobile. He looked like an actor held in a spot light on a darkened stage.

It was all like a scene upon the stage, unreal, inhuman. You felt it could not be true. You felt that the curtain of fire, purring and crackling and sending up hot sparks to meet the kind, calm stars, was only a painted backdrop; that the reports of rifles from the dark ruins came from blank cartridges, and that these trembling shopkeepers and peasants ringed in bayonets would not in a few minutes really die, but that they themselves and their homes would be restored to their wives and children.

You felt it was only a nightmare, cruel and uncivilized. And then you remembered that the German Emperor has told us what it is. It is his Holy War.[121]

78.

Julius Koettgen

from *A German Deserter's War Experience*

It was dark already, and we halted once more. The ground around us was strewn with dead. In the middle of the road were some French batteries and munition wagons, with the horses still attached; but horses and men were dead. After a ten minutes' rest we started again. Marching more quickly, we now approached a small wood in which dismounted cavalry and infantry were waging a desperate hand-to-hand struggle with the enemy. So as to astonish the latter we had to rush in with a mighty yell. Under cover of darkness we had succeeded in getting to the enemy's rear. Taken by surprise by the unexpected attack and our war whoop, most of the Frenchmen lifted their hands and begged for quarter, which was, however, not granted by the infuriated cavalrymen and infantry. When, on our side, now and then the murdering of defenseless men seemed to slacken it was encouraged again by the loud commands of the officers. "No quarter!" "Cut them all down!" Such were the orders of those estimable gentlemen, the officers. . . .

The dead and wounded lay everywhere covered with terrible injuries, and the crying of the wounded, which might soften a stone, but not a soldier's heart, told of the awful pain which those "defenders of their country" had to suffer.

However, not all the soldiers approved of that senseless, that criminal murdering. Some of the "gentlemen" who had ordered us to massacre our French comrades were killed "by mistake" in the darkness of the night, by their own people, of course. Such "mistakes" repeat themselves almost daily, and if I keep silence with regard to many such mistakes which I could relate, giving the exact name and place, the reader will know why.

During that night it was a captain and first lieutenant who met their fate. An infantryman who was serving his second year stabbed the captain through the stomach with his bayonet, and almost at the same time the first lieutenant got a stab in the back. Both men were dead in a few minutes. Those that did the deeds showed not the slightest signs of repentance, and not one of us felt inclined to reproach them; on the contrary, everyone knew that despicable, brutal murderers had met their doom.

In this connection I must mention a certain incident which necessitates my jumping a little ahead of events. When on the following day I conversed with a mate from my company and asked him for the loan of his pocket knife, he drew from his pocket three cartridges besides his knife. I was surprised to find him carrying cartridges in his trousers' pocket and asked him whether he had no room for them in his cartridge case. "There's room enough," he replied, "but those three are meant for a particular purpose; there's a name inscribed on each of them." Sometime after—we had meanwhile become fast friends—I inquired again after the three bullets. He had one of them left. I reflected and remembered two sergeants who had treated us like brutes in times of peace, whom we had hated as one could only hate slave-drivers. They had found their graves in French soil.[122]

79.

E. Alexander Powell

from *Fighting in Flanders*

We were the first foreigners to see Aerschot, or rather what was left of Aerschot after it had been sacked and burned by the Germans. A few days before, Aerschot had been a prosperous and happy town of ten thousand people. When we saw it, it was but a heap of smoking ruins, garrisoned by a battalion of German soldiers, and with its population consisting of half a hundred white-faced women. In many parts of the world I have seen many terrible and revolting things, but nothing so ghastly, so horrifying as Aerschot.

Quite two-thirds of the houses had been burned and showed unmistakable signs of having been sacked by a maddened soldiery before they were burned. Everywhere were the ghastly evidences. Doors had been smashed in with rifle-butts and boot-heels; windows had been broken; furniture had been wantonly destroyed; pictures had been torn from the walls; mattresses had been ripped open with bayonets in search of valuables; drawers had been emptied upon the floors; the outer walls of the houses were spattered with blood and pock-marked with bullets; the sidewalks were slippery with broken wine-bottles; the streets were strewn with women's clothing. It needed no one to tell us the details of that orgy of blood and lust. The story was so plainly written that anyone could read it.

For a mile we drove the car slowly between the blackened

walls of fire-gutted buildings. This was no accidental conflagration, mind you, for scattered here and there were houses which stood undamaged and in every such case there was scrawled with chalk upon their doors, *"Gute Leute. Nicht zu plündern."* (Good people. Do not plunder.) The Germans went about the work of house-burning as systematically as they did everything else. They had various devices for starting conflagrations, all of them effective. At Aerschot and Louvain they broke the windows of the houses and threw in sticks which had been soaked in oil and dipped in sulfur. Elsewhere they used tiny, black tablets, about the size of cough lozenges, made of some highly inflammable composition, to which they touched a match. At Termonde, which they destroyed in spite of the fact that the inhabitants had evacuated the city before their arrival, they used a motor-car equipped with a large tank for petrol, a pump, a hose, and a spraying-nozzle. The car was run slowly through the streets, one soldier working the pump and another spraying the fronts of the houses. Then they set fire to them. Oh, yes, they were very methodical about it all, those Germans.

Despite the scowls of the soldiers, I attempted to talk with some of the women huddled in front of a bakery waiting for a distribution of bread, but the poor creatures were too terror-stricken to do more than stare at us with wide, beseeching eyes. Those eyes will always haunt me. I wonder if they do not sometimes haunt the Germans. But a little episode that occurred as we were leaving the city did more than anything else to bring home the horror of it all. We passed a little girl of nine or ten and I stopped the car to ask the way. Instantly she held both hands above her head and began to scream for mercy. When we had given her some chocolate and money, and had assured her that we were not Germans, but Americans and friends, she ran like a frightened deer. That little child, with her fright-wide eyes and her hands raised in supplication, was in herself a terrible indictment of the Germans.

*   *   *

Half a mile or so out of Sotteghem our road debouched

into the great highway which leads through Lille to Paris, and we suddenly found ourselves in the midst of the German army. It was a sight never to be forgotten. Far as the eye could see stretched solid columns of marching men, pressing westward, ever westward. The army was advancing in three mighty columns along three parallel roads, the dense masses of moving men in their elusive gray-green uniforms looking for all the world like three serpents crawling across the country-side.

The American flags which fluttered from our windshield proved a passport in themselves, and as we approached the close-locked ranks parted to let us pass, and then closed in behind us. For five solid hours, traveling always at express-train speed, we motored between walls of marching men. In time the constant shuffle of boots and the rhythmic swing of gray-clad arms and shoulders grew maddening, and I became obsessed with the fear that I would send the car ploughing into the human hedge on either side. It seemed that the interminable ranks would never end, and so far as we were concerned they never did end, for we never saw the head of that mighty column.

We passed regiment after regiment, brigade after brigade of infantry; then hussars, cuirassiers, uhlans, field batteries, more infantry, more field-guns, ambulances with staring red crosses painted on their canvas tops, then gigantic siege-guns, their grim muzzles pointing skyward, each drawn by thirty straining horses; engineers, sappers and miners with picks and spades, pontoon-wagons, carts piled high with what looked like masses of yellow silk but which proved to be balloons, bicyclists with carbines slung upon their backs hunter-fashion, aeroplane outfits, bearded and spectacled doctors of the medical corps, armored motor-cars with curved steel rails above them as a protection against the wires which the Belgians were in the habit of stringing across the roads, battery after battery of pom-poms (as the quick-firers are descriptively called), and after them more batteries of spidery-looking, lean-barreled machine-guns, more uhlans—the sunlight gleaming on their lance-tips and the breeze fluttering their pennons into a black-and-white cloud above them, and then infantry in spiked and linen-covered helmets, more infantry and still more infantry—all sweeping by, irresistibly as a mighty river, with their faces turned towards France.

This was the Ninth Field Army, composed of the very flower of the German Empire, including the magnificent troops of the Imperial Guard. It was first and last a fighting army. The men were all young, and they struck me as being as keen as razors and as hard as nails. Their equipment was the acme of efficiency, serviceability and comfort. The color of their uniforms was better than any of the shades of khaki; a hundred yards away a regiment seemed to melt into the landscape.[123]

80.

Julius Koettgen

from *A German Deserter's War Experience*

We now advanced quickly, but our participation was no longer necessary, for the whole line of the enemy retired and then faced us again, a mile and a quarter southwest of Sommepy. Sommepy itself was burning for the greater part, and its streets were practically covered with the dead. The enemy's artillery was still bombarding the place, and shells were falling all around us. Several hundred prisoners were gathered in the market-place. A few shells fell at the same time among the prisoners, but they had to stay where they were. An officer of my company, lieutenant of the reserve Neesen, observed humanely that that could not do any harm, for thus the French got a taste of their own shells. He was rewarded with some cries of shame. A Socialist comrade, a reservist, had the pluck to cry aloud, "Do you hear that, Comrades? That's the noble sentiment of an exploiter; that fellow is the son of an Elberfeld capitalist and his father is a sweat-shop keeper of the worst sort. When you get home again do not forget what this capitalist massacre has taught you. Those prisoners are proletarians, are our brethren, and what we are doing here in the interest of that gang of capitalist crooks is a crime against our own body; it is murdering our own brothers!" He was going to continue talking, but the sleuths were soon upon him, and he was arrested. He threw down his gun with great force; then he quietly suffered himself to be led away.

All of us were electrified. No one spoke a word. One suddenly beheld quite a different world. We had a vision which kept our imagination prisoner. Was it true what we had heard—that those prisoners were not our enemies at all, that they were our brothers? That which formerly—O how long ago might that have been—in times of peace had appeared to us as a matter of course, had been forgotten; in war we had regarded our enemies as our friends and our friends as our enemies. Those words of the Elberfeld comrade had lifted the fog from our brains and from before our eyes. We had again a clear view; we could recognize things again.

One looked at the other and nodded without speaking; each one felt that the brave words of our friend had been a boon to us, and none could refrain from inwardly thanking and appreciating the bold man. The man in front of me, who had been a patriot all along as far as I knew, but who was aware of my views, pressed my hand, saying, "Those few words have opened my eyes; I was blind; we are friends. Those words came at the proper time." Others again I heard remark: "You can't surpass Schotes; such a thing requires more courage than all of us together possess. For he knew exactly the consequences that follow when one tells the truth. Did you see the last look he gave us? That meant as much as, Don't be concerned about me; I shall fight my way through to the end. Be faithful workers; remain faithful to your class!"[124]

81.

Mildred Aldrich

from *A Hilltop on the Marne*

Such talks as I listened to that afternoon—only yesterday—at my gate, from such a fluent, amusing, clever French chap—a bicyclist in the ambulance corps—of the crossing of the Meuse and the taking, losing, re-taking, and re-losing of Charleroi. Oddly enough these were the first real battle tales I had heard. . . . But this French lad of the ambulance corps, with his Latin eloquence and his national gift of humor and graphic description, with a smile in his eyes and a laugh on his lips, told me stories that made me see how war affects men, and how often the horrible passes across the line into the grotesque. I shall never forget him as he stood at the gate, leaning on his wheel, describing how the Germans crossed the Meuse—a feat which cost them so dearly that only their superior number made a victory out of a disaster.

"I suppose," he said, "that in the history of the war it will stand as a success—at any rate, they came across, which was what they wanted. We could only have stopped them, if at all, by an awful sacrifice of life. Joffre is not doing that. If the Germans want to fling away their men by the tens of thousands—let them. In the end we gain by it. We can rebuild a country; we cannot so easily re-create a race. We mowed them down like a field of wheat, by the tens of thousands, and tens of thousands sprang into the gaps. They advanced shoulder to shoulder. Our guns could not miss them, but they were too many for us. If you had seen that crossing

I imagine it would have looked to you like a disaster for Germany. It was so awful that it became comic. I remember one point where a bridge was mined. We let the first divisions of artillery and cavalry come right across on to our guns—they were literally destroyed. As the next division came on to the bridge—up it went—men, horses, guns dammed the flood, and the cavalry literally crossed on their own dead. We are bold enough, but we are not so foolhardy as to throw away men like that. They will be more useful to Joffre later."

It was the word "comic" that did for me. There was no sign in the fresh young face before me that the horror had left a mark. If the thought came to him that every one of those tens of thousands whose bodies dammed and reddened the flood was dear to someone weeping in Germany, his eyes gave no sign of it. Perhaps it was as well for the time being. Who knows?

I felt the same revolt against the effect of war when he told me of the taking and losing of Charleroi and set it down as the most "grotesque" sight he had ever seen. "Grotesque" simply made me shudder, when he went on to say that even there, in the narrow streets, the Germans pushed on in "close order," and that the French *mitrailleuses* [machine-guns], which swept the street that he saw, made such havoc in their ranks that the air was so full of flying heads and arms and legs, of boots and helmets, swords and guns, that it did not seem as if it could be real—"it looked like some burlesque"; and that even one of the gunners turned ill and said to his commander, who stood beside him: "For the love of God, Colonel, shall I go on?" and the colonel, with folded arms, replied: "Fire away."[125]

82.

Julius Koettgen

from *A German Deserter's War Experience*

Most of the soldiers made no attempt to conceal the feeling that we poor devils had absolutely nothing to gain in this war, that we had only to lose our lives or, which was still worse, that we should sit at some street corner as crippled "war veterans," trying to arouse the pity of passers-by by means of some squeaking organ. At that moment it was already clear to us in view of the enormous losses that no state, no public benevolent societies, would be able after the war to help the many hundreds of thousands who had sacrificed their health for their "beloved country." The number of the unfortunate wrecks is too great to be helped even with the best of intentions.

*   *   *

It was getting light, and as yet we had not seen much of the enemy. Slowly the mist began to disappear, and now we observed the French occupying positions some hundred yards in front of us. They had made themselves new positions during the night exactly as we had done. Immediately firing became lively on both sides. Our opponent left his trench and attempted an attack, but our great mass of machine-guns literally mowed down his ranks. An infernal firing had set in, and the attack was beaten off after only a few steps had been made by the opposing troops. The

French renewed their attack again and again, and when at noon we had beaten back eight assaults of that kind, hundreds upon hundreds of dead Frenchmen were covering the ground between our trenches and theirs. The enemy had come to the conclusion that it was impossible to break down our iron wall and stopped his attacks.

At that time we had no idea that this was to be the beginning of a murderous exhausting war of position, the beginning of a slow, systematic, and useless slaughter. For months and months we were to fight on in the same trench, without gaining or losing ground, sent forward again and again to murder like raving beasts, and driven back again. Perhaps it was well that we did not know at that time that hundreds of thousands of men were to lose their lives in that senseless slaughter.

The wounded men between the trenches had to perish miserably. Nobody dared help them as the opposing side kept up their fire. They perished slowly, quite slowly. Their cries died away after long hours, one after the other. One man after the other had lain down to sleep, never to awake again. Some we could hear for days; night and day they begged and implored one to assist them, but nobody could help. Their cries became came softer and softer until at last they died away—all suffering had ceased. There was no possibility of burying the dead. They remained where they fell for weeks. The bodies began to decompose and spread pestilential stenches, but nobody dared to come and bury the dead.

If a Frenchman showed himself to look for a friend or a brother among the dead he was fired at from all directions. His life was dearer to him and he never tried again. We had exactly the same experience. The French tried the Red Cross flag. We laughed and shot it to pieces. The impulse to shoot down the "enemy" suppressed every feeling of humanity, and the "red cross" had lost its significance when raised by a Frenchman. Suspicion was nourished artificially, so that we thought the "enemy" was only abusing the flag; and that was why we wanted to shoot him and the flag to bits.

But we ourselves took the French for barbarians because they paid us back in kind and prevented us from removing our own wounded men to safety. The dead remained where they were, and when ten weeks later we were sent to another part of the front they were still there.[126]

83.

Eugen Wiener

On January 22, 1883, my mother's maternal grandmother, Marie Cohen—for whom my mother was named—had a son she named Eugene. As an adult, he was my mother's favorite uncle, and she named me Eugene—my middle name—in his memory. Marie Cohen had emigrated to America when she was eighteen, and by the time Eugene was born she was living with her husband Max and the rest of their family in Brooklyn, where Max worked for Horace Greeley. A year later Marie's sister Rebecca, who was still living in East Prussia, had a son whom she also named Eugene—or Eugen in German—though he was called "Schnuff" as a kid. Rebecca died at 26, when Eugen was just a year and a half old, and he and his younger sister Hedwig were raised in their uncle Hugo's family.

By 1914, Eugen was living in Charlottenburg, an affluent district of Berlin, working in a shop selling women's lingerie. He had married Mietzi Jacob and they had a daughter named Ruth, born on October 31, 1912. Like other Germans, after he finished his compulsory military service he remained in the Reserves, the Landwehr. There's a photograph in the archives of the Jewish Museum in Berlin, showing him with fourteen fellow reservists on summer maneuvers in 1913. There's also a photo of him—taken in 1914—alone, in full uniform, posing with his rifle.[127]

In August 1914, after Russia had begun to mobilize its army to support Serbia against the Austrians, Germany began to mobilize as well, and Eugen was called up along with the rest of the German army.

After the German invasion of France was stopped at the Battle of the Marne, the German army retreated to northern France and made a last desperate attempt to outflank the Allied troops at the English channel in Flanders—part of the so-called Race to the Sea. General Alexander von what was left of the Belgian army—with disastrous results to themselves and the civilian population. Eugen took part in this campaign. His regiment, the 207th Reserve Infantry, was part of the 44th Reserve Division, and the fighting along the Yser was their first engagement of the war.

Eugen Wiener, 1914

After the war, Mietzi married Hugo Simon, and their families were successful in the German ready-to-wear fashion industry, centered in Berlin. They had a summer "estate" in the exclusive Gross Glienicke area and played a part in the world of the German avant-garde, which included Marlene Dietrich and was made familiar to the English-speaking world by Christopher Isherwood's Berlin Stories. In 1940, they managed to escape the Nazis, emigrating to Brazil, where Ruth later joined them—having herself originally fled to South Africa.

Eugen's sister Hedwig married a businessman named Paul Glaserfeld, and they escaped the Nazis by emigrating to America shortly before Pearl Harbor, when the United States had not yet declared war on Germany and Japan. He died in 1955 and after my mother and father moved to New York, she and my mother became quite close. I remember her only as an old woman who spoke with a heavy German accent, and who was always very kind to me.[128]

84.

E. Ashmead-Bartlett

The Battle of Nieuport-Dixmude

Antwerp had fallen and the remnants of the Belgian Army had fallen back until only a few square miles of Belgium soil remained to that unhappy people. The army, under the King, had taken up a strong position with its left resting on the sea at Nieuport, and its right on the town of Dixmude. The front of the army was covered by the river Yser and a network of canals. General Joffre had promised the support of the French troops, but these had not yet come up. South of the Belgians' right at Dixmude there came a great gap in the Allied line which was now being gradually filled up by the arrival of Sir John French's army, which was coming up by degrees from the Aisne. The German General Staff was preparing a giant blow with over a half a million fresh men supported by immense masses of heavy artillery to break through to Calais and seize the Channel coast, thus hoping to dominate our lines of communication with France.

*　　*　　*

The country over which this great struggle took place is absolutely flat. You can motor all over it without ever having to change your gear, in fact there are no elevations. There are numerous good roads connecting the picturesque Flemish towns and villages, for like the whole of Belgium, the countryside is (or rather was) densely populated. For the last two days the German Army, which had been set free by the fall of Antwerp, assisted by fresh corps, which had apparently come up from Brussels, had been making the most desperate efforts to break through the line of the Yser and to turn the Belgians out of the old town of Dixmude.

*   *   *

Imagine a perfectly flat country dotted with towns and villages, all of which were in flames. Imagine your horizon about two miles in front a continuous line of smoke, which completely blotted out all else beyond. Imagine shells screaming and bursting over every one of these villages and farms, and falling into the fields beyond. Everywhere you saw the white puffs of shrapnel and the great black clouds rising in spirals, as the "Jack Johnsons" blew houses, churches, and mother earth into smithereens.

Men are not often visible in modern war, because to make any show at all against the infernal machinations of Messrs. Krupp, Schneider, Creusot and Co. they must bury themselves in the earth, and only rise up to shoot if their enemy is sufficiently foolhardy to show himself. But on this occasion the shell fire from the German batteries was so terrific that the Belgian soldiers and the French marines were continually being blown out of their dugouts and houses and were sent scampering to cover elsewhere. Also little groups of peasants and dwellers in the towns, who had not fled before, were now forced to flee, because even their cellars had begun to fall in.

These unfortunates had to make their way as best they could on foot to the rear, frightened almost to death by the bursting shells. Even children were amongst these refugees, and their cries of alarm were perhaps the saddest incident of this ghastly day.

*   *   *

It was just at this moment before dusk that the Germans chose to deliver their final grand attack, which they hoped would cut through the Allies' left and open the road to Dunkirk. Their artillery redoubled its fire. They could no longer find the Belgian batteries out in the open, and these, taking advantage of this fact, opened a terrible and sustained cannonade on the German infantry.

It seemed as if the Germans were trying to turn Dixmude from the south, and the little village of St. Jacques-Cappelle became the scene of a furious infantry combat. The rifle fire and *mitrailleuses* never ceased for a moment. The bullets seemed to be everywhere. The French supports could not get up for some time, as it was impossible to pass through Dixmude owing to the shells and burning buildings. The wounded came crawling and limping in from the trenches, each with a different tale. Some said the French and Belgians were holding their own, others that it was all over, and that in a few minutes the Germans would have possession of the town.

Suddenly the German artillery fire ceased for a few minutes, and we heard through the gathering darkness shouts which sounded like "Ja, ja." A French soldier told me it was the Germans charging with the bayonet. This was the crisis. The cheers were met by a redoubled rifle fire and the terrible "pat-pat-pat-pat-pat" of the machine-guns. The Belgian batteries fired in salvos, the shells all bursting in groups of red flame over the advancing infantry. The cheers died away and once more the German field batteries and "Jack Johnsons" recommenced their shelling.

It was now 7 p.m. and quite dark. . . . Diksmuide was a red furnace. The flames shot upwards, showing clouds of white smoke above. St. Jacques, farther south, was a smaller furnace. All along the line the shells were no longer bursting in clouds of white and black smoke. All had put on their blood-red mantles. Close at hand everything was bathed in inky darkness; farther off the burning towns and buildings showed up clearer than they had during the day.[129]

85.

Mietzi Jacob

After long, anxious weeks, it was only today that I became sadly certain that my dearly beloved, good husband, the devoted father of my child, our dear son, brother, son-in-law, brother-in-law and nephew, Eugen Wiener, Corporal in Reserve Infantry Regiment No. 207, holder of the Iron Cross, succumbed at the age of 31, in the hospital at Thourout, to the injuries he suffered in the assault on Dixmuiden on October 31st.

In deepest pain, in the name of all those left behind,
Frau Mietze Wiener, née Jacob, Charlottenburg,
Niebuhrstr. 2.
We thank you for your condolences.[130]

Käthe Kollwitz's youngest son, Peter, was also a member of the 207th Reserve Infantry Regiment; he was killed in October 1914 during the fighting along the Yser River. Her famous monument to his memory, and to parental grief, stands in the German war cemetery at Vladslo, near Diksmuide—where the remains of Eugen Wiener are also buried. Eugen died on November 2, 1914, of wounds received in the Battle of Diksmuide on October 31—the same day, sadly, as his daughter Ruth's second birthday.

86.

Arthur Ruhl

from Antwerp to Gallipoli

After breakfast, I ran into a young man whom I had last seen in a white linen uniform, waiting patiently on the orderlies' bench of the American Ambulance [Corps] at Neuilly. The Ambulance [Corps] is as hard to get into as an exclusive club, for the woods are full these days of volunteers who, leading rather decorative lives in times of peace, have been shaken awake by the war into helping out overtaxed embassies, making beds in hospitals, doing whatever comes along with a childlike delight in the novelty of work. This young man wore a Red Cross button now and paused long enough to impart the following—characteristic of the things we non-combatants hear daily, and which, authentic or not, help to a make life interesting: an English general just down from the front had told him that four thousand soldiers had been sent out as a burial party after the fighting along the Yser, and had buried, by actual count, thirty-nine thousand Germans.

* * *

I found myself the other evening, after zigzagging all over Berlin with an address given me at a typewriter agency, in a little apartment on the outskirts of the town. The woman who lived there had been a stenographer in the city until the war cut off her business, and she was now supporting herself with the six marks (one dollar and fifty cents) weekly war benefit given by the municipality, and by making soldiers' shirts for the War Department at fifty pfennigs (twelve and one-half cents) a shirt. She was glad to get typewriting, and without words on either side at once got to work. So we proceeded for a page or two until something was said about an Iron Cross stuck inside a soldier's coat.

"That is the Iron Cross of the second class," she interrupted; "they put that inside. The first class they wear outside," and, as if she could keep still no longer, she suddenly flung out, almost without a pause:

"My brother has the Iron Cross. I have seven brothers in the army. Three are in the east and three are in the west, and one is in the hospital. He was shot three times in the leg—here—and here—and here. They hope to save his leg, but he will always be lame. He got the Iron Cross. He was at Diksmuide. They marched up singing Deutschland über Alles. They were all shot down. There were three hundred of them, and every one fell. They knew they must all be shot, but they marched on just the same, singing *Deutschland über Alles*. They knew they were going against the English, and nothing could stop them. . . .

"I told you," she said, "when you first came in, that I was German. And I asked you if you were an American, because I know that dreadful things have been said in America about our Kaiser, and I will not have such things said to me. Our Kaiser did not want the war—he did everything he could to prevent the war—no ruler in the world ever did more for his people than our Kaiser has done, and there is not a man, woman, or child in Germany who would not fight for him." And this, you must remember, was from a woman whose support was cut off by the war and who was making a living by sewing shirts at twelve and a half cents a shirt.[131]

87.

Julius Koettgen

from *A German Deserter's War Experience*

Those soldiers who had been in the war from the start who had not been wounded, but had gone through all the fighting, were gradually all sent home on furlough for ten days. Though our company contained but fourteen unwounded soldiers it was very hard to obtain the furlough. We had lost several times the number of men on our muster-roll, but all our officers were still in good physical condition.

It was not until September that I managed to obtain furlough at the request of my relations, and I left for home with a resolve that at times seemed to me impossible to execute. . . .

After the first hours of meeting all at home again had passed I found myself provided with faultless underwear and had taken the urgently needed bath. Once more I could put on the civilian dress I had missed for so long a time. All of it appeared strange to me. I began to think. Under no conditions was I going to return to the front.

*   *   *

Julius never does return to the army. He acquires false identification papers from a friend and barely avoids being arrested in a hotel close to the border. After hiding in the woods he manages to evade a routine patrol and successfully crosses to the Netherlands. From there he makes his way to New York City.

*   *   *

I hid in the thick underwood; open country was in front of me. I remained at that spot for three days and nights. It rained and at night it was very chilly. On the evening of the third day I resolved to execute my plan that night.

Regularly every fifteen minutes a patrol of from three to six soldiers arrived. When it had got dark I changed my place for one more to the right, some five hundred yards from the frontier. I said to myself that I would have to venture out as soon as it got a little lighter. In the darkness I could not see anything. It would have to be done in twilight. I had rolled my overcoat into a bundle to avoid making a noise against the trees. I advanced just after a patrol had passed. I went forward slowly and stepped out cautiously without making a noise. Then I walked with ever increasing rapidity. Suddenly a patrol appeared on my right. The frontier was about three hundred yards away from me. The patrol had about two hundred yards to the point of the frontier nearest to me. Victory would fall to the best and swiftest runner. The patrol consisted of five men; they fired several times. That did not bother me. I threw everything away and, summoning all my strength, I made in huge leaps for the frontier which I passed like a whirlwind. I ran past the pointed frontier stone and stopped fifty yards away from it. I was quite out of breath, and an indescribable happy feeling took hold of me. I felt like crying into the world that at last I was free.[132]

88.

Mary Heaton Vorse

from *A Footnote to Folly*

I drove through a smiling, fruitful country over whose surface graves were everywhere scattered—they died fast along these country roads. In the grain were crosses, in the dooryards of what had once been peasants' houses, more crosses. Here and there in the pleasant wood, trees had been mown down as by a scythe—and when the road led to a town, one found heaps of brick, tortured ironwork, and shapeless mounds of stone. In strange contrast to the general desolation, scattered seemingly at random, were occasional wooden houses—temporary dwellings which the English Quakers, in cooperation with the French government, had been building.

Paris was terrible, but far worse was the lovely northern country. There was a sense of emptiness, as if terror still hushed the normal, cheerful noises of mankind. The people had lost everything, their houses were burnt, their animals were gone even to the rabbits, their farm implements were shapeless pieces of grotesquely melted iron. They lived in temporary patched shelters and in the houses built by the Society of Friends, or crowded together in some near-by village that had escaped destruction at the hands of the Crown Prince's retreating army.

After a time in this quiet silent country I got the sense that destruction was normal. Tears started to my eyes at the sight of an undestroyed French village, sitting in the sun. So changed were all the values that I could feel nothing strange in the words of a woman who said, "Fortunately my husband is a hunchback." Through the quiet countryside came soldiers, or a band of wounded men staggered and groped their way on their first walk forth from the hospital gates. Except for these, from one week's end to another, one would see no young men....

Next day I met one of the heroic schoolmistresses, who had been nicknamed "Mayor of Soissons." In the village which was recorded "totally destroyed," one house had been rebuilt. This one house served as schoolhouse and *mairie* [town hall]. The schoolmistress was a youngish woman, frail and delicate, lines of anxiety and overwork on her intelligent face. She and an assistant teacher instructed eighty children. It was her energy and resourcefulness that caused the reconstruction of this one house. She also acted as mayor of the village—the mayor himself was mobilized, as was the *curé*; this meant that she took upon herself much of the relief work that the *curé* would naturally have performed....

"Two thousand French soldiers fell in the battlefield over there"—she nodded toward the open window—"and I am, of course, still answering the inquiries of their families."

I looked out the window. Here indeed was the Biblical word fulfilled—"Not one stone shall remain upon another." What had been an orderly French village was a heap of stones and rubble; only rearing their heads, fireless amid the general destruction, were the chimneys and the hearthstones, as though the foyer—the heart of France—refused to be destroyed. Beside this, Pompeii was habitable—it looked as if some great natural calamity, known as an act of God, had passed over it. So it seemed.

Then came to me the intolerable thought: Man did this thing! No incredible cataclysm of nature, but man.

I looked from this work of man to the toil-burdened schoolmistress, who, in the midst of this desolation, had assembled her children, and I contrasted her work with that for which the men of Europe had been preparing, and one nation so supremely well and with such loving care.

The careful Germans had brought with them solid petroleum cans with which to burn the villages through which they passed. An old man standing in his flowering garden showed me the can that had escaped in the general conflagration; he called it the "little souvenir which the Prussians had left" him. The Germans even brought paraffin with which to burn the manure heaps, so that in case they should not hold the land the civil population might suffer to the utmost.

Nearby I found an old woman working in her flower garden. No dwelling of man was now near that garden, only the shapeless ruins of what had once been houses. All about was the quiet of the country and fields—fields studded with graves, graves and ruins—and that garden bright with peonies and other flowering things, and the old woman working it. She looked up from her weeding to offer me flowers.

"Of course, my garden is not what it may be another year," she told me, "for I have walked eight miles to get here, and I cannot always come; but I cannot bear the thought of losing them altogether; flowers, you know, require cultivation."

*   *   *

As I went about on this strange sightseeing . . . there came to me a knowledge of what a war means to the civil population.

Day by day among the *sinistrés* [refugees] I heard stories of flight from burning villages, until such a flight seemed a usual experience. I heard tales of lost relations. I saw women searching for old mothers. I saw refugees who had lost little children. I listened to the dreadful prattle of children who talked of killing. I saw the listless girls who had witnessed the death of all dear to them. I saw women sitting with folded hands, their means of livelihood gone, their husbands gone, their reason for living gone.

I saw little children below the age of speech who had been found wandering on the roads by soldiers, Belgian children who had been found in the very trenches where they had fled terrified during the bombardment. No one can ever know who they are, their mothers will never see them again.[133]

89.

Robert Dunn

from *Five Fronts*

The Cholera Trail to Przemysl

Przemysl, Galicia (Austrian Poland), October 25–November 3.
Remember, that for all one reads of France and Belgium,
this eastern war theatre is by far the greater both in length of firing
line and numbers engaged. The line extends from the Baltic Sea
to Rumania, now that the German and Austrian armies are joined.
Here three nations with some six million men in arms face one
another in unending battle.

But a nearer marvel lies in the contrast, both human and
military, between the war here and the war in the west; and in that
difference there is a resemblance of significance for Americans.
Yesterday as we pushed our car over the high divide between two
forks of the San, no veteran of our War of the Secession could have
stood among those yellowing birches and believed his eyes. Arms
bandaged in slings, limping, bracing themselves with sticks, the
wounded slipped and tottered down the hills—afoot, mind you,
in muddy gray uniforms and high-fronted caps, almost the exact
color and design of the South's. It was 1864, not 1914. It was as if
the years between had profited mankind nothing, the world had
not moved since then. . . .

By three o'clock in the afternoon we had passed seven
trains. In one I counted twenty-seven cars, with but a single sur-

geon aboard. And from the battlefields in this region alone at least three lines of rail are open. Ever since the war began I have been haunted with the thought that no human agencies could, with all justice to modern altruism and science, cope with the masses of wounded. Here, for the first time, the truth of such a speculation hit me concretely. As the jammed cars ground westward, the great red crosses on them, the "Kranke" in black letters underneath, began to dance in the back of my mind. Vanished, those shadowy crosses still flew over the weeping willows of the roadsides, over the high thatchings, green with moss, of the peasants' log hovels. And you knew that over with the Russians the same pitiful cargoes were trundling eastward.

Still they passed us. Arms were thrust out from bandages, holding caps, which we showered with cigarettes. The men shouted and scrambled for them. Tied to the button on each man's right shoulder was a small white tag, noting the nature and location of his hurt. Occasionally at a halt some grimed and hairy fellow would step off for a moment upon the lime of the white trail, dragging after him a bandaged foot. And your one thought was: It all cannot last long—it never, never can last. . . .

We followed the route of the Russian retreat. By ten o'clock we had overtaken and passed three trains of supply wagons headed for the front, in all 469 rigs, and not one motor-truck. You were in a different world, a different age, from the war in France. Long and narrow, on very small wheels, with in-sloping sides of woven willow withes, the soiled, hooded coverings of these carts suggested a toy emigrant train of our West. From every hilltop they wound forward, an endless coil of evenly spaced, whitish dots along the road. We threaded them, the heaps of hay high on each tailboard. Vacant peasant faces under round sheep-wool caps stole cowed and wondering stares at us, as they urged on the bony horses to the creak of countless little wheels in the glut of mud. You felt the amazing, searching force of organization that war demands; ability in administration against grim, far-flung odds beside which the most complex commercial enterprises must be child's play. No. It could never, never last, this war. What of the wives, daughters, mothers, of those sturdy drivers? Barefoot in the sodden fields they hoed over the muck for potatoes no bigger than walnuts.

*   *   *

Dead Radymno

We turned through the main street. Not a door nor window-sash remained in any house. Within their oblongs, among the charred walls and naked chimneys, could be seen no recognizable belonging of home or shop. Only ashes, sodden straw where horses had been stabled, twisted metal things. Here before a doorway was a heap of brass belt-buckles, from dead Austrian soldiers by the double eagles holding the globe and sword designed on each; there, a litter of blood-soaked underclothing, a heap of broken rifles, warped bayonets, knapsacks. From torn cornices reached down long tentacles of tin roofing, sometimes draping a second-story balcony. They quivered in the raw wind with ghostly sounds, and regularly as the shells passed overhead—in threes now, at about five-minute intervals, giving out their silky-metallic waves of sound—every sliver creaked with an added vigor. You heard the tinkle-tinkle of glass splinters falling, as if by some magic out of the terrible pulsations of that blank, dark sky.

*   *   *

Retreat from Przemysl

Mitrovitz, Slavonia (Hungary), November 20.
Forced a fortnight ago to leave Przemysl, one makes an odyssey through Hungary, and at last lands in Serbia, which lies just across the River Sava from here. . . .
This journey has only crystallized into a final understanding the inevitable amazement of any traveler through the Germanic countries in this war. Once away from the "front," one has continually to nudge himself to believe that the great conflict is a reality. At home we do not realize how militarism, long prepara-

tion of the popular mind for war, has disciplined and discounted its stress and excitement. These lands find themselves facing the tragedy with a calmness and self-control easier than they or the world can have anticipated. Hungary, though only lately ridden of the enemy, was, except for the Red Cross trains and the groups of reserves ladling goulash from the steaming cauldron in each station yard, the same quiet plain of maize fields and huge-skirted peasant women that it is in times of peace. The one sinister touch lay in the endless way of anti-cholera lime along the tracks; and even this took on a gaiety by its whiteness and the figure of some bright-jacketed peasant on every platform, swinging a watering-pot that seemed to stream out milk.

*　　*　　*

A Glorious Catacomb

Crna Bara, Serbia, November 25.
Here again one was in the war zone. In the commonplace of uniforms it was Galicia once more, except that white, long-horned oxen, instead of stubby ponies, drew the ceaseless streams of supply carts going and coming from the front; and leaves still clung to the sycamores of a fatter land. Every hour through the night sentries shouted the watchword, medievally, on the ramparts of the fort. . . .

Thirty miles of desolation, glimpsed through the swirl of snow or drizzle; and in all that area to have been not once out of sight of a sod grave and cross, from artillery positions that were but warrens of bomb-proofs roofed with timber and straw; from the labyrinths of connecting trenches strewn with the wrack of the deads' equipment; from shattered, looted farmhouses, wrapped in a ghoulish silence! Between this village and the junction of the Sava and Drina Rivers, where the fight was hardest in the last weeks of September and the first of October—some 120,000 engaged upon each side—I counted on a single battlefield eight lines of trenches, few more than two hundred yards apart, with the ground between rough as a nutmeg grater from broken shrapnel.[134]

Part Three: The War Saps All One's Energy

I read this paragraph yesterday in a Paris-American journal:

"The body of a woman was found floating in the Seine off Suresnes. As the fingers of the body were covered with costly rings and the neck and breast with very expensive necklaces and brooches it is evident that she was a woman of culture."

It isn't. A culture that is founded on the activities of the applied scientist, the financier, the commercial engineer is not only very little elevated above the state of savagedom but is foredoomed. Armageddon, as it was called, came upon us because of those activities. We fought so as to determine which set of savages should decorate the corpses of its women with the more costly rings and the neck and breasts with the most expensive necklaces and brooches.

—Ford Madox Ford[135]

When two dogs fight in the street, no one supposes that anything but instinct prompts them, or that they are inspired by high and noble ends. But if they were capable of what is called thought, if they had been taught that Dog is a rational animal, we may be sure that a superstructure of belief would grow up in them during the combat. They fight really because something angers them in each other's smell. But if their fighting were accompanied by intellectual activity, the one would say he was fighting to promote the right kind of smell (kultur), and the other to uphold the inherent canine right of running on the pavement (democracy).

—Bertrand Russell[136]

From Archangel to Baghdad, from Carnarvon to Vladivostok there is not one to whom an impersonal entity known as THE STATE may not suddenly come and say, "You shall leave your wife and children and the tasks to which you have devoted your life, immediately, and put yourself obediently at my orders. The task which I assign to you is to kill certain men; as many as possible, whether you think them right or whether you think them wrong. Kill; or be killed."

—Norman Angell[137]

What the Civilian Saw

Kensington High Street

It is all shiny and black, like bombazine or taffeta,
Or the satin of my grandmother's gown, that stood alone
It was so thick;
A screen between us and knowledge,
That sometimes, when we are very good, gets on to the
      placards.

Past the screen of the dark the rain glissades,
Flowing down the straight damp palisades of the dark.

Faces against the screen,
Lamps of living flesh hung out in the storm
That has draped the world in black. . . .
Here by the station an iridescent sheen,
Dazzling, not gay. And news,
Special; oh, "Special"!
What have they let through to us from over there—
For once?

Faces, news, on the screen,
And the hungry crowds weltering in the dark!
Here is the English translation
Of what goes on over there,
There where hangings are not black but red,
And the king of England is lying on the ground. . . .

—Violet Hunt[138]

90.

from the *Little Review*

Richard Aldington

The Zeppelins Over London

The war saps all one's energy. It seems impossible to do any creative work in the midst of all this turmoil and carnage. Of course you know that we had the Zeppelins over London? Let me give you my version of the affair.

It was just after eleven. We were sitting in our little flat, which is on the top floor of a building on the slope of Hampstead Hill. We were reading—I was savoring, like a true decadent, that over-sweet honied Latin of the early Renaissance in an edition of 1513! Could anything be more peaceful? Our window was shut— so the silence was absolute. Suddenly there was a Bang! and a shrill wail. "That was pretty close," said I. Bang—whizz! Bang—whizz! Shrapnel from the anti-aircraft guns which are not five hundred yards from our house! (Of course, like boobies, we thought they were bombs.) I jumped up and got my coat, and grabbed the door-key. It took hours to put out the light! (All the time Bang—whizz!) It seemed interminable, that descent of those four flights of stairs, all the time with the knowledge that any second might see the whole damn place blown to hell. We could see the flashes of the guns and the searchlights as we passed the windows—they were *pointed straight at us*! That meant that the Zeppelin was either right overhead or coming there! Some excitement, I tell you. I shiver

294

with excitement when I think of it. We stood at the porch for a few seconds—very long seconds—wondering what to do. You are supposed to get into the cellars, but we haven't got cellars; and it's very risky in the streets from the flying shrapnel. We could see the long searchlights pointing to a spot almost overhead and the little red pin-pricks of bursting shells. A man came down from one of the flats—very calm, with field glasses, to have a look at the animal! Suddenly we saw it, clear overhead, with shells from three of four guns making little rose-colored punctures in the air underneath it. One shell went near, very near, the Zeppelin swerved, tilted— "They've got it! It's coming down!" we all exclaimed. In the distance we could hear faint cheering. But the Zeppelin righted itself, waggled a little, and scenting danger made for the nearest cloud! Apparently, a piece of shell had hit the pilot, for there was no apparent damage to be seen through the glasses. There were a few more bangs from the guns, followed by the cat-squeals of the shells and the little explosions in the air. Then silence as the Zeppelin got into a cloud; the searchlights looked wildly for it, for ten minutes. Then they all went out and in the resulting darkness we could see the glow of the fires in London.[139]

91.

Ford Madox Ford

Review of Ezra Pound's *Cathay*, June 1915

The poems in *Cathay* are things of a supreme beauty. What poetry should be, that they are. And, if a new breath of imagery and of handling can do anything for our poetry, that new breath these poems bring.

In a sense they only back up a theory that poetry consists in so rendering concrete objects that the emotions produced by the objects shall arise in the reader—and not in writing about the emotions themselves. What could be better poetry than the first verse of "The Beautiful Toilet"?

> Blue, blue is the grass about the river
> And the willows have overfilled the close garden.
> And within, the mistress, in the midmost of her youth,
> White, white of face, hesitates, passing the door:
> Slender, she puts forth a slender hand.

Or what could better render the feelings of protracted war than "The Song of the Bowmen of Shu"?

> Here we are, picking the first fern-shoots
> And saying: When shall we get back to our country?
> Our defense is not yet made sure, no one can let his friend
>   return.

We grab the old fern-stalks.
We say: Will we be let to go back in October?
Whose chariot? The General's.
Horses, his horses even, are tired. They were strong.
We have no rest, three battles a month.
By heaven, his horses are tired.
The Generals are on them, the soldiers are by them;
The horses are well trained, the generals have ivory arrows
      and quivers ornamented with fish-skin.
The enemy is swift, we must be careful:
When we set out, the willows were drooping with spring;
We come back in the snow,
We go slowly, we are hungry and thirsty,
Our mind is full of sorrow, who will know of our grief?

Or where have you had better rendered, or more permanently a rendering of, the feelings of one of those lonely watchers, in the outposts of progress, whether it be Ovid in Hyrcania, a Roman sentinel upon the Great Wall of this country, or merely ourselves in the lonely recesses of our minds, than the "Lament of the Frontier Guard"?

By the North Gate, the wind blows full of sand,
Lonely from the beginning of time until now!
Trees fall, the grass goes yellow with autumn.
I climb the towers and towers to watch out the barbarous
      land:
Desolate castle, the sky, the wide desert:
There is no wall left to this village.
Bones white with a thousand frosts,
High heaps covered with trees and grass;
Who brought this to pass?
Who has brought the flaming imperial anger?
Who has brought the army with drums and with kettle-
      drums?
Barbarous Kings.
A gracious spring, turned to blood-ravenous autumn,

A turmoil of warsmen, spread over the Middle Kingdom,
Three hundred and sixty thousand
And sorrow, sorrow like rain,
Sorrow to go, and sorrow, sorrow returning,
Desolate, desolate fields,
And no children of warfare upon them,
No longer the men for offense and defense.
Ah, how shall you know the dreary sorrow at the North
        Gate,
With Rihoku's name forgotten,
And we guardsmen fed to the tigers.

Rihaku[140]

Yet the first two of these poems are over two thousand
years old and the last more than a thousand. And Mr. Pound's little
volume is like a door in a wall, opening suddenly upon fields of an
extreme beauty, and upon a landscape made real by the intensity
of human emotions.

We are accustomed to think of the Chinese as arbitrary or
uniform in sentiment, but these poems reveal them as being just
ourselves. I do not know that that matters much, but what does
matter to us immediately is the lesson in the handling of words
and in the framing of emotions. Man is to mankind a wolf—*homo
homini lupus*—largely because the means of communication between man and man are very limited. I daresay that if words direct
enough could have been found, the fiend who sanctioned the use
of poisonous gases in the present war could have been so touched
to the heart that he would never have signed that order, calamitous, since it marks a definite retrogression in civilization such as
had not yet happened in the Christian era.

Beauty is a very valuable thing; perhaps it is the most valuable thing in life; but the power to express emotion so that it shall
communicate itself intact and exactly is almost more valuable. Of
both of these qualities Mr. Pound's book is very full. Therefore I
think we may say that this is much the best work that he has yet
done, for, however closely he may have followed his originals—

and of that most of us have no means whatever of judging—there is certainly a good deal of Mr. Pound in this little volume.[141]

92.

William Allen White

Endings

In the year 1915 the European war was beginning to dominate American politics. It dominated somewhat, I suppose, because the war was beginning to change our national economy. . . . War orders were speeding up the wheels in a thousand mills and lighting the fires in ten thousand furnaces. Accelerated business was increasing our national income. Labor and agriculture were getting more money, if not a larger share of the income, than they had had during the decade and a half before. War was producing in the United States its own intoxication, a kind of economic inflation that had spiritual reflexes. People felt happy because they were busy and seemed to be making money. . . .

The Bull Moose party, which was founded upon a demand for distributive justice, using government as an agency of human welfare, lost its cause. Prosperity was cheering up the farmers and the workers.

* * *

Many Progressives heard Roosevelt's war drums with distaste and uneasiness; but they did make a tremendous clamor, and finally the uproar was so definite that the Democratic national organization and the Democrats in Congress feared that Wilson might lose his leadership. I heard him recant [his previous stance on neutrality], at a dinner arranged by the Manhattan Club at a New York hotel. . . .

When he rose to talk his glum face was a douser on the applause, for it was perfunctory. His voice was strained when he began. It relaxed a little as he went on, and by the time he had come to his climax, announcing the national intention to rearm for national defense, he had cast off his black mantle, and his voice was vibrant and his face was radiant for a few moments. . . . I may have imagined it, but that night, as I watched the President . . . I felt he had entered a new phase of leadership. Neutrality had gone out of his heart. He was a partisan of the Allies against Germany. He took the country with him eventually.

*   *   *

Not long after that I saw the President again, from a window of the Macmillan Building on lower Fifth Avenue, marching at the head of the Preparedness Parade. He was in Presidential regalia: silk hat and cutaway coat of the period, dark striped trousers, appropriate tie—a fine figure of a man. His head was thrown back in exultation, for he received a tremendous ovation during the mile and more of the march at the head of the bands, the drum corps, the soldiers, sailors, and civic organizations. And cheers along the line rose to greet him like a flowing wave of deep emotion that seemed to carry him along as one tiptoeing upon clouds. It was a happy day for him, and he turned a happy face to the multitude.

*   *   *

When Woodrow Wilson spoke for preparedness at the Manhattan Club and when he had marched on New York's Fifth Avenue in the long Preparedness Parade, the bell tolled for social reform in the United States. The struggle for industrial economic justice and progressive political change had ended. Not that President Wilson had consciously put the period at the close of fifteen years of liberal advance. The war did that. But when he—the liberal leader—was forced away from his liberal goal into the business of rallying his country into the quickstep of war . . . we poor panting crusaders for a just and righteous order were left on a deserted battlefield, our drums punctured, our bugles muted, our cause forgotten.

∗   ∗   ∗

    I realize, of course, that ways of thinking and patterns of political conduct do not come bang-up against a certain year or month or day, and then suddenly turn or dissolve or shape new courses, but looking back it seems to me that what may be called the liberal movement in the United States came to a rather definite and catastrophic climax in that summer of 1916.[142]

Preparedness

The editors and ex-Presidents will not do the fighting, nor will our bellicose lawyers, bankers, stock brokers and other prominent citizens, who mess at Delmonico's, bivouac in club windows, and are at all times willing to give to their country's service the last full measure of conversation. No, the people themselves will do the fighting, and they will pay the bill.

—Amos Pinchot[143]

93.

President Wilson's Third Annual Message

December 7, 1915.

Gentlemen of the Congress:

Since I last had the privilege of addressing you on the state of the Union the war of nations on the other side of the sea, which had then only begun to disclose its portentous proportions, has extended its threatening and sinister scope until it has swept within its flame some portion of every quarter of the globe ... and now presents a prospect of reorganization and reconstruction such as statesmen and peoples have never been called upon to attempt before.

No one who really comprehends the spirit of the great people for whom we are appointed to speak can fail to perceive that their passion is for peace, their genius best displayed in the practice of the arts of peace. Great democracies are not belligerent. ... But just because we demand unmolested development and the undisturbed government of our own lives upon our own principles of right and liberty, we resent, from whatever quarter it may come, the aggression we ourselves will not practice. We insist upon security in prosecuting our self-chosen lines of national development. ...

It is with these ideals in mind that the plans of the Department of War for more adequate national defense were conceived which will be laid before you, and which I urge you to sanction and put into effect as soon as they can be properly scrutinized and discussed. They seem to me the essential first steps, and they seem to me for the present sufficient.

They contemplate an increase of the standing force of the regular army . . . by the addition of fifty-two companies of coast artillery, fifteen companies of engineers, ten regiments of infantry, four regiments of field artillery, and four aero squadrons, besides seven hundred and fifty officers required for a great variety of extra service, especially the all-important duty of training the citizen force of which I shall presently speak. . . . By way of making the country ready to assert some part of its real power promptly and upon a larger scale, should occasion arise, the plan also contemplates supplementing the army by a force of four hundred thousand disciplined citizens, raised in increments of one hundred and thirty-three thousand a year throughout a period of three years. This it is proposed to do by a process of enlistment under which the serviceable men of the country would be asked to bind themselves to serve with the colors for purposes of training for short periods throughout three years, and to come to the colors at call at any time throughout an additional "furlough" period of three years. . . .

At least so much by way of preparation for defense seems to me to be absolutely imperative now. We cannot do less.

The program which will be laid before you by the Secretary of the Navy is similarly conceived. . . . If this full program should be carried out we should have built or building in 1921 . . . an effective navy consisting of twenty-seven battleships of the first line, six battle cruisers, twenty-five battleships of the second line, ten armored cruisers, thirteen scout cruisers, five first class cruisers, three second class cruisers, ten third class cruisers, one hundred and eight destroyers, eighteen fleet submarines, one hundred and fifty-seven coast submarines, six monitors, twenty gunboats, four supply ships, fifteen fuel ships, four transports, three tenders to torpedo vessels, eight vessels of special types, and two ammunition ships. This would be a navy fitted to our needs and worthy of our traditions. . . .

The plans for the armed forces of the nation which I have outlined, and for the general policy of adequate preparation for mobilization and defense, involve of course very large additional expenditures of money—expenditures which will considerably exceed the estimated revenues of the government. . . .

How shall we obtain the new revenue? We are frequently reminded that there are many millions of bonds which the Treasury is authorized under existing law to sell. . . . But I, for one, do not believe that the people of this country approve of postponing the payment of their bills. . . . The people of the country are entitled to know just what burdens of taxation they are to carry, and to know from the outset, now. The new bills should be paid by internal taxation. . . .

By somewhat lowering the present limits of exemption and the figure at which the surtax shall begin to be imposed, and by increasing, step by step throughout the present graduation, the surtax itself, the income taxes as at present apportioned would yield sums sufficient to balance the books of the Treasury at the end of the fiscal year 1917 without anywhere making the burden unreasonably or oppressively heavy.[144]

94.

STARTS OPEN FIGHT AGAINST PREPAREDNESS

Anti-Militarism Committee Plans to Block Attempts "to Stampede the Nation."

WASHINGTON, Dec. 21 [1915].—What is announced as the beginning of a nation-wide fight against the huge war budget and the "cult of preparedness" which is sweeping the country was launched here today with the formation of the Anti-Militarism Committee, which has opened local headquarters in the Munsey Building and is said to be in close conference with the anti-preparedness minority in both the Senate and the House.

The members of the committee are Lillian Wald of the Nurses' Settlement, New York City; Paul U. Kellogg, editor of the Survey; Rev. John Haynes Holmes and Rabbi Stephen S. Wise of New York City, Mrs. Florence Kelley of the National Consumers' League, Professor George E. Kirchwey of Columbia University, Mrs. Crystal Eastman Benedict, L. Hollingsworth Wood, Louis P. Lochner, Miss Alice Lewisohn, Max Eastman, and Allan Benson.

L. Hollingsworth Wood, 43 Cedar Street, New York City, is Treasurer of the committee; Mrs. Crystal Eastman Benedict is Secretary in charge of the organization work, and Charles T. Hallinan of Chicago is "Editorial Director." The committee says that it wants to raise a budget which will permit it to put speakers into the field to meet the propagandas of the various "preparedness" organizations.

—*New York Times*, December 22, 1915

95.

John Reed

At the Throat of the Republic

The process of frightening people into "an heroic mood" is an old game. Europe was in "an heroic mood" in August, 1914. We Americans used to know all about that; before the war our newspapers and magazines used to comment with amused contempt upon "the European peoples staggering under a huge weight of senseless armaments," and there was much sympathy for "the poor conscript, forced to fight a tyrant's battles, whether he wants to or not." Do you remember how we laughed when Parliament discovered that the Coventry Ordnance Co. was spreading lies about Germany's naval program, in order to boost English "preparedness"; when the Reichstag discovered that the Krupps and the Waffenfabrik were bribing Paris newspapers to publish false information about French armament increases, in order to boost German "preparedness"; when, during the last two years, the great Japanese scandals burst, revealing monstrous corruption of army and navy officers by the munition-makers? We laughed when we read how the Navy Leagues of Germany and England had been proved to be the tools of the armor-plate makers and the shipbuilders. We knew it all.

And knowing these things, suddenly the American people went mad. Denouncing "Prussian militarism," we suddenly began to shout for Universal Military Service, and to applaud General John O'Ryan, commander of the New York National Guard, when he said:

We must get our men so that they are machines, and this can only be done as the result of a process of training.

When the feeling of fear—the natural instinct of self-preservation—comes over a man, there must be something to hold him to his duty. We have to have our men trained so that the influence of fear is overpowered by the peril of an uncompromising military system, often backed up by a pistol in the hands of an officer. We must make the men unconsciously forget their fear. All these matters of standing at attention and "Sir, I have the honor to report," are valuable to put him through the biological and social process by which he becomes a soldier.

The recruits have got to put their heads into the military noose. They have got to be "jacked up"—they have got to be "bawled out."

*   *   *

We shudder over "the horrors of war"—and yet once a month regularly (sometimes oftener), Colonel Theodore Roosevelt calls everyone who prefers peace to war a "coward" or a "white worm.". . . And of later date, that it is—"through strife and the readiness for strife that a nation must win greatness."

Of course that is bosh, and the public knows it. If all the Preparedness advocates used that line of argument their cause would be lost. But they don't. They appeal for a gigantic standing army and navy, universal conscription, tremendous fortifications, "for defense." Defense against what? . . .

Military experts tell us that no overseas nation would attempt an invasion of the United States with less than four hundred thousand men. Does the public realize what it means to transport such a force, its guns and supplies, across three thousand miles of ocean, and land them in the face of a modern navy, submarines, mines, or even coast defenses alone? Just refresh your memory with the story of what happened to England at the Dardanelles. . . .

General Nelson A. Miles has had more military experience than any other officer in the United States Army; and in January,

1916, he said before a Senate committee:

"The placing of an army on American soil is the last thing any European government would attempt; it could never be re-embarked. It would dissolve like snow beneath the midday sun. Whenever it has been attempted it has resulted in disaster."

Then the General burst out:

"These overseas expeditions spring from the minds of men writing about preparedness, who know less about preparedness than anything else!"...

*   *   *

Reader, have you listened to the recent calumny heaped upon our Army, Navy and Coast Defenses? Are you not astonished to suddenly discover that the military and naval establishments of the United States, only two years ago declared to be so efficient, so powerful, are now "contemptible," "inadequate" and "ridiculous"?

This is an interesting question. Let's look into it.

Take the Navy, for example. . . . Admiral Fletcher, commander of the Atlantic Squadron, stated under oath before the House Committee on Naval Affairs in December, 1914, that England is the only nation with a navy that we could not successfully resist; and that the last five American battleships constructed were immensely more powerful than the last five English battleships. How can two years, in which we have spent vastly increasing sums of money on the Navy, have so altered its status among the navies of the world? . . .

There still remains the Army proper. What's the matter with it? It's cost more than England's army. According to the Preparedness shouters, the only trouble with our Army is, that it is too small.

*   *   *

Let us examine some of the organizations who are flooding the country with panic-breeding lies in the campaign for an enormous Army and Navy. Perhaps we can discover the reason why they are frightening America, as Europe was frightened, into "an heroic mood."

The National Security League shouts for a Big Army. One of its most valuable propagandists is Mr. Hudson Maxim, inventor and now manufacturer of war-munitions. He wrote a book called "Defenseless America," painting an appalling picture of what would happen to the United States if attacked by a foreign nation; and Colonel Theodore Roosevelt heartily endorsed the book. . . .

Next in order is the Navy League, with its grandiloquent program of five hundred million dollars' worth of bonds to be issued to build a colossal Navy and Army—"for defense." . . .

As we have seen in the case of Mr. Hudson Maxim and the National Security League, so the Navy League is also controlled by men who have something to sell—war munitions. Of the 19 persons listed as "founders" of the Navy League, the majority are connected with concerns and establishments which directly, and through interlocking directorates, monopolize the manufacture of war-munitions in the United States.

*　　*　　*

Rear-Admiral French C. Chadwick, of the United States Navy, said at Clark University, on December 17, 1915:

"Navies and Armies are the insurance for capital owned abroad by the leisure class of a nation. It is for them that empires and spheres of influence exist. The great war now raging is the culmination of efforts to extend those spheres."

Back of all this crude agitation on the part of the munitions-makers is a more grandiose reason for Preparedness—a conspiracy of the great financial interests, so enormous that its prospective loot makes the war-profits look like petty larceny. The real power behind the National Security League, the Navy League and other such organizations, is Wall Street. Wall Street does not talk of "defense." No. Wall Street is getting ready to launch the United States upon a gigantic adventure in World Imperialism, for the benefit of the big financial speculators. And in order to do this, Wall Street must have a great army and navy to protect its foreign investments.

*   *   *

All financial roads lead to Morgan or Rockefeller, broadly speaking; and these are now almost indistinguishably interlocked. On one side the Preparedness shouters are usually munition-makers, with something to sell; on the other side they are imperialist bankers, who create the demand for munitions. They take a profit coming or going.[145]

96.

HOSTS IN CHICAGO ON DEFENSE PARADE

More Than 130,000 March to Voice Their Desire for Preparedness.

MANY WOMEN ARE IN LINE

Precision and Seriousness Mark Outpouring— Demonstrations in Other Cities.

CHICAGO. June 3 [1916]. — The greatest parade ever held in Chicago, finished tonight after 130,214 persons, one-sixth of them women, had filed through the streets in the preparedness demonstration. The parade was eleven and a half hours in passing. The night division was made up largely of military organizations.

The parade was said by Major General Thomas H. Barry, Commander of the Central Department of the United States Army, who sat in the reviewing stand, to be the greatest and most inspiring spectacle he had ever seen.

The great parade, in close order, massed from curb to curb, rolled like a tide through the streets all day. It was as if the great skyscrapers were the banks of a river, and the marching thousands, each with an American flag, the current moving between them. . . .

The precision with which the parade moved was itself said to be a lesson in preparedness, for it was handled by Captain Raymond Sheldon of the regular army, by a system of telephones. The demonstration started promptly at 9 a.m. upon a salute of twenty-one guns. When a gap would open between divisions the fact was reported from one of the 120 sub-stations and upon word from Captain Sheldon the division leader sounded a whistle, whereupon the untrained patriots did their best at a double quick and closed up the interval. . . .

About twenty-five percent of these were women. The weather left nothing to be desired.

—*New York Times*, June 4, 1916

97.

Harold Stearns

from *Liberalism in America*

In London during the first few weeks of the war I remember that the spontaneous impulse of Americans when we met each other was to offer silent congratulations. Whatever else happened in a world which had fallen to pieces, we were out of it. We were safe behind the broad stretches of the Atlantic; we had a sanity and a sense of humor that contrasted only too sharply with the strain and nervousness of our foreign friends. It seemed literally impossible that we should ever get into the war ourselves. The very notion was grotesque. We conceived America's natural function as that of a mediator, the great neutral to whom both sides would appeal, and not in vain, for an impartial settling of their claims when the passions of fighting had exhausted themselves.

Coming home on the liner this notion was confirmed. Rumors flew thick and fast when we went on board at Liverpool, but it was then too early for the submarine menace. There was talk, of course, of mines, although once past the Irish coast, there could possibly be no danger. Random German raiders had no terrors for us. We were an American ship. Other friends on English boats had told us gloomily that they had a dull voyage ahead of them—no lights at night, no music, curtains covering all the port holes, reprimands if you lighted a cigarette on deck after nightfall. With us, after the first day, it was a gay voyage. We danced and flirted and after dinner crowded the smoker to exchange experiences over a friendly glass. We were flying the American flag and nothing could happen to disturb our security. For after a fashion our boat was itself a symbol of American isolation and self-complacency.

Of course this was naive and of course it was an attitude which reckoned too lightly upon the economic interlacing of the world which had taken place since the Spanish war. Intellectually it was an attitude difficult to defend. Yet it was an attitude which had its emotional roots very deep in our national traditions. In spite of the terrific pro-Entente propaganda which was immediately let loose upon the United States, in spite of our sympathy with France and Belgium as invaded countries (in our international traditions there has always been an element of sportsmanship that led us spontaneously to back what we considered the losing side), in spite of the atrocity stories which were certain of a popular appeal, the genuine emotional neutrality of the country could hardly be doubted.

*   *   *

In trying to understand the emotional break-down before the war-hysteria of 1917, it is necessary to realize our spiritual unpreparedness for the war when it actually came, and, indeed, our actual hostility to it. Although our official policy as a nation began to swerve towards a "benevolent" neutrality policy with respect to the Entente as early as 1914, the great mass of American citizens were wholly unaware of it. The Middle West in particular, aside from the interested German-Americans and the Irish who could never espouse a cause of England's, was completely indifferent to what policy we were pursuing so long as that policy kept us prosperous and at peace. Furthermore, from time to time the newspapers would publish our diplomatic protests against violation of our trade rights by Great Britain, and editorial comment against that country's flagrant and unwarranted interference with our mails was usually severe, even the most Anglophile metropolitan newspapers not venturing to defend it. Consequently it was easy to persuade the average citizen that we were neutral in fact as well as in popular inclination. . . .

Yet if the average American was consciously caught unprepared for the war, a campaign of preparedness was constantly being waged, all the more insidious and emotionally disturbing because its methods were indirect and adroitly disguised. Ostensibly, it was waged in the name of patriotism and good citizenship, although in the end it came to be officially known as the "preparedness" campaign. Beginning with professional military men who saw in the European war only a confirmation of their militaristic philosophy, the movement then enlisted the support of large munition and war-material manufacturing interests, which for obvious economic reasons were willing that the country should commit itself to the policy of a large standing army. . . . Then as our loans to the Allies became greater and greater, the bankers instinctively encouraged the development of a weapon which might, in the unhappy contingency of ourselves going in, be employed to guarantee the loans or—in the opposite contingency—to make sure that Germany would not, by a crushing military victory, destroy the Entente's ability to pay. The whole upper social class, natural haters of Wilson because of his vacillating pacifism and suspected democracy, natural defenders of England because of social connections and caste sympathy, speedily flung its support to the campaign. The last to fall in line—and here, I am glad to say, there were many honorable exceptions—were the intellectuals and the college professors. . . .

Now even this cursory description makes it clear that the preparedness campaign was an upper class movement. In the region west of the Alleghanies, in the whole Mississippi Valley, in the flourishing grain country of the Northwest, on the Pacific Coast, war even as late as 1917 seemed an alien and impossible thing. President Wilson had sensed the feeling of the country . . . [and] had preached peace and not war. Even when he had advocated preparedness he had adroitly turned this advocacy into preparedness for defense only, had preached it as a condition necessary for the maintenance of that peace which we cherished. The temper of the country was pacific. There can be no doubt that whatever the local and temporary conflicting causes, the outstanding reason for the success of the President in his re-election was because he was identified with the slogan, "He kept us out of war." Even as late as January 13, 1917, the *New Republic* could write—and was correct in its interpretation—"the man who thinks conscription can be applied today in America hasn't even an elementary grasp of the political situation." Taken as a whole, the country was mentally unprepared for the war. The actual declaration came as something of a shock.

*　*　*

Nevertheless the preparedness campaign had done its work. If its advocates constituted only a minority, the minority was a powerful and aggressive one. It was organized and articulate. It controlled the press and the popular magazines. It could dominate the moving-picture industry. It held the government practically at its mercy. It had the support of substantially all of the financial interests. It spoke from the pulpits. It captured the colleges and schools. Hardly a single recognized leader in the economic or social or intellectual world dared to risk his prestige by speaking against it. It was a minority which began to function actively with the day of the declaration of war. Who cannot recall the parades and "loyalty" pledges? the invitations to turn amateur spy and report to the secret service any person making a statement calculated to upset members of the National Security League? the patriotic orations? the sudden flood of "atrocity" moving-pictures? the cartoons?

The American people may have been apathetic and indifferent, but this minority had not been. When the war actually came it was in a position to swing public opinion in the belligerent direction it desired. Senators might filibuster . . . Congressmen might feel reluctant to vote for war (and it is well known that many of them, solely under the pressure of what they thought was the mass of opinion, voted for war against their personal convictions); the American Society Opposed to Militarism and other pacific organizations might protest; here and there might be found a skeptical writer of some standing; the younger generation of rebels might threaten to sabotage the whole war scheme; the radicals might howl in rage, as they did in the St. Louis platform of the Socialist party. All was useless. The way had been "prepared" in a very real sense.[146]

98.

from the *Little Review*

Emma Goldman

The Road to Universal Slaughter

Ever since the beginning of the European conflagration the people of Europe have thrown themselves into the flames of war like panic-stricken cattle. And now America, pushed to the very brink by unscrupulous politicians, by ranting demagogues, and by military sharks, is preparing for the same terrible fate. In the face of this approaching disaster it behooves men and women not yet overcome by the war madness to raise their protest, to call the attention of the people to the crime and outrage which are about to be perpetrated upon them.

America is essentially the melting pot. No national unit composing it is in a position to boast of superior race purity, particular historic mission, or higher culture. Yet the jingoes and war speculators are filling the air with the sentimental slogan of hypocritical nationalism, "America for Americans," "America first, last, and all the time." This cry has caught the popular fancy from one end of the country to the other. In order to maintain America, military preparedness must be engaged in at once. A billion dollars of the people's sweat and blood is to be expended for dreadnaughts and submarines, for the army and the navy, all to protect this precious America.

The pathos of it all is that the America which is to be protected by a huge military force is not the America of the people, but the America of the privileged class; the class which robs and exploits the masses, and controls their lives. And it is no less pathetic that so few people realize that preparedness never leads to peace, but is indeed the road to universal slaughter.

*   *   *

Forty years ago Germany proclaimed the slogan: "Germany above everything. Germany for the Germans, first, last and always. We want peace; therefore we must prepare for war. Only a well-armed and thoroughly-prepared nation can maintain peace, can command respect, can be sure of its national integrity." And Germany continued to prepare, thereby forcing the other nations to do the same. The European war is the fruition of the gospel of military preparedness.

Since the war began, miles of paper and oceans of ink have been used to prove the barbarity, the cruelty, the oppression of Prussian militarism. Conservatives and radicals alike are giving their support to the Allies for no other reason than to help crush that militarism, in the presence of which, they say, there can be no peace or progress in Europe. But though America grows fat on the manufacture of munitions and war loans to the Allies to help crush Prussianism, the same cry is now being raised in America which, if carried into national action, will build up an American militarism far more terrible than German or Prussian militarism could ever be; because nowhere in the world has capitalism become so brazen in its greed as in America, and nowhere is the State so ready to kneel at the feet of Capital.

Like a plague, the mad spirit of militarism is sweeping the country, infesting the clearest heads and staunchest hearts. National security leagues, with cannon as their emblem of protection, naval leagues with women in their lead, have sprung up all through the United States. Americanization societies with well-known liberals as members, they who but yesterday decried the patriotic clap-trap of today, are now lending themselves to the befogging of the minds of the people, to the building-up of the same destructive institutions in America which they are directly and indirectly helping to pull down in Germany—militarism, the destroyer of youth, the raper of woman, the annihilator of the best in the race, the very mower of life.

Even Woodrow Wilson, who not so long ago talked of "a nation too proud to fight," who in the beginning of the war ordered prayers for peace, who in his proclamations spoke of the necessity of watchful waiting—even he has been whipped into line. He has now joined his worthy colleagues in the jingo movement, echoing their clamor for preparedness and their howl of "America for Americans." The difference between Wilson and Roosevelt is this: Roosevelt, the bully, uses the club; Wilson, the historian, the college professor, wears the smooth polished university mask, but underneath it he, like Roosevelt, has but one aim: to serve the big interests, to add to those who are growing phenomenally rich by the manufacture of military preparedness.

Woodrow Wilson, in his address before the Daughters of the American Revolution, gave his case away when he said: "I would rather be beaten than ostracized." To stand out against Bethlehem, DuPont, Baldwin, Remington, Winchester metallic cartridges, and the rest of the armament ring means political ostracism and death. Wilson knows that; therefore he betrays his original position, goes back on the bombast of "too proud to fight," and howls as loudly as any other cheap politician for preparedness and national glory.

*   *   *

To uphold the institutions of our country—that is it: the institutions which protect and sustain a handful of people in the robbery and plunder of the masses; the institutions which drain the blood of the native as well as of the foreigner and turn it into wealth and power; the institutions which rob the alien of whatever originality he brings with him and in return give him cheap Americanism, whose glory consists in mediocrity and arrogance. The very proclaimers of "America first" have long before this betrayed the fundamental principles of real Americanism, of the kind of Americanism Jefferson had in mind when he said that the best government is that which governs least; the kind of an America David Thoreau worked for when he proclaimed that the best government is the one that doesn't govern at all; or the other truly great Americans who aimed to make of this country a haven of refuge, who hoped that all the disinherited and oppressed coming to these shores would give character, quality, and meaning to the country. That is not the America of the politicians and the munition speculators. Their America has been powerfully portrayed by a young New York sculptor I know; he has made a hard cruel hand with long lean merciless fingers, crushing in over the heart of the foreigner, squeezing out its blood in order to coin dollars.

*   *   *

Preparedness is directed not only against the external enemy; it aims much more at the internal enemy. It is directed against that element of labor which has learned not to hope for anything from our institutions, that awakened part of the working people who have realized that the war of the classes underlies all wars among nations, and that if war is justified at all it is the war against economic dependence and political slavery, the two dominant issues involved in the struggle of the classes.

Already militarism has been acting its bloody part in every economic conflict, with the approval and support of the State. Where was the protest from Washington when "our men, women and children" were killed in Ludlow? Where was that high-sounding outraged protest contained in the note to Germany? Or is there any difference in killing "our men, women and children" in Ludlow or on the high seas? Yes, indeed. The men, women, and children at Ludlow were working people, belonging to the disinherited of the earth, foreigners who had to be given a taste of the glories of Americanism, while the passengers of the *Lusitania* represented wealth and station; therein lies the difference.

It will be with preparedness as it has been with all the other institutions in our confused life which were created for the good of the people and which have accomplished the very reverse. Supposedly, America is to prepare for peace; but in reality it will prepare for the cause of war. It has always been so and it will continue to be so until nation refuses to fight against nation, and until the people of the world stop preparing for slaughter. Preparedness is like the seed of a poisonous plant; placed in the soil, it will bear poisonous fruit. The European mass destruction is the fruit of that poisonous seed. It is imperative that the American workers realize this before they are driven by the jingoes into the madness that is forever haunted by the specter of danger and invasion; they must know that to prepare for peace means to invite war, means to unloose the furies of death over land and sea.

You cannot build up a standing army and then throw it back into a box like tin soldiers. Armies equipped to the teeth with highly-developed instruments of murder and backed by their military interests have their own dynamic functions. We have but to examine into the nature of militarism to realize the truth of this contention.

Militarism consumes the strongest and most productive elements of each nation. Militarism swallows the largest part of the national revenue. Even in times of peace almost nothing is spent on education, art, literature, and science in comparison with the amount devoted to militarism; while in times of war everything else is set at naught: all life stagnates, all effort is curtailed, the very sweat and blood of the masses are used to feed this insatiable monster—militarism. Under such circumstances it must become more arrogant, more aggressive, more bloated with its own importance. . . . Therefore it will find an enemy or create one artificially. In this civilized purpose militarism is sustained by the State, protected by the laws of the land, fostered by the home and the school, and glorified by public opinion. In other words, the function of militarism is to kill. It cannot live except through murder.[147]

99.

Margaret Anderson & Emma Goldman in Chicago

Margaret Anderson

from *My Thirty Years' War*

Emma Goldman had written how much she appreciated my article on anarchism. Now she wrote again that she was passing through Chicago and would like to see me.

I was exalted. To know the great martyred leader! I thought the lake and the empty apartment would be soothing to her so I asked her to stay with us while she was in Chicago.

She answered, thanking me graciously, but explaining that she never visited families, that she couldn't adapt herself to bourgeois life even for a few days. I replied that we weren't exactly bourgeois perhaps—that we ought to be very congenial to her, being without furniture. But she didn't believe it, I think. She wanted to see.

She asked me to come to the Lexington Hotel to talk with her, which I quickly did. As my elevator reached her floor she was standing near it, waiting for me. She wore a flowered summer dress and a straw hat with a ribbon. She was made all of one piece. When I stepped from the elevator she turned her back on me. I was amazed and hurt. I decided that I probably looked so frivolous she was scorning me. But I took courage and asked her if she weren't Miss Goldman, and she turned a welcoming face to me, saying she had been sure it wasn't I. Later she explained that this was because

I looked too chic. She hadn't been prepared for it.

She had some people in her room—the fantastic Dr. Ben Reitman (who wasn't so bad if you could hastily drop all your ideas as to how human beings should look and act) and a beautiful woman with white hair who resembled a czarina. She had an ailing heart and made me think of Yeats' poem to Aubrey Beardsley's sister. She was flamingly revolted by everything and, though she had been born in a conventional world, had lived her life highly and thought anarchists and I.W.W.'s a little tame. She was never precise about what should be done to the offending bourgeois but it was always something unthinkably scathing. We became great friends.[148]

* * *

Emma Goldman

from *Living My Life*

During my stay [in Chicago] I came upon the new literary publication called the *Little Review*, and shortly afterwards I met its editor, Margaret C. Anderson. I felt like a desert wanderer who unexpectedly discovers a stream of fresh water. At last a magazine to sound a note of rebellion in creative endeavor! The *Little Review* lacked clarity on social questions, but it was alive to new art forms and was free from the mawkish sentimentality of most American publications. Its main appeal to me lay in its strong and fearless critique of conventional standards, something I had been looking for in the United States for twenty-five years. "Who is this Margaret Anderson?" I inquired of the friend who had shown me a copy of the magazine. "A charming American girl," he replied, "and she is anxious to interview you." I told him I did not care to be interviewed, but that I did want to meet the editor of the *Little Review*.[149]

* * *

Margaret Anderson

Emma Goldman surprised me by being more human than she had seemed on the platform. When she lectured she was as serious as the deep Russian soul itself. In private she was gay, communicative, tender. Her English was the peculiar personal idiom favored by Russian Jews and she spoke only in platitudes—which I found fascinating. Her eyes were a clear strong blue which deepened as she talked.

She asked me to lunch the next day and we went into the Auditorium Hotel. It was Sunday and there were few people. I wanted stories of her life and loved her way of telling them. I asked for the McKinley story. So she told me of the fair-haired blue-eyed boy she had met one day in a library in Cleveland. She had been startled when he presented himself, looking like an angel and explaining that he had read her philosophy of anarchism. She never saw him again, never heard from him, never heard of him again until "the country was ringing" with the assassination. She was almost mobbed and narrowly escaped being held responsible for the crime. I asked her how she explained such acts.

Who knows the human soul? she asked slowly.

I couldn't continue calling her Miss Goldman and her request to be called Emma was beyond me. I don't believe I could call any human being Emma. I suggested naming her "E.G.," which pleased her. She was by this time entirely reassured as to my unbourgeois nature, and eager to see the empty apartment.

I went to the Lexington to fetch her and her bag (it deserves mention, being so big) and as we stood at the door of the hotel waiting for a trolley car a proletarian chose that moment to fall off a truck he was driving. He slid down from his high seat and floundered among the horses' feet with horrible noises. E.G.'s coordination was something to remark—her cry and act were simultaneous. She pulled the man from under the horses before anyone else on the street could move and administered first aid with such a grim face that I felt she might be planning to hit him on the jaw as soon as she had revived him. But I learned later that she was always grim when distressed. I have seen beggars in the street ask her for money and my instinct was always to conceal myself under the sidewalk until the bout was over—she looked as if she would knock out the universe.

The truckman wasn't ruined and we went on to the North Side. E.G. was grim all the way. She relaxed when she saw the apartment and saw that I hadn't exaggerated about the furniture. I urged her to have a chair (piano stool) and not to worry about capitalism while she was with us. She laughed and said she saw none to worry about.

Harriet Dean came in to meet her. Harriet had such an emphatic handshake, such a Rooseveltian smile, and was in such haste to assure E.G. of her impulse to knock the blocks off tyrants and oppressors that E.G. adopted her at once. We dined lightly (on superlative coffee made by E.G.) and then walked on the beach as the night came down. No one else was there. E.G. sang Russian folk songs in a low and husky voice. We were immensely moved. And then the great anarchist could control her enthusiasm no longer. She telephoned to Reitman and a few "comrades" to come out.

It's divine here, she cried.

They came and also found it divine.

You look rejuvenated, Emma, they exclaimed, rushing through the apartment with violence. I was glad there was no furniture.[150]

∗   ∗   ∗

Emma Goldman

In a large apartment facing Lake Michigan I found, besides Miss Anderson, the latter's sister with her two children, and a girl named Harriet Dean. The entire furniture consisted of a piano, piano-stool, several broken cots, a table, and some kitchen chairs. However this strange ménage managed to pay the undoubtedly large rent, there was evidently no money for anything else. In some mysterious way, though, Miss Anderson and her friend procured flowers, fruit, and dainties for me.

Harriet Dean was as much a novel type to me as Margaret, yet the two were entirely unlike. Harriet was athletic, masculine-looking, reserved, and self-conscious. Margaret, on the contrary, was feminine in the extreme, constantly bubbling over with enthusiasm. A few hours with her entirely changed my first impression and made me realize that underneath her apparent lightness was depth and strength of character to pursue whatever aim in life she might choose. Before long I saw that the girls were not actuated by any sense of social injustice, like the young Russian intelligentsia, for instance. Strongly individualized, they had broken the shackles of their middle-class homes to find release from family bondage and bourgeois tradition. I regretted their lack of social consciousness, but as rebels for their own liberation Margaret Anderson and Harriet Dean strengthened my faith in the possibilities of my adopted country.[151]

*   *   *

Margaret Anderson

Bill Haywood was with them but as always gave the impression of being alone. He didn't inspect the apartment. He sat powerfully on a window ledge and talked of small dogs.

Can you stand seeing rich women with lapdogs? he asked. I can't. When I think of the thousands of children who are in want—and then those women with their dogs—well, it makes me sick.

This was almost his only remark. Someone recited Whitman's "Come lovely and smiling death," and he bowed his head in approval. He had only one eye and at that moment it was full of tears.

Play for us, E.G. demanded. And I, feeling unselfconscious for the first time in my life, played the piano for an hour. They all sat silent.

You're a great artist, said E.G. authoritatively.

It was the first time in my magazine-cover existence that I had been taken at another valuation. I was filled with gratitude.

Two days later the agent of our building came to see me with a determined face.

We've had complaints that Emma Goldman has been here. We can't allow such a thing.

I was charmed to enlighten him. I made him sit on the piano stool. I produced pamphlets on anarchism. I read passages. I explained the difference between philosophical and bomb-throwing anarchism. I stated that it was an honor to have Emma Goldman in the house as contrasted with the bridge-playing protoplasms that infested the rest of the building. I was working up to my climax when he seemed to get bored. He left and never came back.

I became increasingly anarchistic. I began to find people of my own class vicious, people in clean collars uninteresting. I even accepted smells, personal as well as official. Everyone who came to the studio smelled either of machine oil or herring.

Anarchism was the ideal expression for my ideas of freedom and justice. The knowledge that people could be put into prisons and kept there for life had the power to torture me. That human beings could be sentenced to death by other human beings was a fact beyond human imagination. I decided that I would make my life a crusade against inhumanity.

One day the papers announced that the governor of Utah had refused to pardon an anarchist condemned to death for—I've forgotten what—nothing at all as I remember, like Sacco and Vanzetti. I wrote an editorial ending with the cry: Why doesn't someone shoot the governor of Utah?

Detectives came to the studio. I happened not to be there (to my regret). A man from New York—an influential person I had met at dinner the night before, who had been enormously intrigued with the idea of the *Little Review*—did happen to be there. He took the detectives with him to some important city office and persuaded the powers that I was a flighty society girl who meant nothing she said. I discovered this later, after I had sat in the studio for two days patiently waiting for the detectives to come back.

And now we were very poor. Subscriptions kept coming in but advertising had fallen off on account of anarchism. We had taken a cheaper studio in the Fine Arts Building—room 834 on the Renaissance court where the fountain and the pianos tinkled all day.[152]

100.

Ellen N. La Motte

Pour la Patrie

This is how it was. It is pretty much always like this in a field hospital. Just ambulances rolling in, and dirty, dying men, and the guns off there in the distance! Very monotonous, and the same, day after day, till one gets so tired and bored. Big things may be going on over there, on the other side of the captive balloons that we can see from a distance, but we are always here, on this side of them, and here, on this side of them, it is always the same. The weariness of it—the sameness of it! The same ambulances, and dirty men, and groans, or silence. The same hot operating rooms, the same beds, always full, in the wards. This is war. But it goes on and on, over and over, day after day, till it seems like life. Life in peace time. It might be life in a big city hospital, so alike is the routine. Only the city hospitals are bigger, and better equipped, and the ambulances are smarter, and the patients don't always come in ambulances—they walk in sometimes, or come in street cars, or in limousines, and they are of both sexes, men and women, and have ever so many things the matter with them—the hospitals of peace time are not nearly so stupid, so monotonous, as the hospitals of war. Bah! War's humane compared to peace! More spectacular, I grant you, more acute—that's what interests us—but for the sheer agony of life—oh, peace is way ahead!

War is so clean. Peace is so dirty. There are so many foul diseases in peace time. They drag on over so many years, too. No, war's clean! I'd rather see a man die in the prime of life, in war time, than see him doddering along in peace time, broken hearted, broken spirited, life broken, and very weary, having suffered many things—to die at last, at a good, ripe age! How they have suffered, those who drive up to our city hospitals in limousines, in peace time. What's been saved them, those who die young, and clean and swiftly, here behind the guns. In the long run it adds up just the same. Only war's spectacular, that's all.

Well, he came in like the rest, only older than most of them. A shock of iron-gray hair, a mane of it, above heavy, black brows, and the brows were contracted in pain. Shot, as usual, in the abdomen. He spent three hours on the table after admission—the operating table—and when he came over to the ward, they said, not a dog's chance for him. No more had he. When he came out of ether, he said he didn't want to die. He said he wanted to live. Very much. He said he wanted to see his wife again and his children. Over and over he insisted on this, insisted on getting well. He caught hold of the doctor's hand and said he must get well, that the doctor must get him well. Then the doctor drew away his slim fingers from the rough, imploring grasp, and told him to be good and patient.

"Be good! Be patient!" said the doctor, and that was all he could say, for he was honest. What else could he say, knowing that there were eighteen little holes, cut by the bullets, leaking poison into that gashed, distended abdomen? When these little holes, that the doctor could not stop, had leaked enough poison into his system, he would die. Not today, no, but day after tomorrow. Three days more.

So all that first day, the man talked of getting well. He was insistent on that. He was confident. Next day, the second of the three days the doctor gave him, very much pain laid hold of him. His black brows bent with pain and he grew puzzled. How could one live with such pain as that?

That afternoon, about five o'clock, came the General. The one who decorates the men. He had no sword, just a riding whip, so he tossed the whip on the bed, for you can't do an accolade with anything but a sword. Just the *Médaille Militaire*. Not the other one. But the *Médaille Militaire* carries a pension of a hundred francs a year, so that's something. So the General said, very briefly: "In the name of the Republic of France, I confer upon you the *Médaille Militaire*." Then he bent over and kissed the man on his forehead, pinned the medal to the bedspread, and departed.

There you are! Just a brief little ceremony, and perfunctory. We all got that impression. The General has decorated so many dying men. And this one seemed so nearly dead. He seemed half-conscious. Yet the General might have put a little more feeling into it, not made it quite so perfunctory. Yet he's done this thing so many, many times before. It's all right, he does it differently when there are people about, but this time there was no one present— just the doctor, the dying man, and me. And so we four knew what it meant—just a widow's pension. Therefore there wasn't any reason for the accolade, for the sonorous, ringing phrases of a dress parade—

We all knew what it meant. So did the man. When he got the medal, he knew too. He knew there wasn't any hope. I held the medal before him, after the General had gone, in its red plush case. It looked cheap, somehow. The exchange didn't seem even. He pushed it aside with a contemptuous hand sweep, a disgusted shrug.

"I've seen these things before!" he exclaimed. We all had seen them too. We all knew about them, he and the doctor, and the General and I. He knew and understood, most of all. And his tone was bitter.

After that, he knew the doctor couldn't save him, and that he should not see his wife and children again. Whereupon he became angry with the treatment, and protested against it. The *picqures* hurt—they hurt very much, and he did not want them. Moreover, they did no good, for his pain was now very intense, and he tossed and tossed to get away from it.

So the third day dawned, and he was alive, and dying, and knew that he was dying. Which is unusual and disconcerting. He turned over and over, and black fluid vomited from his mouth into the white enamel basin. From time to time, the orderly emptied the basin, but always there was more, and always he choked and

334

gasped and knit his brows in pain. Once his face broke up as a child's breaks up when it cries. So he cried in pain and loneliness and resentment.

He struggled hard to hold on. He wanted very much to live, but he could not do it. He said: "*Je ne tiens plus.*"

Which was true. He couldn't hold on. The pain was too great. He clenched his hands and writhed, and cried out for mercy. But what mercy had we? We gave him morphia, but it did not help. So he continued to cry to us for mercy, he cried to us and to God. Between us, we let him suffer eight hours more like that, us and God.

Then I called the priest. We have three priests on the ward, as orderlies, and I got one of them to give him the Sacrament. I thought it would quiet him. We could not help him with drugs, and he had not got it quite in his head that he must die, and when he said, "I am dying," he expected to be contradicted. So I asked Capolarde to give him the Sacrament, and he said yes, and put a red screen around the bed, to screen him from the ward. Then Capolarde turned to me and asked me to leave. It was summertime. The window at the head of the bed was open, the hay outside was new cut and piled into little haycocks. Over in the distance the guns rolled. As I turned to go, I saw Capolarde holding a tray of Holy Oils in one hand, while with the other he emptied the basin containing black vomitus out the window.

No, it did not bring him comfort, or resignation. He fought against it. He wanted to live, and he resented Death, very bitterly. Down at my end of the ward—it was a silent, summer afternoon—I heard them very clearly. I heard the low words from behind the screen.

"*Dites: 'Dieu je vous donne ma vie librement pour ma patrie'*" (God, I give you my life freely for my country). The priests usually say that to them, for death has more dignity that way. It is not in the ritual, but it makes a soldier's death more noble. So I suppose Capolarde said it. I could only judge by the response. I could hear the heavy, labored breath, the choking, wailing cry.

"*Oui! Oui!*" gasped out at intervals. "*Ah mon Dieu! Oui!*" Again the mumbling, guiding whisper. "*Oui—oui!*" came sobbing, gasping, in response.

So I heard the whispers, the priest's whispers, and the stertorous choke, the feeble wailing, rebellious wailing in response. He was being forced into it. Forced into acceptance. Beaten into submission, beaten into resignation.

"*Oui, oui!*" came the protesting moans. "*Ah, oui!*"

It must be dawning upon him now. Capolarde is making him see.

"*Oui! Oui!*" The choking sobs reach me. "*Ah, mon Dieu, oui!*" Then very deep, panting, crying breaths:

"*Dieu—je—vous—donne—ma—vie—librement—pour— ma—patrie!*"

"*Librement! Librement! Ah, oui! Oui!*" He was beaten at last. The choking, dying, bewildered man had said the noble words. "God, I give you my life freely for my country!"

After which came a volley of low toned Latin phrases, rattling in the stillness like the popping of a mitrailleuse.

Two hours later he was still alive, restless, but no longer resentful. "It is difficult to go," he murmured, and then: "Tonight, I shall sleep well." A long pause followed, and he opened his eyes. "Without doubt, the next world is more chic than this," he remarked smiling, and then:

"I was mobilized against my inclination. Now I have won the *Médaille Militaire*. My Captain won it for me. He made me brave. He had a revolver in his hand."[153]

Richard Aldington

from *Life for Life's Sake*

It would be tedious to enumerate at length all my lucky chances and escapes, but consider these facts. It was by chance that I was given just one night off in a period of two months and that night happened to be one when a shell dropped on a group of our officers and runners, killing or wounding all except Carl and his officer. It was by chance that I lowered my head just as a shell burst beside me in a mine crater, so that instead of hitting my face a splinter merely crashed my tin hat. It was by chance that I shifted my foot a fraction of a second before a bullet neatly took the toe from my boot instead of smashing my ankle. It was by chance that, standing in a trench, I turned my head to speak to the man behind me exactly at the moment a large chunk of shell whizzed so close to my cheek that I felt its harsh and horrid breath. It was by chance that in the last attack of the war my field glasses shifted round over my stomach—when I went to use them I found they had been smashed and bent. And finally (though by no means completely) it was by chance that I missed the worst phase of two of the worst battles of the war. If that isn't what novelists used to call "a charmed life," what is?

*   *   *

There is a superstition that drowning men live over all their lives again as vividly as they first endured them. If this be true, I hope I don't die by drowning, for I shouldn't like to live the war—that little, old-fashioned war I knew—over again. It no longer haunts me against my will, as it did for years. Deliberately what I have set down here has been the trifling, not the tragical. To have re-lived it all once in the making of another book was more than strain enough.

But memory is a faculty not understood, a capricious responder to strange calls. Unexpectedly, in a flash, it may break through that laboriously built wall of forgetfulness. Certain smells, sounds, and sights are the battering rams which suddenly demolish the wall and let the memories escape.

The smell of old wood burning brings back to my lungs and nostrils the hot frowsty air from a dugout on a winter's night. I can see the rough chalk steps going down through darkness to the candle-glimmer, the trench in which I stand, the dark patient sentry beside me, and overhead the cold stars dimmed suddenly by a Very light. The scent of new-mown hay is no longer delicious to me. It is like phosgene, and brings up a picture of dawn over a ruined village and stretcher-bearers bringing down gasping foam-mouthed bodies in stretchers. And that stuff women use to take the pink from their nails is very like tear gas, so that pink nails make me think of masked men groping along muddy trenches. In the vaults of the Escorial I smelled again that awful stench of corrupting corpse. I was with my old friend, Hal Glover, and simultaneously and without argument we both agreed to drop sight-seeing and retire to the nearest cafe for brandy and coffee. We had both smelt battlefields.

Sounds next. The drone of an airplane high up (not near) brings a blue sky filled with the little white cauliflowers of bursting shells. A distant train whinging away into silence on a frosty night brings back the sad whine of shells flying away death-laden to burst, unheard by us, among the unseen and mysterious Enemy. An impatient motorcyclist warming up his engine is no friend of mine; he echoes the more deadly machine-gun. Yet thunder is harmless to memory; it is so much milder than a barrage.

Sight is much fainter. Pavé roads and fields of beet bring

back the dead horses, with huge starting eyeballs of terror, heads reared back like the horse from the Parthenon, and large pools of dark blood. The New England woods, wrecked by the hurricane, brought back other wreckage of trees and many men's bodies.

The thought that all this must again be endured and perhaps worse, and that it may be repeated until this malicious and foolish species has gone, is a thought not to be borne.

⁕   ⁕   ⁕

They say I am bitter. The trouble is that I am not bitter enough. Tragedy upon tragedy, destruction upon destruction, another generation lost—and in my "bitterness" I dimly foresaw it: "And trouble deaf heaven with our bootless cries."

It is only after a war that the experience of the individual survivor seems to have either interest or value. During a war civilians can think only in terms of "our side" and "their side." All they ask of their men is that they shall win. The individual suffering and cost are veiled behind military phrases, which cushion the abrupt shocks of reality. How much human misery and unrepeatable calamity lie hidden behind such words and phrases as "curtain fire," "local bombardment," "clashes of patrols," "strategic retreat," "heavy fighting," "advance held up," "aerial bombing," "casualties"! We cease to think of Jack, Jean, and Johann, and talk of Divisions and Corps. We even rejoice—it is horrible—at "enemy casualties." Delicate women look pleased when they hear that "the ground in front of our positions is heaped with enemy dead." And yet they are shocked by the simple-minded and practical cannibal who makes a meal of his enemy or his grandmother. We should not say, "as savage as a wild beast," but "as savage as civilized man." How can we look on ourselves and our species with anything but disgust?[154]

102.

Robert Graves

from *Goodbye to All That*

At least one in three of my generation at school died, because they all took commissions as soon as they could, most of them in the infantry and Royal Flying Corps. The average life expectancy of an infantry subaltern on the Western Front was, at some stages of the war, only about three months, by which time he had been either wounded or killed. The proportions worked out at about four wounded to every one killed. Of these four, one got wounded seriously, and the remaining three more or less lightly. The three lightly wounded returned to the front after a few weeks or months of absence, and again faced the same odds. Flying casualties were even higher. Since the war lasted for four and a half years, it is easy to see why most of the survivors, if not permanently disabled, got wounded several times.

*   *   *

The regimental spirit persistently survived all catastrophes. Our First Battalion, for instance, was practically annihilated within two months of joining the British Expeditionary Force. Young Orme, who joined straight from Sandhurst, at the crisis of the first battle of Ypres, found himself commanding a battalion reduced to only about forty rifles. With these, and another small force, the remnants of the Second Battalion of the Queen's Regiment, reduced to thirty men and two officers, he helped to recapture three lines of lost trenches and was himself killed. The reconstituted battalion saw heavy fighting at Bois Grenier in December, but got smashed up at the Aubers Ridge and Festubert in the following May, and again at Loos in September, when only one combatant officer survived the attack—a machine-gun officer on loan from the South Staffordshire Regiment. The same sort of thing happened time after time in fighting at Fricourt, the Quadrangle, High Wood, Delville Wood, and Ginchy on the Somme in 1916, and again at Puisieux and Bullecourt in the spring fighting of 1917, and again, and again, until the Armistice. In the course of the war, at least fifteen or twenty thousand men must have passed through each of the two line battalions [of the Royal Welch Fusiliers], whose fighting strength never stood at more than eight hundred. After each catastrophe the ranks were filled up with new drafts from home, with the lightly wounded from the disaster of three or four months before, and with the more seriously wounded of earlier ones.

*   *   *

Sergeant Smith, my second sergeant, told me of the officer who had commanded the platoon before I did. "He was a nice gentleman, Sir, but very wild. Just before the Rue du Bois show, he says to me: 'By the way, sergeant, I'm going to get killed tomorrow. I know that. And I know that you're going to be all right. So see that my kit goes back to my people. You'll find their address in my pocket-book. You'll find five hundred francs there too. Now remember this, Sergeant Smith, you keep a hundred francs yourself and divide up the rest among the chaps left.' He says: 'Send my pocket-book back with my other stuff, Sergeant Smith, but for God's sake burn my diary. They mustn't see that. I'm going to get it here!' He points to his forehead. And that's how it was. He got it through the forehead all right. I sent the stuff back to his parents. I divided up the money and I burned the diary."

One day, walking along a trench at Cambrin, I suddenly dropped flat on my face, two seconds later a whizz-bang struck the back of the trench exactly where my head had been. The sergeant who was with me, walking a few steps ahead, turned round: "Are you killed, Sir?" The shell was fired from a battery near Les Briques Farm, only a thousand yards away, so that I must have reacted simultaneously with the explosion of the gun. How did I know that the shell would be coming my way?

At Béthune, I saw the ghost of a man named Private Challoner, who had been at Lancaster with me, and again in F Company at Wrexham. When he went out with a draft to join the First Battalion, he shook my hand and said: "I'll meet you again in France, Sir." In June he passed by our C Company billet, where we were just having a special dinner to celebrate our safe return from Cuinchy—new potatoes, fish, green peas, asparagus, mutton chops, strawberries and cream, and three bottles of Pommard. Private Challoner looked in at the window, saluted, and passed on. I could not mistake him, or the cap-badge he wore, yet no Royal Welch battalion was billeted within miles of Béthune at the time. I jumped up, looked out of the window, and saw nothing except a fag-end smoking on the pavement. Challoner had been killed at Festubert in May.[155]

103.

Henri Gaudier-Brzeska

Letters from the Front

[To Ezra Pound]
December 18th [1914].

The poems [of Rihaku] depict our situation in a wonderful way.... Before Rheims we had dug hibernating trenches which we had accommodated with all possible care, and we only slept once in this seeming comfort to be ousted over here. I was spying a German through a shooting cranny and loading my rifle when the order came to pack up and get ready to start on a night march. We did not know the destination: some were sure we went to rest some 20 miles behind the lines, others said we were led to the assault of a position, and this seemed confirmed when they took away our blankets to lessen the weight of the knapsack. Anyway, no one foresaw the awful ground we had to defend. We must keep two bridges and naturally as usual "until death." We cannot come back to villages to sleep, and we have to dig holes in the ground which we fill with straw and build a roof over, but the soil is so nasty that we find water at two feet six inches depth; and even if we stop at a foot, which is hardly sufficient to afford cover, we wake up in the night through the water filtering up the straw. We have been busy these last nights bringing in lots of materials, stoves, grates, etc., to make decent abodes, and unhappily they will be done just in time for us to go, as we are relieved of the post within three weeks. The beastly regiment which was here before us remained three months, and as they were all dirty northern miners used to all kind of dampness they never did an effort to better the place up a bit. When we took the trenches after the march it was a sight worthy of Dante, there was at the bottom a foot deep of liquid mud in which we had to stand two days and two nights, rest we had in small holes nearly as muddy, add to this a position making a V point into the enemy who shell us from three sides, the close vicinity of 800 putrefying German corpses, and you are at the front in the marshes of the Aisne.

It has been dry these last three days and the 1st Battalion has cleansed up the place, I believe. Anyway we are going back tonight, and we shall finish the work.

I got a sore throat in this damned place and lost my knife while falling down to avoid bullets from a stupid German sentry, whom I subsequently shot dead, but the stupid ass had no knife on him to replace mine, and the bad humor will last another week until I receive a new one from my people.

Anyway the three weeks here will pass away soon. I take the opportunity to wish you and your wife a Merry Xmas and a prosperous 1915.[156]

✶   ✶   ✶

[To Olivia Shakespear]
April 11th.
The war won't be over for another year. . . . You can tell me anything you like about the rumors you talk of, there's no censure on letters. . . . For the present I should like to see some love poems: seven months' campaign give desires which seem very commonplace in usual times, and sensualists have for once my whole sympathy. . . .

Ezra has sent me the Chinese poems. I like them very much. I keep the book in my pocket, indeed I use them to put courage in my fellows. I speak now of the "Bowmen" and the "North Gate" which are so appropriate to our case.

I shall never be a colonel but I expect to be promoted lieutenant very soon, and that will be the end of the carrière; 60 men are quite enough for my strength. I have now about 30 to command and it is much more amusing than being commanded by a grocer or a pawnbroker. My lieutenant is a baron of the old stock, a very brave man, intelligent and a fine education, so that I am happy. . . .

I am going back to the trenches in 3 days now. We have been annoying them first rate: we bombarded a wood and the infantry finished up all the wounded, bringing back only 5 prisoners. About 400 boches passed off. It's not enough yet, as the brutes shoot the prisoners they make [of] us. My best regards to the family.

May 14th.

Our woods are magnificent. I am just now quartered in trenches in the middle of them, they are covered with lily of the valley, it grows and flowers on the trench itself. In the night we have many nightingales to keep us company. They sing very finely and the loud noise of the usual attacks and counter-attacks does not disturb them in the least. It is very warm and nice out of doors, one does not mind sleeping out on the ground now.

I have heard W[alter] Rummel already, at your house once, and Chopin and Beethoven are my preferred musicians. Needless to say that here we can have nothing of the kind, we have the finest futurist music Marinetti can dream of, big guns, small guns, bomb-throwers' reports, with a great difference between the German and the French, the different kinds of whistling from the shells, their explosion, the echo in the woods of the rifle fire, some short, discreet, others long, rolling, etc.; but it is all stupid vulgarity, and I prefer the fresh wind in the leaves with a few songs from the birds.

In case I should be wounded I would let you know from the hospital some time afterwards. If I was killed of course there could be no direct news, but then you could write to my captain:

Capitaine B. Menager
commandant la 7-ème. cie.
129 regt. infanterie

but only after a very long silence on my part.

Really the English fleet can't be so serious as we imagined: these U boats seem to be allowed to tramp the seas at their own will. That the English are not careful enough on sea and land is the feeling among us. I knew Sir Hugh Lane. We got the news of the *Lusitania* the very day it happened, and we were in the trenches then; we also know day by day what happens on the front. I am very far off the English and Indian troops, so can never see them. Compliments to Max.

May 29th.

It was a pleasure to have news: we had our correspondence very late, 8 to 10 days without letters, and the place where I get it is anything but delightful for a stay in the country: the foremost trench element near Neuville, St.!—a continual bombardment, and endless inferno. I have been buried twice in the trench, have had a shell bursting in the middle of a dozen hand grenades, which miraculously did not explode, and men nastily wounded whom I must give the first aid. We are betting on our chances, whose turn it is next. The boches are restless, but we pay them well, they dared attack the day before yesterday. It has been a lurid death dance. Imagine a dull dawn, two lines of trenches and in between explosion upon explosion with clouds of black and yellow smoke, a ceaseless crackling noise from the rifles, a few legs and heads flying, and me standing up among all this like to Mephisto—commanding: "*Feu par salve à 250 metres—joue—feu!*" then throwing a bomb, and again a volley—until the Germans had enough of it. We give them nice gas to breathe when the wind is for us. I have magnificent little bombs, they are as big as an ostrich egg, they smell of ripe apples, but when they burst your eyes weep until you can't see, you are suffocated, and if the boche wants to save his skin he has to scoot. Then a good little bullet puts an end to his misery. This is not war, but a murderer hunt, we have to bring these rascals out of their holes, we do it and kill them remorselessly when they do not surrender.

Today is magnificent, a fresh wind, clear sun and larks singing cheerfully. The shells do not disturb the songsters. In the

Champagne woods the nightingales took no notice of the fight either. They solemnly proclaim man's foolery and sacrilege of nature. I respect their disdain. Many thanks for the explanation about the fleet, tell me what comes out of the enquiry if you please. . . . (I become rather interrupted because of the enemy. I tell you they'll end by wounding me.)

All I can give you from here is a buttercup, the only flower that grows on the trench (we are in meadows) and not a very nice flower, but it is a souvenir from the hard fights at the Neuville. (Again broken off, there's a machine gun rattling away in the village. I must look above the trench to see if they are not coming.) It has stopped . . . false alarm.[157]

*　　*　　*

The following letter is dated 3/5/1915, but my recollection is that I received it after the one dated May 25th. The post-mark is faint but seems to indicate "6," i.e. June. It is the only letter in which he shows any premonition of death. I have further verification that it was sent in June, not May.—Ezra Pound

Dear Ezra,

I have written to Mrs. Shakespear in what a nice place I was. It becomes worse and worse. It is the 10th day we are on the first line, and the 10th day we are getting shells on the cocoanut without truce. Right and left they lead Rosalie to the dance, but we have the ungrateful task to keep to the last under a hellish fire.

Perhaps you ignore what is Rosalie? It's our bayonet, we call it so because we draw it red from fat Saxon bellies. We shall be going to rest sometime soon, and then when we do come back it will be for an attack. It is a gruesome place all strewn with dead, and there's not a day without half a dozen fellows in the company crossing the Styx. We are betting on our mutual chances. Hope all this nasty nightmare will soon come to an end.

What are you writing? Is there anything important or even interesting going on in the world? I mean the "artistic London." I read all the "poetries" in one of the *Egoists* Mrs. Shakepear sent along. Away from this and some stories of Guy de Maupassant and E. Rod, I have read nothing, a desert in the head a very inviting place for a boche bullet or a shell, but still it had better not chose this place, and will be received in the calf for instance. . . .

(The Germans are restless, machine-gun crackling ahead, so I must end this in haste.)

*   *   *

His premonition of a head wound is curious, for this letter was written I believe only two days before his death. His sister tells me that years ago in Paris, when the war was undreamed of, he insisted that he would die in the war.—Ezra Pound[158]

*   *   *

Mort pour la Patrie

After ten months of fighting, and two promotions for gallantry on the field, Henri Gaudier-Brzeska, in a charge at Neuville St. Vaast, June 5th, 1915. [159]

104.

James Stephens

from *The Insurrection in Dublin*

To the editor of the *Nation*
New York, May 12, 1916
Nothing more lamentable in the course of the war now raging has
come to pass than the act of bloody vengeance by the English Government. . . . The shooting of the Irish insurrectionists is too much
like the shooting of prisoners of war, too much like taking a leaf
from the German classic of Schrecklichkeit [frightfulness]; and in
giving way to her vengeance England has roused the moral sense
of mankind against her. What a pity, what an infinite pity!

—William Dean Howells[160]

We believe these fundamental things: First, that every people has
a right to choose the sovereignty under which they shall live. Like
other nations, we have ourselves no doubt once and again offended against that principle when for a little while controlled by
selfish passion, as our franker historians have been honorable
enough to admit; but it has become more and more our rule of life
and action. Second, that the small states of the world have a right
to enjoy the same respect for their sovereignty and for their terri-
torial integrity that great and powerful nations expect and insist
upon. And, third, that the world has a right to be free from every

disturbance of its peace that has its origin in aggression and disregard of the rights of peoples and nations.

—Woodrow Wilson[161]

The British government, that "friend of small nationalities," has been discovered; what has been foreordained has now come to pass. The government that has been the curse of humanity for centuries, the high-priest of commercial and economic exploitation, that was responsible for the birth of militarism, has been exposed in all its nakedness and brutality; it is well that this exposure has been made by the Irish revolutionary movement.

—Jim Larkin[162]

MONDAY
This has taken everyone by surprise. It is possible, that, with the exception of their Staff, it has taken the Volunteers themselves by surprise; but, to-day, our peaceful city is no longer peaceful; guns are sounding, or rolling and crackling from different directions, and, although rarely, the rattle of machine guns can be heard also.

TUESDAY
A sultry, lowering day, and dusk skies fat with rain.
I left for my office, believing that the insurrection was at an end. At a corner I asked a man was it all finished. He said it was not, and that, if anything, it was worse.
On this day the rumors began, and I think it will be many a year before the rumors cease....
On the previous day the Volunteers had proclaimed the Irish Republic. This ceremony was conducted from the Mansion House steps, and the manifesto was said to have been read by Pearse, of St. Enda's. The Republican and Volunteer flag was hoisted on the Mansion House. The latter consisted of vertical colors of green, white and orange. Kerry wireless station was re-

ported captured, and news of the Republic flashed abroad. These rumors were flying in the street.

It was also reported that two transports had come in the night and had landed from England about 8,000 soldiers. An attack reported on the Post Office by a troop of lancers who were received with fire and repulsed. It is foolish to send cavalry into street war. . . .

At eleven o'clock the rain ceased, and to it succeeded a beautiful night, gusty with wind, and packed with sailing clouds and stars. We were expecting visitors this night, but the sound of guns may have warned most people away. Three only came, and with them we listened from my window to the guns at the Green challenging and replying to each other, and to where, further away, the Trinity snipers were crackling, and beyond again to the sounds of war from Sackville Street. The firing was fairly heavy, and often the short rattle of machine guns could be heard.

One of the stories told was that the Volunteers had taken the South Dublin Union Workhouse, occupied it, and trenched the grounds. They were heavily attacked by the military, who, at a loss of 150 men, took the place. The tale went that towards the close the officer in command offered them terms of surrender, but the Volunteers replied that they were not there to surrender. They were there to be killed. The garrison consisted of fifty men, and the story said that fifty men were killed.

WEDNESDAY

It was three o'clock before I got to sleep last night, and during the hours machine guns and rifle firing had been continuous.

This morning the sun is shining brilliantly, and the movement in the streets possesses more of animation than it has done. The movement ends always in a knot of people, and folk go from group to group vainly seeking information, and quite content if the rumor they presently gather differs even a little from the one they have just communicated.

The first statement I heard was that the Green had been taken by the military the second that it had been re-taken the third that it had not been taken at all. The facts at last emerged that the

Green had not been occupied by the soldiers, but that the Volunteers had retreated from it into a house which commanded it. This was found to be the College of Surgeons, and from the windows and roof of this College they were sniping. A machine gun was mounted on the roof; other machine guns, however, opposed them from the roofs of the Shelbourne Hotel, the United Service Club, and the Alexandra Club. Thus a triangular duel opened between these positions across the trees of the Park.

THURSDAY

Again, the rumors greeted one. This place had fallen and had not fallen. Such a position had been captured by the soldiers recaptured by the Volunteers, and had not been attacked at all. But certainly fighting was proceeding. Up Mount Street, the rifle volleys were continuous, and the coming and going of ambulance cars from that direction were continuous also. Some spoke of pitched battles on the bridge, and said that as yet the advantage lay with the Volunteers.

At 11:30 there came the sound of heavy guns firing in the direction of Sackville Street. I went on the roof, and remained there for some time. From this height the sounds could be heard plainly. There was sustained firing along the whole central line of the City, from the Green down to Trinity College, and from thence to Sackville Street, and the report of the various types of arm could be easily distinguished. There were rifles, machine guns and very heavy cannon. There was another sound which I could not put a name to, something that coughed out over all the other sounds, a short, sharp bark, or rather a short noise something like the popping of a tremendous cork. . . .

This night also was calm and beautiful, but this night was the most sinister and woeful of those that have passed. The sound of artillery, of rifles, machine guns, grenades, did not cease even for a moment. From my window I saw a red flare that crept to the sky, and stole over it and remained there glaring; the smoke reached from the ground to the clouds, and I could see great red sparks go soaring to enormous heights while always, in the calm air, hour after hour there was the buzzing and rattling and thudding of guns, and, but for the guns, silence.

It is in a dead silence this Insurrection is being fought, and one imagines what must be the feeling of these men, young for the most part, and unused to violence, who are submitting silently to the crash and flame and explosion by which they are surrounded.

FRIDAY

This morning there are no newspapers, no bread, no milk, no news. The sun is shining, and the streets are lively but discreet. All people continue to talk to one another without distinction of class, but nobody knows what any person thinks. . . .

None of these people were prepared for Insurrection. The thing had been sprung on them so suddenly that they were unable to take sides, and their feeling of detachment was still so complete that they would have betted on the business as if it had been a horse race or a dog fight.

Many English troops have been landed each night, and it is believed that there are more than sixty thousand soldiers in Dublin alone, and that they are supplied with every offensive contrivance which military art has invented. . . .

From the roof there comes the sound of machine guns. Looking towards Sackville Street one picks out easily Nelson's Pillar, which towers slenderly over all the buildings of the neighborhood. It is wreathed in smoke. Another towering building was the D.B.C. Café. Its Chinese-like pagoda was a landmark easily to be found, but today I could not find it. It was not there. . . .

During the night the firing was heavy from almost every direction and in the direction of Sackville Street a red glare told again of fire.

It is hard to get to bed these nights. It is hard even to sit down, for the moment one does sit down one stands immediately up again resuming that ridiculous ship's march from the window to the wall and back. I am foot weary as I have never been before in my life, but I cannot say that I am excited. No person in Dublin is excited, but there exists a state of tension and expectancy which is mentally more exasperating than any excitement could be. The absence of news is largely responsible for this. We do not know what has happened, what is happening, or what is going to happen, and the reversion to barbarism (for barbarism is largely a lack of news) disturbs us.

Each night we have got to bed at last murmuring, "I wonder will it be all over tomorrow," and this night the like question accompanied us.

SATURDAY

This morning also there has been no bread, no milk, no meat, no newspapers, but the sun is shining. It is astonishing that, thus early in the Spring, the weather should be so beautiful. It is stated freely that the Post Office has been taken, and just as freely it is averred that it has not been taken. The approaches to Merrion Square are held by the military, and I was not permitted to go to my office. . . .

The rifle fire was persistent all day, but, saving in certain localities, it was not heavy. Occasionally the machine guns rapped in. There was no sound of heavy artillery. The rumor grows that the Post Office has been evacuated, and that the Volunteers are at large and spreading everywhere across the roofs. The rumor grows also that terms of surrender are being discussed, and that Sackville Street has been levelled to the ground.

At half-past seven in the evening calm is almost complete. The sound of a rifle shot being only heard at long intervals.

I got to bed this night earlier than usual. At two o'clock I left the window from which a red flare is yet visible in the direction of Sackville Street. The morning will tell if the Insurrection is finished or not, but at this hour all is not over. Shots are ringing all around and down my street, and the vicious crackling of these rifles grow at times into regular volleys.

SUNDAY

The Insurrection has not ceased.

There is much rifle fire, but no sound from the machine guns or the eighteen pounders and trench mortars.

From the window of my kitchen the flag of the Republic can be seen flying afar. This is the flag that flies over Jacob's Biscuit

Factory, and I will know that the Insurrection has ended as soon as I see this flag pulled down. . . .

It is half-past three o'clock, and from my window the Republican flag can still be seen flying over Jacob's factory. There is occasional shooting, but the city as a whole is quiet. At a quarter to five o'clock a heavy gun boomed once. Ten minutes later there was heavy machine gun firing and much rifle shooting. In another ten minutes the flag at Jacob's was hauled down. During the remainder of the night sniping and military replies were incessant, particularly in my street.

The raids have begun in private houses.

THE INSURRECTION IS OVER!

The finest part of our city has been blown to smithereens, and burned into ashes. Soldiers amongst us who have served abroad say that the ruin of this quarter is more complete than anything they have seen at Ypres, than anything they have seen anywhere in France or Flanders. A great number of our men and women and children, Volunteers and civilians confounded alike, are dead, and some fifty thousand men who have been moved with military equipment to our land are now being removed therefrom. The English nation has been disorganized no more than as they were affected by the transport of these men and material. That is what happened, and it is all that happened.[163]

105.

from *Poetry: A Magazine of Verse*

Harriet Monroe

New Banners

What are we to do with war—all these wars and rumors of wars which absorb man's interests and energies, waste his treasure, and interrupt his proper modern business—the business of making a more habitable world, and more beautiful and noble men and women to live in it? What are we to do with this stupid and violent interruption, which fills our eyes with ruin, our ears with noise, our nostrils with sickening stenches, and our minds with pompous and brutal melodrama? War which, as it destroys and maims and kills, is in no other detail so disgusting as in its monstrous pretense of heroism. Heroism!—the big bully merely shows us how many heroes we have by destroying them; merely brings out tragic evidence of the heroism which existed in its victims before the guns mangled them, heroism which should have been preserved for the slow struggles of peace.

"Europe will be born again through this war"—thus I have heard people rhapsodize; "she will rise purified and illumined"—etc., etc., in minute detail. Ah, when the artificial stimulus ceases that produced all the bitter rapture and agony, will not men and nations have to resume their old tasks, their old lives, but with heavier burdens to carry, and under harsher conditions than before?

*   *   *

So there is more joy in heaven over one little sweat-shop sewing girl who rebels than over ninety-and-nine V.C.'s won at the point of a bayonet. And there is more hope for humanity in the present very definite movement for increase of beauty and joy in our lives, than in the triumphant march of a thousand armies.

One conspicuous phase of this movement—the many-sided struggle to abolish poverty—may not be in *Poetry*'s province; but another phase, the impulse toward civic beauty, is the beginning of a richer life in this country which will bring a renaissance of all the arts. Therefore the sense of joy, of spiritual expansion, which came to me during a recent visit, one fine summer Sunday, to Chicago's new Municipal Recreation Pier, seemed to bear a direct relation to *Poetry*. Here, in this beautiful assemblage of vast halls and towers, outdoor courts and colonnades, reaching out into the cool blue lake as a spacious refuge from dust and heat, from toil and struggle and ugliness—here was the proof of a new movement in our democracy, proof that the people are beginning to express in definite, concrete form their demand for beauty. . . .

The organization of society for rapid, effective and beautiful movement in peace, as hitherto it has frequently been organized for such movement in war—that is the modern problem, a problem worth the devotion of our best minds, our richest treasure. Such devotion will destroy war at last by stripping it of its ancient glamour. Men live by dreams, by the ever elusive dream of beauty. Give them dreams more beautiful and heroic than their long-cherished vision of the glory of war, and they will put away war like a worn-out garment, and unite for conquests really glorious, for the advance toward justice and beauty in the brotherhood of nations.[164]

106.

Margaret Anderson

from *My Thirty Years' War*

At this moment the most interesting thing that had happened to the *Little Review*— the most interesting thing that ever happened to it—took place in February.

Jane Heap appeared.

...There is no one in the modern world whose conversation I haven't sampled, I believe, except Picasso's. So I can't say it isn't better than Jane Heap's. But I doubt it in spite of his reputation. I felt in 1916 and feel today that Jane Heap is the world's best talker. It isn't a question of words, facility, style. It isn't a question of erudition. It isn't even a question of truth. (Who knows whether what she says is true?) It is entirely a question of ideas. No one can find such interesting things to say on any subject. I have often thought I should like to give my life over to talk-racing, with my money on Jane. No one else would ever win—you can't win against magic. What it is exactly—this making of ideas—I don't know. Jane herself doesn't know.

Things become known to me, she says.

She talks usually in monosyllables, with here and there an important word placed so personally as to give it a curious personal significance. It is impossible to quote her. You can hear that done, with appropriate disaster, by anyone who tries it. I will try.

Take a group of people discussing sophistication, for example. You hear every possible definition of sophistication—you already know them all. Then Jane says:

A really sophisticated person? I should say a person who is used to being a human being. . . .

A phrase of Jane's I have always remembered was one she found as a tribute to someone who (briefly) understood her:

A hand on the exact octave that is me. . . .

This was the kind of perception I liked. Jane's impersonal judgment of people was always unexpected—and always creative. I decided that it must be presented in the *Little Review*.[165]

*   *   *

Margaret Anderson and Jane Heap moved to California in the summer of 1916 for an extended sojourn at a "ranch" in Muir Woods. The war having had its way with the quality of submissions to the magazine, the two of them—"maddened by . . . the lack of interest in the manuscripts that came in"—put out an issue of the Little Review *consisting of sixty-four empty pages, which stated "that since no art was being produced we would make no attempt to publish any." There were two pages of cartoons by Jane—"Mason and Hamlin, anarchist meetings, horse-back riding, fudge breakfasts and intellectual combats. These filled the two pages in the center, and all the other pages were reproachfully blank." In late autumn they returned to Chicago.*[166]

*   *   *

We arrived in Chicago and at once I knew we should go to New York. This was an inconvenient thought. Also an unhappy one for Jane, who would never in those days leave any place she loved. Besides I had no reasons to give. It was just "the time to go." . . .

Chicago had had all it wanted from us, we had had all that it could give. It was time to touch the greatest city of America. It would then be time for Europe. The only way to make the *L.R.* the international organ I had planned was to publish it from New York, where our position would be more commanding. We hadn't yet met all the interesting people in the world. Some of them were in New York. Some were in London and Paris—the greatest artists of the modern age. I loved Chicago forever, I could never forget it, I would come back to it . . . but I must go on.

*　　*　　*

We prepared to say farewell to Chicago. . . . I told everyone good-by—including the Fine Arts Building. I went to walk through its corridors which always seemed to me filled with flowers—its shops, which gave me the emotion of a perpetual Christmas. I talked for the last time with the elevator boys, the head starter, the night watchman. They assured me that the Fine Arts wouldn't be the same without me, that Chicago wouldn't be the same. I went to buy a rose from the flower woman around the corner, where my single rose purchases at five cents had left a great tenderness. . . .

Coming back to the Fine Arts Building I met Ben Hecht. After you have gone, he announced, I'm going to have an electric sign put across this building:

Where is Athens now?[167]

Epilogue: And the War Came to America

It is almost certain that Wilson could have carried majorities in Congress and among the public with him in virtually any direction he chose. Why Wilson decided upon intervention at the end of March, 1917, still remains something of a puzzle. He continued to express misgivings even after issuing a call for Congress to meet to consider further action in the crisis.

—John Milton Cooper[168]

Like all true-hearted Americans. he hoped that the United States would not be drawn into the war; but he was of Scotch and English blood, and by inheritance, tradition and rearing at all times the friend of the Allies.

—T. W. Gregory[169]

Old Timers

I am an ancient reluctant conscript.

On the soup wagons of Xerxes I was a cleaner of pans.

On the march of Miltiades' phalanx I had a haft and head;
I had a bristling gleaming spear-handle.

Red-headed Caesar picked me for a teamster.
He said, "Go to work, you Tuscan bastard!
      Rome calls for a man who can drive horses."

The units of conquest led by Charles the Twelfth,
The whirling whimsical Napoleonic columns:
They saw me one of the horseshoers.

I trimmed the feet of a white horse Bonaparte swept
      the night stars with.
Lincoln said, "Get into the game; your nation takes you."
And I drove a wagon and team and I had my arm shot off
At Spottsylvania Court House.

I am an ancient reluctant conscript.

—Carl Sandburg[170]

107.

Randolph Bourne

The War and the Intellectuals

To those of us who still retain an irreconcilable animus against war, it has been a bitter experience to see the unanimity with which the American intellectuals have thrown their support to the use of war-technique in the crisis in which America found herself. Socialists, college professors, publicists, new-republicans, practitioners of literature, have vied with each other in confirming with their intellectual faith the collapse of neutrality and the riveting of the war-mind on a hundred million more of the world's people.

And the intellectuals are not content with confirming our belligerent gesture. They are now complacently asserting that it was they who effectively willed it, against the hesitation and dim perceptions of the American democratic masses. A war made deliberately by the intellectuals! A calm moral verdict, arrived at after a penetrating study of inexorable facts! Sluggish masses, too remote from the world-conflict to be stirred, too lacking in intellect to perceive their danger! An alert intellectual class, saving the people in spite of themselves, biding their time with Fabian strategy until the nation could be moved into war without serious resistance! An intellectual class, gently guiding a nation through sheer force of ideas into what the other nations entered only through predatory craft or popular hysteria or militarist madness! A war free from any taint of self-seeking, a war that will secure the triumph of democracy and internationalize the world! This is the picture which the more self-conscious intellectuals have formed of themselves, and which they are slowly impressing upon a population which is being led no man knows whither by an indubitably intellectualized President. And they are right, in that the war certainly did not spring from either the ideals or the prejudices, from the national ambitions or hysterias, of the American people, however acquiescent the masses prove to be, and however clearly the intellectuals prove their putative intuition.

Those intellectuals who have felt themselves totally out of sympathy with this drag toward war will seek some explanation for this joyful leadership. They will want to understand this willingness of the American intellect to open the sluices and flood us with the sewage of the war spirit. We cannot forget the virtuous horror and stupefaction which filled our college professors when they read the famous manifesto of their ninety-three German colleagues in defense of their war. To the American academic mind of 1914 defense of war was inconceivable . . . little dreaming that two years later would find it creating its own cleanly reasons for imposing military service on the country and for talking of the rough rude currents of health and regeneration that war would send through the American body politic. They would have thought anyone mad who talked of shipping American men by the hundreds of thousands—conscripts—to die on the fields of France. Such a spiritual change seems catastrophic when we shoot our minds back to those days when neutrality was a proud thing. But the intellectual progress has been so gradual that the country retains little sense of the irony. The war sentiment, begun so gradually but so perseveringly by the preparedness advocates who came from the ranks of big business, caught hold of one after another of the intellectual groups. With the aid of Roosevelt, the murmurs became a monotonous chant, and finally a chorus so mighty that to be out of it was at first to be disreputable and finally almost obscene.[171]

108.

Max Eastman

from *Love and Revolution*

I had had a friendly relation with Wilson dating back to 1912, when we addressed together a banquet of the Chamber of Commerce in Syracuse, New York. We sat side by side through an eight-course dinner and talked searchingly about everything under the sun, starting with woman suffrage. Knowing that I had spoken in favor of it, he asked me earnestly and with a flattering deference for "instruction" on the subject. . . . I pride myself that our conversation led him some way along toward his belated decision to support the Nineteenth Amendment. It led at any rate to a friendly feeling between us, which survived until the summer of 1916 when I turned up at the White House with a group of liberals protesting against increased military appropriations.

Recalling our conversation at the banquet, Wilson greeted me with special warmth. He was not impressed by our arguments, but impressed us rather with his gift of suave and perfect diction. . . He called us "we," and imparted to us his private and exciting plan to stay out of the war in Europe until both sides were exhausted and then step in with a proposal of peace and an association of nations to prevent future wars. This was a radical proposal in those days and fell in pat with my own anti-Marxist views on the war problem. For that reason—much to the disgust of the dogmatic pundits of the Socialist Party—I spoke up for Wilson in the November elections. Neither his personality, which seemed a little off-on-a-mountain to me, nor the slogan "He kept us out of war," would have swerved me that far from my "revolutionary" course. But that he had a plan—the very plan I had been advocating—for ending war altogether, swung me strongly to his side. When in January 1917, he made his famous "peace without victory" speech, I was enraptured.

"The histories of all the nations will hold a venerated record of that address," I wrote in the *Masses*. "Peace without victory, and the United States not involved in the quarrel, but standing with all her impartial power for international union—that is the highest hope and purpose for us and for the world."

Three months later Wilson threw the whole thing over, and entered the fight, heart, soul, and ideology, on the side of the Allies. To us of the antiwar party this looked treacherous and capricious, and his biographers still wrestle over the causes of it. We did not know that the slogan "He kept us out of war" had been launched by his campaign managers, and that he had tried to call it back.[172] But even if we had, the change from *Peace Without Victory and a League of Nations* to *War for Democracy and No Mention of Peace Terms*, was too much for us. It shattered the pattern of perception with which we were making a hero of Wilson, or reshuffled it with all his weak points in the focus.

In an editorial on his speech of April 2, 1917, demanding the declaration of war against Germany, I paid an ironical tribute to his "talent for mobilizing noble ideas in behalf of whatever he has decided to do." His speech began, I pointed out, by citing the *defense of our national rights* as both cause and justification of our entering the war, but ended, with serene indifference to logic, by representing us as having joined a *crusade for democracy*. I asked that this seeking out of "ideological forms" under which we were to fight be replaced by a concrete statement of the purposes for which we were fighting. I recalled the President's statement three months before: "The singularity of the present war is that its origin and objects have never been disclosed. They have obscure European roots which we do not know how to trace." And I asked him, before conscripting American citizens to fight in a war whose roots are unknown and objects undisclosed, to state at least what his own objects were. . . .

The *Masses* was not alone, of course, in attacking Wilson's war policy. We had the whole Socialist Party and the I.W.W. with us, the pacifists, many of the humanitarian uplifters, most of the Quakers and deep-feeling Christian ministers, the Irish, the "hyphenated Americans," the old-fashioned patriots still faithful to George Washington's Farewell Address, and millions of plain folks whose hearts were in it when they sang a song that swept the country in those days:

> I didn't raise my boy to be a soldier,
> I brought him up to be my pride and joy . . .

Better for us, if we *had* been alone in opposing the war policy. For this immense opposition, this nation-wide conflict of passionate opinion, created a state of mind in which laws were unable to protect the liberties or lives of the citizens. In nations as well as individuals, hysteria is caused by inner conflict, and the United States on entering the First World War suffered a violent attack of this disease. No other such event in our history is comparable to the nation-wide witch hunt of those mad days.

In spite of a ruling by the Attorney General that "the constitutional right of free speech, free assembly, and petition exist in wartime as in peacetime," nearly two thousand men and women were jailed for their opinions during the First World War, their sentences running as high as thirty years. . . .

"For my part," I wrote, "I do not recognize the right of a government to draft me to a war whose purpose I do not believe in. But to draft me to a war whose purposes it will not so much as communicate to my ear seems an act of tyranny discordant with the memory even of the decent kings."[173]

109.

Scott Nearing

War Fever

During the first two years of the war the United States public was overwhelmingly anti-war and isolationist. Irish-Americans were anti-British and therefore opposed to American entrance on the side of England. German-Americans were pro-German and therefore against American participation on the side of the Allies. Far more important than these nationalist segments was the population of the immense Mississippi Valley, which proclaimed, "Kansas has no sea coast; what do we care for 'over there.'" Even as late as November 1916 President Woodrow Wilson won his re-election on the slogan, "He kept us out of war." And in January 1917, in a speech at the Waldorf Astoria in New York City, he proclaimed: "One thing this country never will endure is a system that can be called militarism."

Three months later, in April 1917, the same President Wilson led the American people into the war "to make the world safe for Democracy." What had happened in the meantime? For one thing, the war had become stalemated. If there was any choice, the Germans had the edge. Then again, United States business interests had lined up more and more solidly behind the British and their Allies. President Wilson was consistently pro-British if not outright anti-German. Carefully written propaganda made the Germans and their Kaiser the symbols of cruelty and tyranny while the British and their German-sired royal family were hailed as the symbols of freedom and democracy.

As it became more and more evident that the outcome of stalemated war could be determined by the American decision to join one side or the other, the propaganda battle grew in intensity. I remember the parades, the bands, the fervent speeches, the cheering crowds. I also remember the anxieties, the whipped-up fears and hatreds. Likewise I remember the sturdy opposition, the demonstrations, the mobs, the beatings, jailings, lynchings which come with war fever. . . .

On any basis of judgment, at the time of the Victorian Jubilee in 1897, the United States was a second- or third-rate power. Two decades later Washington had won its title to world power-hood by playing a decisive role among the Allied governments. All of the European powers took a beating. By accident, design, or intuition, President Wilson (and the American Oligarchy for which he was then the chief political spokesman) hit on a long-accepted axiom: where several dogs are fighting for a bone, the wisest dog will let the others tire themselves out in the melee, then snatch the bone and make off with it. Wilson and Washington waited and grabbed the bone.[174]

110.

The German Ambassador in Washington (Bernstorff) to the Secretary of State (Lansing)

On January 31, 1917, the German Foreign Office sent a note to the United States announcing the resumption of unrestricted submarine warfare, which they had suspended in May 1916, following an ultimatum from the U.S. government—the end result of a year-long diplomatic pas-de-deux after the sinking of the Cunard liner Lusitania *on May 7, 1915.*

(Translation)
Washington, January 31, 1917.

Since two years and a half England is using her naval power for a criminal attempt to force Germany into submission by starvation. In brutal contempt of international law the group of powers led by England does not only curtail the legitimate trade of their opponents but they also by ruthless pressure compel neutral countries either to altogether forego every trade not agreeable to the Entente powers or to limit it according to their arbitrary decrees. The American Government knows the steps which have been taken to cause England and her allies to return to the rules of international law and to respect the freedom of the seas. The English Government, however, insists upon continuing its war of starvation, which does not at all affect the military power of its opponents, but compels women and children, the sick and the aged to suffer, for their country, pains and privations which endanger the vitality of the nation. Thus British tyranny mercilessly increases the sufferings of the world indifferent to the laws of humanity, indifferent to the protests of the neutrals whom they severely harm, indifferent even to the silent longing for peace among England's own allies. Each day of the terrible struggle causes new destruction, new sufferings. Each day shortening the war will, on both sides, preserve the life of thousands of brave soldiers and be a benefit to mankind.

The Imperial Government could not justify before its own conscience, before the German people, and before history the neglect of any means destined to bring about the end of the war. . . . [and] is now compelled to continue the fight for existence . . . with the full employment of all the weapons which are at its disposal.

(Enclosure)

Memorandum

Germany has, so far, not made unrestricted use of the weapon which she possesses in her submarines. Since the Entente powers, however, have made it impossible to come to an understanding based upon equality of rights of all nations, as proposed by the Central powers, and have instead declared only such a peace to be possible which shall be dictated by the Entente allies and shall result in the destruction and humiliation of the Central powers, Germany is unable further to forego the full use of her submarines. . . .

Under these circumstances Germany will meet the illegal measures of her enemies by forcibly preventing after February 1, 1917, in a zone around Great Britain, France, Italy, and in the eastern Mediterranean all navigation, that of neutrals included, from and to England and from and to France, etc., etc. All ships met within that zone will be sunk.[175]

III.

Count Johann von Bernstorff

Resumption of Submarine Warfare

After the 31st of January, 1917, Mr. Wilson was incapable of an impartial attitude towards Germany. He saw red whenever he thought of the Imperial Government, and his repugnance against it knew no bounds. . . .

Had Mr. Wilson, after January, 1917, really come to the definite conclusion that he held the proofs of Germany's war guilt and lust of world empire? Whereas, theretofore he had considered the question of war guilt impartially, he now agreed that the Germans would have been able to obtain a reasonable peace through his mediation, but had rejected it and chosen to declare the U-boat war instead, in order to achieve a complete victory. Consequently, the Germans had not been concerned all this time with bringing about a reasonable peace, but with gaining the empire of the world, a conclusion from which their war guilt was also to be inferred. It was as the result of these ideas that Mr. Wilson preached the crusade against militaristic and autocratic Germany, who wanted to achieve the mastery of the world. Only by means of the belief in a crusade could the peace-loving American people be prevailed upon to wage war.[176]

112.

Woodrow Wilson

Address to a Joint Session of Congress on the Severance of Diplomatic Relations with Germany

February 3, 1917.

The Imperial German Government on the thirty-first of January announced to this Government and to the governments of the other neutral nations that on and after the first day of February, the present month, it would adopt a policy with regard to the use of submarines against all shipping seeking to pass through certain designated areas of the high seas to which it is clearly my duty to call your attention. . . .

I think that you will agree with me that, in view of this declaration, which suddenly and without prior intimation of any kind deliberately withdraws the solemn assurance given in the Imperial Government's note of the fourth of May, 1916, this Government has no alternative consistent with the dignity and honor of the United States but to take the course which, in its note of the eighteenth of April, 1916, it announced that it would take in the event that the German Government did not declare and effect an abandonment of the methods of submarine warfare which it was then employing and to which it now purposes again to resort.

I have, therefore, directed the Secretary of State to announce to His Excellency the German Ambassador that all diplomatic relations between the United States and the German

Empire are severed, and that the American Ambassador at Berlin will immediately be withdrawn; and, in accordance with this decision, to hand to His Excellency his passports.[177]

113.

Senator Robert M. LaFollette

On Neutrality

On the 2nd of November, 1914, only three months after the beginning of the war, England issued a proclamation, the most ruthless and sweeping in its violation of neutral rights that up to that time had ever emanated from a civilized government engaged in prosecuting a war, announcing that on three days' notice all of the North Sea, free under international law to the trade of the world, would be entered by our merchant ships at their peril. She based her action upon the assertion that the German government had been scattering mines in waters open to the world's commerce. . . .

The North Sea, a great stretch of the Atlantic Ocean, extending from Scotland to Iceland, was barred to the commerce of the world, the neutral commerce that had the same right there that you have to walk down Pennsylvania Ave. . . .

Now we come to the most unfortunate part of our record. The present administration agreed to this lawless act of Great Britain. I make this statement deliberately and fully appreciating its consequences. If we had entered into a contract with Great Britain, signed and sealed under the great seals of the respective countries, agreeing that she should commit the act of piracy involved in mining the North Sea, we would not more completely have been bound by such contract than we are bound by the conduct of the present administration. . . .

If our ships had been sent into [England's] forbidden high-sea war zone, as they have into the proscribed area Germany marked out on the high seas as a war zone, we would have had the same loss of life and property in the one case as in the other. But because we avoided doing that in the case of England, and acquiesced in her violation of law, we have not only a legal but a moral responsibility for the position in which Germany has been placed by our collusion and cooperation with Great Britain.

By suspending the rule with respect to neutral rights in Great Britain's case, we have been actively aiding her in starving the civil population of Germany. We have helped to drive Germany into a corner, her back to the wall, to fight with what weapons she can lay her hands on to prevent the starving of her women and children, her old men and babes. . . .

Days, weeks, and months went by, and still no protest came from the American government against this unlawful act on the part of Great Britain. . . . Germany then did as a matter of retaliation and defense what Great Britain had done months previously purely as an offensive measure—established a war zone or war area. She included in it portions of the sea about the British islands, and gave notice that ships coming within it would be destroyed by mines or submarines, even as English mines in the North Sea destroyed the ships which entered there.

It is Germany's insistence upon her right to blindly destroy with mines and submarines in the area she has declared as a war zone all ships that enter there, that causes the whole trouble existing between us and Germany today. . . .

The English mines are intended to destroy without warning every ship that enters the war zone she has proscribed, killing or drowning every passenger that cannot find some means of escape. It is neither more nor less than that which Germany tries to do with her submarines in her war zone. We acquiesced in England's action without protest. . . .

The present administration has assumed and acted upon the policy that it could enforce to the very letter of the law the principles or international law against one belligerent and relax them as to the other.

That thing no nation can do without losing its character as

a neutral nation and without losing the rights that go with strict and absolute neutrality. . . .

Jefferson asserted that we could not permit one warring nation to curtail our neutral rights if we were not ready to allow her enemy the same privileges, and that any other course entailed the sacrifice of our neutrality.[178]

114.

Frederic C. Howe

Portrait of Woodrow Wilson

At Johns Hopkins, Woodrow Wilson fell under the spell of Walter Bagehot, one of the greatest of British essayists. He urged his students to read and reread Bagehot as he himself had done. His *Congressional Government* was said to have been inspired by Bagehot's *British Constitution*, as were many of his essays on public men. Bagehot gave the student Wilson that which his mind wanted, a picture of what a great constitutional statesman should be. Through Bagehot's eyes he saw British statesmen as he saw himself. They were drawn from the best families, trained from youth for the service of the state. They grew up in the atmosphere of Oxford and Cambridge, and were exalted by traditions of disinterested public service. They had no private ends to serve; because of their independent wealth they were influenced only by the welfare of the empire. They were the natural rulers of the constitutional state. England was a gentlemen's country. And Mr. Wilson believed in gentlemen, in selected men, in the platonic sense of the term. To Woodrow Wilson the scholar it was easy to idealize a country that put its scholars in politics and kept them there as it kept Arthur Balfour, James Bryce, and other men of his own type.

A love of English institutions was strong in Mr. Wilson even during his student days. He organized then a debating society known as the University Commons, modeled after the Oxford

Union. Its proceedings were carried on as are the proceedings in the House of Commons. There was a ministry and an opposition. Weekly debates were staged on current political issues, and ministries rose or fell on votes of confidence. As a dissertation for his doctor's degree Mr. Wilson had written *Congressional Government*, which was considered the best book written by an American on our form of government. It treated the British constitution with its responsible ministries sitting in Parliament as better fitted than our own for popular government.

Woodrow Wilson loved England as the mother of civil liberty and of parliamentary government. She had given us the Magna Carta, the Bill of Rights, and the Petition of Rights. She had exiled the Stuarts for their betrayal of English liberties and had called in Cromwell and William of Orange to re-establish them. In his mind England was the literal mother of America. From her we had taken our political institutions. Also our system of jurisprudence. His chief criticisms of the American Constitution related to those features which failed to follow the British parliamentary model. It was this love for British forms that led him to read his messages to Congress in person and to treat himself as a Premier rather than as a President. As a matter of fact he was better fitted by temperament to serve as a parliamentary leader than as a President, and he would have felt much more at home at Westminster than in Washington.

Mr. Wilson gave us no glimpse of the economic background of the English ruling class. There was always the assumption that these public men were not moved by private gain. It was never hinted in his lecture-room that the British landed gentry, bankers, and business men enacted laws to protect their own class and group; looked out, in short, for their own interests. Nor that the House of Lords was in the nature of a private corporation representative of special interests even more than the United States Senate. He was not interested in economics.

Woodrow Wilson prized the blood of his forebears. It was the blood of the Washingtons, Jeffersons, Madisons, Lees which flowed back in its purity to old England. During the Peace Conference Mr. Wilson went to Buckingham Palace, to the old Guildhall, to Carlisle with a pride of birth, which the British never failed to keep alive before his eyes. He was the kin, the equal, of the men he sat among from the British Parliament. He loved England as did they. His blood was the same as theirs. He knew her history better than did most of his English associates, and he was proud of the service which he had been able to render to the mother country.

Another university influence permanently affected Woodrow Wilson. At Johns Hopkins history was studied from original sources, from American State Papers, from *The Federalist*, from the writings of the Fathers; the textbook was secondary. We were directed to read and reread the writings of the Presidents, especially of Washington, Jefferson, and Madison. We read the debates of the Constitutional Convention, the letters of these early men. This reverence for State Papers lived on in President Wilson as it did in all of his contemporaries. It exalted the written word; it made him careful of his official addresses and communications to Congress. Just as he gathered his pictures of men out of their public utterances so subsequent historians would judge him from the same source. His other addresses may pass away; his *History of the United States* may be forgotten; the things he did may be condemned; but generations hence students in the universities and statesmen at the Capital will find the Woodrow Wilson of his own reveries the Woodrow Wilson that he wanted preserved in the State Papers written by him to his contemporaries.

Woodrow Wilson the President is to be found in these early influences. He never outgrew them. He lived in a world of dreams rather than with men. His reveries were of English and American statesmen, himself among the number; they were the reveries of the student, of the admiring biographer, of the historian of the Victorian age, when men were measured by ideological standards rather than by the more realistic standards of today. He was always religious, Calvinistic. He loved Virginia, the Mother of Presidents, and esteemed great documents as the most enduring of deeds. His heroes had phrased liberty, had inspired movements, had given the world charters of freedom. They had won great victories by the pen.[179]

115.

Telegram: The Ambassador in Great Britain (Page) to the Secretary of State (Lansing)

London, March 5, 1917, 1 p.m. (Received March 6, 3.20 a.m.)

The financial inquiries made here reveal an international condition most alarming to the American financial and industrial outlook. England is obliged to finance her allies as well as to meet her own war expenses. She has as yet been able to do these tasks out of her own resources. But in addition to these tasks she cannot continue her present large purchases in the United States without shipments of gold to pay for them and she cannot maintain large shipments of gold for two reasons: first, both England and France must retain most of the gold they have to keep their paper money at par; and second, the submarine has made the shipping of gold too hazardous, even if they had it to ship. The almost immediate danger, therefore, is that Franco-American and Anglo-American exchange will be so disturbed that orders by all the Allied Governments will be reduced to the lowest minimum and there will be almost a cessation of transatlantic trade. This will, of course, cause a panic in the United States.

The world will be divided into two hemispheres, one of which has gold and commodities and the other, which needs these commodities, will have no money to pay for them and practically no commodities of their own to exchange for them. The financial and commercial result will be almost as bad for one as for the other. This condition may soon come suddenly unless action is quickly taken to prevent it. France and England must have a large enough credit in the United States to prevent the collapse of world trade and of the whole of European finance.

If we should go to war with Germany the greatest help we could give the Allies would be such a credit. In that case our Government could, if it would, make a large investment in a Franco-British loan or might guarantee such a loan. All the money would be kept in our own country, trade would be continued and enlarged till the war ends, and after the war, Europe would continue to buy food and would buy from us also an enormous supply of things to re-equip her peace industries. We should thus reap the profit of an uninterrupted, perhaps an enlarging, trade over a number of years and we should hold their securities in payment.

But if we hold most of the money and Europe cannot pay for re-equipment there may be a world-wide panic for an indefinite period.

Unless we go to war with Germany our Government of course cannot make such a direct grant of credit. . . . It is a danger for us more real and imminent, I think, than the public on either side of the ocean realizes. If it be not averted before its symptoms become apparent it will then be too late to avert it. I think that the pressure of this approaching crisis has gone beyond the ability of the Morgan Financial Agency for the British and French Governments. The need is becoming too great and urgent for any private agency to meet. . . .

Perhaps our going to war is the only way in which our present preeminent trade position can be maintained and a panic averted. The submarine has added the last item to the danger of a financial world crash.[180]

116.

Admiral William S. Sims

Germany Was Winning the War

Whenever I think of the naval situation as it existed in April, 1917, I always have before my mind two contrasting pictures—one that of the British public, as represented in their press and in their social gatherings in London, and the other that of British officialdom, as represented in my confidential meetings with British statesmen and British naval officers. For the larger part the English newspapers were publishing optimistic statements about the German submarine campaign. In these they generally scouted the idea that this new form of piracy really threatened in any way the safety of the British Empire. They accompanied these rather cheerful outgivings by weekly statistics of submarine sinkings; figures which, while not particularly reassuring, hardly indicated that any serious inroads had yet been made on the British mercantile marine. . . .

Such figures were worthless, for they did not include neutral ships and did not give the amount of tonnage sunk, details, of course, which it was necessary to keep from the enemy. The facts which the Government thus permitted to come to public knowledge did not indicate that the situation was particularly alarming. . . . The generally prevailing feeling both in the press and in general discussions of the war seemed to be that the submarine campaign had already failed, that Germany's last desperate attempt to win the war had already broken down, and that peace would probably not be long delayed. . . . This same atmosphere of cheerful ignorance I found everywhere in London society. The fear of German submarines was not disturbing the London season, which had now reached its height; the theatres were packed every night; everywhere, indeed, the men and women of the upper classes were apparently giving little thought to any danger that might be hanging over their country.

Before arriving in England I myself had not known the gravity of the situation. I had followed the war from the beginning with the greatest interest; I had read practically everything printed about it in the American and foreign press, and I had had access to such official information as was available on our side of the Atlantic. The result was that, when I sailed for England in March, I felt little fear about the outcome. All the fundamental facts in the case made it appear impossible that the Germans could win the war. Sea power apparently rested practically unchallenged in the hands of the Allies; and that in itself, according to the unvarying lessons of history, was an absolute assurance of ultimate victory. The statistics of shipping losses had been regularly printed in the American press, and, while such wanton destruction of life and property seemed appalling, there was apparently nothing in these figures that was likely to make any material change in the result. Indeed it appeared to be altogether probable that the war would end before the United States could exert any material influence upon the outcome. My conclusions were shared by most American naval officers whom I knew, students of warfare, who, like myself, had the utmost respect for the British fleet and believed that it had the naval situation well in hand.

Yet a few days spent in London clearly showed that all this confidence in the defeat of the Germans rested upon a misapprehension. The Germans, it now appeared, were not losing the war—they were winning it. The British Admiralty now placed before the American representative facts and figures which it had not given to the British press. These documents disclosed the astounding fact that, unless the appalling destruction of merchant tonnage which was then taking place could be materially checked, the unconditional surrender of the British Empire would inevitably take place within a few months.[181]

117.

Edith Bolling Wilson

from *My Memoir*

March 4th falling on Sunday, the oath of office was taken without formality. . . . My husband arose, standing beside the littered desk where he had been signing papers. The Clerk handed him the Bible he had used four years before, and also when he became Governor of New Jersey. The Chief Justice administered the oath.

This simple ceremony (I was the only woman present) was more to our taste than the formal Inauguration which followed on Monday, March 5th. Though the day came in darkly, at ten o'clock the sun appeared, which I prayed might be an augury of the lifting of the cloud of war.

*   *   *

At noon on March 7th the President came in from the Executive Offices so wretched with a cold that I telephoned Dr. Grayson with the result that he ordered his patient to bed. He remained abed, or in the house, for ten days. The seclusion rested and restored him somewhat, freeing him from profitless interruptions for the contemplation of more important matters. . . .

Mr. Lansing, especially, saw no hope for peace and urged that we proceed on the theory that we should soon be at war with Germany. This was on the 8th and 9th. The 11th, Sunday, found

Woodrow better and I had Mother, Bertha, and Randolph to dinner. To amuse my husband I suggested that he and Randolph try the Ouija board. They did, and who should announce himself as present but Lord Nelson, saying he wished to discuss submarine warfare. We were all interested by what he said, for it was entirely logical.

*   *   *

March 15, 1917: Thrilling news from Russia regarding an almost bloodless Revolution. Overthrow of the Government and taking control by the people.

The tidings of the Czar's abdication, contained in a dispatch from Ambassador Francis, and the hope for a democratic Russia, seemed to give new strength to the President's conception of a war against autocracy.[182] Immediate preparation was made to recognize the new Russian Government.

*   *   *

[March] 19th brought word of the sinking of three American ships by German submarines. "The shadow of war," reads my diary, "is stretching its dark length over our own dear country."

On March 21st the President summoned Congress to meet in extraordinary session on April 2nd to consider "grave questions of national policy." This meant war.

My diary: "March 30, 1917: Perfect day, but W. felt he must work on his message to Congress. So we closed the door and gave orders no one was to disturb him. We lunched alone and I took him for an hour's ride in the park."

*   *   *

The Message was finished on Sunday, April 1st, after we had returned from services at Mr. Wilson's church. The President had asked Frank I. Cobb, editor of the *New York World*, to come down. He simply wanted a friend to talk to. Due to a delay in receiving the invitation, Mr. Cobb did not arrive until one in the

386

morning. The President was waiting up. They talked for an hour or so.[183]

118.

Woodrow Wilson

Interview with Frank Cobb

Though Frank Cobb never published an account of his talk with Wilson, he did, according to Arthur Link, give Maxwell Anderson "a long narration of a conversation that he said he had had with Woodrow Wilson at 1:00 a.m. on April 2, 1917, the very day on which Wilson went before a joint session of Congress to ask for a declaration of war against the German Empire."[184]

I have never been so uncertain about anything in my life as that decision. A declaration of war would mean that Germany would be beaten and so badly beaten that there would be a dictated peace, a victorious peace. It means an attempt to reconstruct a peace-time civilization with war standards, and at the end of the War there will be no bystanders with sufficient power to influence the terms. There won't be any peace standards left to work with. There will be only war standards. It would mean that we should lose our heads, along with the rest, and stop weighing right and wrong. It would mean that a majority of people on this hemisphere would be war-mad, quit thinking and devote their energies to destruction.

We couldn't fight Germany and maintain the ideals of government that all thinking men share. I shall try it but it will be too much for us. Once lead this people into war and they'll forget there ever was such a thing as tolerance. To fight, you must be brutal . . .

and the spirit of ruthless brutality will enter into the very fiber of our national life, infecting Congress, the courts, the policemen on the beat, the man in the street. Conformity will be the only virtue. And every man who refuses to conform will have to pay the penalty.[185]

119.

Edith Wilson

from *My Memoir*

April 2, 1917: Momentous day. . . . When we reached the Capitol the crowd outside was almost as dense as Inauguration Day, but perfectly orderly. Troops were standing on guard round the entire building, which stood out white and majestic in the indirect lighting which was used for the first time this eventful night. When I reached the gallery, after leaving my husband in the room always reserved for him, I found every seat taken and people standing in every available place both on the floor and in the galleries. . . . When my husband came in and all rose to their feet my very heart seemed to stop its beating.

After the first applause there was utter silence as the President read—until he pronounced the words: "We will not choose the path of submission." Whereupon Chief Justice White, an ex-Confederate soldier, rose to his feet and cheered. The response from the galleries and the floor was deafening.[186]

*   *   *

And thus it was that America, as Henry Adams had predicted, moved from Republic to Empire—a destiny affirmed on April 6, 1917, when the United States formally declared war on Germany.[187]

Coda

We are told that the peasants in Flanders, whose fields border upon the very trenches, disconsolately came back to them last spring and continued to plough the familiar soil, regardless of the rain of shrapnel falling into the fresh furrows; that the wine growers of Champagne last autumn insistently gathered their ripened grapes, though the bombs of rival armies were exploding in their vineyards.

—Jane Addams[188]

Just think: we may be on the eve of the discovery of the secret of the release of atomic energy. Such a discovery would multiply overnight the wealth of the world very many times. If man knew how to use such a discovery he could liberate himself once and for ever from poverty and soul destroying toil. But the instrument will simply use him: it will kill him in ever increasing numbers if our present ideas in international relationships, our present attitude in certain large human issues continue, if we continue to believe that "ordeal by battle" is the right method of settling differences between peoples. . . . For there would be a real danger that man would use such an instrument for collective suicide.

—Norman Angell[189]

120.

Jane Heap

The War, Madmen!

Honor:
> Speculations in misery, forced famines, sweat shops, child labor, suppression of free speech, leaks, lynchings, frame-ups, prisons. . . .

Protection:
> Millions for munitions: Starvation for millions. . . .

Justice:
> The death sentence for no crime and without trial: Conscription. . . .

Freedom:
> The right to be free: Prison. . . .

Glory:
> Parades, cheers, flags: Wooden limbs, blindness, widows orphans, poverty, soldiers' homes, asylums. . . .[190]

121.

Richard Aldington

The Road [1917]

To have watched all night at the feast where Socrates spoke of love, letting fall from tranquil fingers white violets in the cold black wine; or to have listened while some friend of Bembo talked of the groves of Academe and made golden flesh for us the ghosts of dead Greece—who would shrink from so exquisite a vigil? Then indeed not to sleep would be divine, and dawn—the first birds among the trees in the misty park, the first gold flush—would fill us perhaps with regret, certainly with exultation.

But there is no exultation for those who watch beside the Road, the road some know too bitterly and some will never know, the road which is the Place of Skulls—for it starts from a graveyard and passes through graveyards and ends in a graveyard.

By day the road is empty and desolate; no boot or wheel marks its mud, no human figure is reflected in its deep shell-pools. By day the road is silent. But by night it is alive with a harsh monotonous epic. Along that muddy trail move the rattling transport limbers, the field-guns, the ammunition wagons; the Red Cross cars lurch and sway on their springs over its deep ruts. Down that road come the weary battalions, platoon after platoon, heroic in their mud and silence; up that road go the fresh battalions, platoon after platoon, heroic in their cleanliness and silence. Down that road come the dead men on their silent wheeled stretchers. All that goes up that road is young and strong and alive; all that comes down is weary and old or dead. Over that road shriek and crash the shells; the sharp bullets strike gold sparks from its stones; the mortars tear craters in it. And just before dawn when the last limber rattles away and the last stretcher has gone back to the line, then the ghosts of the dead armies march down, heroic in their silence, battalion after battalion, brigade after brigade, division after division; the immeasurable forces of the dead youth of Europe march down the road past the silent sentry by the ruined house, march back, march home.[191]

Postscript

The *Little Review* departed Chicago for New York City during the winter of 1917 (the March issue was the first to have a 14th Street address), and Eunice Tietjens wrote that "some irresistible glory left with Margaret."[192] In the April issue Margaret Anderson announced that Ezra Pound—having tired of Harriet Monroe and *Poetry*—would henceforth be the "foreign editor" of the magazine:

> This means that he and T. S. Eliot will have an American organ (horrible phrase) in which they can appear regularly once a month, where James Joyce can appear when he likes, and where Wyndham Lewis can appear if he comes back from the war. . . . It means that a great deal of the most creative work of modern London and Paris will be published in these pages.[193]

In June, the *Egoist* in London announced that T. S. Eliot would be taking over the duties of literary editor from H. D., who for the past year had been filling in for Richard Aldington while he was away, fighting in France. Thus, with Pound and Eliot in the editorial chairs of two of the most influential little magazines of the Modernist era, the stage was set for what has become known as High Modernism, characterized—certainly in the postwar years—by what Hazel Hutchison has termed "disillusionment, irony, fragmentation of viewpoint and of language, alongside a keen sense of the futility of human endeavor."[194]

As Stanley Coffman wrote in his history of Imagism, "America's entry into the war put . . . a temporary halt to the surging interest in the arts that had almost reached the proportions of

[Pound's] desired risorgimento; not until the twenties would the renaissance appear in full strength."[195]

✳   ✳   ✳

Looking back later from the 1950s, Margaret Anderson would sum it all up in *The Little Review Anthology*:

> In 1929, in Paris, I decided that the time had come to end the *Little Review*. Our mission was accomplished; contemporary art had 'arrived'; for a hundred years, perhaps, the literary world would produce only: repetition. ... Ben Hecht wrote [in the last issue of the magazine]: "I never pass the Fine Arts Building in Michigan Avenue, Chicago, where the *Little Review* once lived, but youthful and exuberant ghosts say hello to me."[196]

Meanwhile, *Poetry* still soldiers on: vol. 200, no. 1, was published in April 2012—supported now by the vast resources of the Poetry Foundation. Harriet Monroe and her original guarantors, who signed on to support the magazine for five years, at $50 per year, would be proud.

About the Author

Robert Alexander (1949–2023) grew up in Massachusetts. He attended the University of Wisconsin–Madison and for several years taught in the Madison public schools. After receiving his Ph.D. from the University of Wisconsin–Milwaukee, he worked for many years as a freelance editor. From 1993 to 2001, he was a contributing editor at New Rivers Press, serving for the final two years as New Rivers' creative director. Alexander is the founding editor of the Marie Alexander Poetry Series at White Pine Press. He divided his time between southern Wisconsin and the Upper Peninsula of Michigan.

Selected Bibliography

Adams, Henry. *The Education of Henry Adams: An Autobiography*.
    Boston: Houghton Mifflin, 1918.

Addams, Jane. *Peace and Bread in Time of War*.
    New York: Macmillan, 1922.
———. *The Long Road of Woman's Memory*.
    New York: Macmillan, 1917.

Aldington, Richard. *Life for Life's Sake: A Book of Reminiscences*. New
    York: Viking, 1941.
———. *War and Love, 1915–1918*. Boston: Four Seas, 1919.
———. "The Road." *Egoist* 5.7 (Aug. 1918): 97–98.
———. "The Zeppelins over London." *Little Review* 2.8
    (November 1915): 4.
———. "Modern Poetry and the Imagists." *Egoist* 1.11 (1 June
    1914): 201–203.

Aldington, Richard, et al. *Some Imagist Poets, 1917: An Annual
    Anthology*. Boston: Houghton Mifflin, 1917.
———. *Some Imagist Poets, 1916: An Annual Anthology*. Boston:
    Houghton Mifflin, 1916.
———. *Some Imagist Poets: An Anthology*.
    Boston: Houghton Mifflin, 1915.

Aldrich, Mildred. *A Hilltop on the Marne: Being Letters Written
    June 3–September 8, 1914*. Boston: Houghton Mifflin, 1915.

Allerfeldt, Kristofer, ed. *The Progressive Era in the USA, 1890-1921*.
    Aldershot, UK: Ashgate, 2007.

Anderson, Margaret, ed. *The Little Review Anthology*. New York:
    Hermitage House, 1953.
———. *My Thirty Years' War: An Autobiography*. New York: Covici
    Friede, 1930.

―――. "Armageddon." *Little Review* 1.6 (Sept. 1914): 3–4.

Anderson, Sherwood. *Sherwood Anderson's Memoirs*. Edited by Paul Rosenfeld. New York: Harcourt, Brace and Co., 1942.
―――. "The New Note." *Little Review* 1.1 (March 1914): 23.

Angell, Norman. *After All: The Autobiography of Norman Angell*. London: H. Hamilton, [1951].
―――. *The British Revolution and the American Democracy: An Interpretation of British Labour Programmes*. New York: Huebsch, 1919.
―――. *The Great Illusion: A Study of the Relation of Military Power to National Advantage*. New Edition. London: Heinemann, 1914.

Antin, Mary. *The Promised Land*. Boston: Houghton Mifflin, 1912.

Baggett, Holly A. *The Buzz and the Sting: Margaret Anderson, Jane Heap, and the Little Review* (n.p.: n.p., forthcoming).
―――. " 'Someone to Talk Our Language': Jane Heap, Margaret Anderson, and the Little Review in Chicago." In *Modern American Queer History*, edited by Allida M. Black, 24–35. Philadelphia: Temple Univ. Press, 2001.
―――. " 'Aloof from Natural Laws': Margaret C. Anderson and the Little Review." Ph.D. diss., University of Delaware, 1992.

Bagnold, Enid. *A Diary without Dates*. Boston: John W. Luce and Co., 1918.

Baker, Ray Stannard. *American Chronicle: The Autobiography of Ray Stannard Baker*. New York: Scribner's, 1945.
―――. *Facing War, 1915–1917*. Vol. 6 of *Woodrow Wilson: Life and Letters*. Garden City, NY: Doubleday, Doran, 1937.
―――. "Gathering Clouds along the Color Line." *The World's Work* 32.2 (June 1916): 232–236.
―――. *Seen in Germany*. New York: McClure, Philips, 1901.

Ashmead-Bartlett, Ellis. *Some of My Experiences in the Great War*. London: Newnes, 1918.

Bernstorff, Count [Johann Heinrich von]. *My Three Years in America*. New York: Scribner's, 1920.

Beveridge, Albert J. *What Is Back of the War*. Indianapolis: Bobbs-Merrill, 1915.

Borden, Mary. *The Forbidden Zone*. London: Heinemann, 1929.

Bourne, Randolph S. *The War and the Intellectuals: Collected Essays, 1915–1919*. Edited by Carl Resek. Indianapolis: Hackett, 1999.

Brailsford, Henry Noel. *Belgium and "The Scrap of Paper."* London: The Independent Labour Party, 1915.
———. *The Origins of the Great War*. London: Union of Demo cratic Control, [1914].

Brandeis, Louis D. *Other People's Money and How the Bankers Use It*. New York: Frederick A. Stokes, 1914.

Brooker, Peter. *Bohemia in London: The Social Scene of Early Modernism*. New York: Palgrave Macmillan, 2007.

Brooks, Van Wyck. *America's Coming of Age*. New York: Huebsch, 1915.

Brown, Milton W. *The Story of the Armory Show*. New York: Abbeville Press, 1988.

Bryan, William Jennings. To the Editor. *New York Times* (23 Aug. 1915).
———. To Woodrow Wilson, 9 June 1915. *The Commoner* 15.6 (June 1915).
———. *A Tale of Two Conventions: Being an Account of the Republican*

and Democratic National Conventions of June, 1912, with an Outline of the Progressive National Convention of August in the Same Year. New York: Funk & Wagnalls, 1912.

Bryer, Jackson R. "'A Trial-Track for Racers': Margaret Anderson and the *Little Review.*" Ph.D. diss., University of Wisconsin –Madison, 1965.

Bryher [Winifred Ellerman]. *The Heart to Artemis: A Writer's Memoirs.* New York: Harcourt, Brace, 1962.

Carr, Helen. "Imagism: A Hundred Years On." Introduction to *Imagism: Essays on its Initiation, Impact and Influence,* edited by John Gery, Daniel Kempton, and H. R. Stoneback, 19–31. New Orleans: Univ. of New Orleans Press, 2013.
———. *The Verse Revolutionaries: Ezra Pound, H.D. and the Imagists.* London: Jonathan Cape, 2009.
———. "Imagism and Empire." In *Modernism and Empire,* edited by Howard J. Booth and Nigel Rigby, 65–92. Manchester, UK: Manchester Univ. Press, 2000.

Chace, James. *1912: Wilson, Roosevelt, Taft and Debs: The Election That Changed the Country.* New York: Simon & Schuster, 2004.

Chamberlain, John. *Farewell to Reform: The Rise, Life and Decay of the Progressive Mind in America.* Chicago: Quadrangle Books, 1965. Originally published in 1932.

Churchill, Suzanne W. *The Little Magazine Others and the Renovation of Modern American Poetry.* Aldershot, UK: Ashgate, 2006.

Churchill, Suzanne W., and Adam McKible, eds. *Little Magazines and Modernism: New Approaches.* London: Routledge, 2016.

Clark, Christopher. *The Sleepwalkers: How Europe Went to War in 1914.* New York: HarperCollins, 2013.

Cobb, Irvin S. *Paths of Glory: Impressions of War Written at and Near the Front*. New York: Doran, 1915.

Coffman, Stanley K. *Imagism: A Chapter for the History of Modern Poetry*. Norman: Univ. of Oklahoma Press, 1951.

Congressional Record. Vols. 54 and 55. Washington, DC: Government. Printing Office, 1917.

Cooper, John Milton Jr. *Pivotal Decades: The United States, 1900–1920*. New York: Norton, 1990.
———. *The Vanity of Power: American Isolationism and the First World War, 1914–1917*. Westport, CT: Greenwood Publishing, 1969.

Cournos, John. *Autobiography*. New York: Putnam's, 1935.

Creel, George. *Rebel at Large: Recollections of Fifty Crowded Years*. New York: Putnam's, 1947.

Cronon, William. *Nature's Metropolis: Chicago and the Great West*. New York: W. W. Norton, 1991.

Crunden, Robert M. *American Salons: Encounters with European Modernism, 1885–1917*. New York: Oxford Univ. Press, 1993.

D[oolittle], H[ilda]. *End to Torment: A Memoir of Ezra Pound*. New York: New Directions, 1979.
———. *Sea Garden*. London: Constable, 1916.

Daniels, Josephus. *The Wilson Era: Years of Peace, 1910–1917*. Chapel Hill: Univ. of North Carolina Press, 1944.

Davis, Richard Harding. *With the Allies*. New York: Scribner's, 1914.

Dayer, Roberta A. "Strange Bedfellows: J. P. Morgan & Co.,

Whitehall and the Wilson Administration During World War I." *Business History* 18.2 (July 1976): 127–151.

Dell, Floyd. *Essays from the* Friday Literary Review, *1909–1913*. Edited by R. Craig Sautter. Highland Park, IL: December Press, 1995.

———. *Homecoming: An Autobiography*. New York: Farrar & Rine hart, 1933.

Dickinson, G. Lowes. *The European Anarchy*. London: Allen & Unwin, 1916.

Doenecke, Justus D. *Nothing Less Than War: A New History of America's Entry into World War I*. Lexington: Univ. Press of Kentucky, 2011.

Dorr, Rheta Childe. *What Eight Million Women Want*. Boston: Small, Maynard, 1910.

Dreiser, Theodore. *A Book about Myself*. New York: Boni & Liveright, 1922.

Du Bois, W. E. Burghardt. *The Souls of Black Folk: Essays and Sketches*. Chicago: McClurg, 1903.

Duffey, Bernard. *The Chicago Renaissance in American Letters: A Critical History*. East Lansing: Michigan State College Press, 1954.

Dunn, Robert. *Five Fronts: On the Firing-Lines with English-French, Austrian, German and Russian Troops*. New York: Dodd, Mead, 1915.

Eastman, Max. *Love and Revolution: My Journey through an Epoch*. New York: Random House, 1964.

———. *Enjoyment of Living*. New York: Harper & Brothers, 1948.

Eliot, T. S. *Prufrock and Other Observations*. London: The Egoist, 1917.

———. "Reflections on Vers Libre." *New Statesman* 8.204 (3 March 1917): 518–519. Reprinted in *T. S. Eliot, To Criticize the Critic*, 183–189. Lincoln: Univ. of Nebraska Press, 1991.

Everdell, William R. *The First Moderns: Profiles in the Origins of Twentieth-Century Thought*. Chicago: Univ. of Chicago Press, 1997.

Fess, Simeon D. *The Submarine Controversy*. Part One of *The Problems of Neutrality When the World Is at War: A History of Our Relations with Germany and Great Britain as Detailed in the Documents that Passed between the United States and the Two Great Belligerent Powers*. Washington, DC: Government Printing Office, 1917.

Fleming, D. F. "Our Entry into the World War in 1917: The Revised Version." *The Journal of Politics* 2.1 (Feb. 1940): 75–86.

Fletcher, John Gould. *Life is my Song: The Autobiography of John Gould Fletcher*. New York: Farrar & Rinehart, 1937.

———. *Breakers and Granite*. New York: Macmillan, 1921.

———. "Vers Libre and Advertisements." *Little Review* 2.2 (April 1915): 29–30.

Flint, F[rank] S. *Cadences*. London: Poetry Bookshop, [1915].

———. "The History of Imagism." *Egoist* 2.5 (1 May 1915): 70–71.

———. "Imagisme." *Poetry* 1.6 (March 1913): 198–200.

———. "Contemporary French Poetry." *Poetry Review* 1.8 (August 1912): 355–414. Reprinted in *The Road from Paris: French Influence on English Poetry, 1900–1920*, edited by Cyrena N. Pondrom, 84–145. Cambridge: Cambridge Univ. Press, 1974.

———. "Recent Verse." *New Age* [n.s.] 4.5 (26 November 1908): 95–97.

Ford, Ford Madox (named changed from F. M. Hueffer in 1919):

———. *It Was the Nightingale*. London: Heinemann, 1934.

———. *Return to Yesterday*. New York: Liveright, 1932.

———. "Those Were the Days." Foreword to *Imagist Anthology 1930, 13–21*. New York: Covici, Friede, 1930.

———. *Thus to Revisit: Some Reminiscences*. New York: Dutton, 1921.

———. *On Heaven, and Poems Written on Active Service*. London: John Lane, 1918.

———. *When Blood Is Their Argument: An Analysis of Prussian Culture*. New York: Hodder & Stoughton, 1915.

———. "From China to Peru." *Outlook* [London] 35 (19 June 1915): 800–801.

———. "Les Jeunes and *Des Imagistes*." *Outlook* [London] 33 (9 May and 16 May 1914): 636–637, 683.

———. *Collected Poems*. London: Max Goschen, 1914.

Frank, Florence Kiper. "The Moving-Picture Show." *Little Review* 2.5 (August 1915): 11–12.

Frank, Waldo. *Our America*. New York: Boni & Liveright, 1919.

Frost, Robert. *North of Boston*. New York: Henry Holt, 1914.

Fussell, Paul. *The Great War and Modern Memory*. New York: Oxord Univ. Press, 1975.

Garrison, William Lloyd. "Letter from Mr. William Lloyd Garrison, Boston," 226–227. In *Proceedings of the National Negro Conference, 1909: New York, May 31 and June 1*. [N.p.]: [n.p.], [n.d.].

Gerard, James W. *My Four Years in Germany*. New York: Doran, 1917.

Glaspell, Susan. *The Road to the Temple*. New York: Frederick A. Stokes, 1927.

Goldman, Emma. *Living My Life*. New York: Knopf, 1934.
———. "Preparedness: The Road to Universal Slaughter." *Little Review* 2.9 (Dec. 1915): 7–12.

Goldring, Douglas. *South Lodge: Reminiscences of Violet Hunt, Ford Madox Ford and the* English Review *Circle*. London: Constable, 1943.

Grattan, C. Hartley. *Why We Fought*. Indianapolis: Bobbs-Merrill, 1968. Originally published in 1929.

Graves, Robert. *Goodbye to All That*. Revised Edition. London: Cassell, 1957.
———. *Fairies and Fusiliers*. New York: Knopf, 1918.

Greasley, Philip A., ed. *Dictionary of Midwest Literature*. Volume One: *The Authors*. Bloomington: Indiana Univ. Press, 2001.

Green, Martin. *New York, 1913: The Armory Show and the Paterson Strike Pageant*. New York: Scribner's, 1988.

Gregory, Ross. *The Origins of American Intervention in the First World War*. New York: Norton, 1971.

Hahn, Emily. *Romantic Rebels: An Informal History of Bohemianism in America*. Boston: Houghton Mifflin, 1967.

Hansen, Harry. *Midwest Portraits: A Book of Memories and Friendships*. New York: Harcourt, Brace, 1923.

Hapgood, Hutchins. *A Victorian in the Modern World*. New York: Harcourt, Brace, 1939.

Harris, Frank. *England or Germany?* New York: The Wilmarth Press, 1915.

Haywood, William D. *Bill Haywood's Book: The Autobiography of William D. Haywood*. New York: International Publishers, 1929.

Heap, Jane. "The War, Madmen!" *Little Review* 3.9 (March 1917): 15.

Hecht, Ben. *A Child of the Century*. New York: Simon & Schuster, 1954.
———. *1001 Afternoons in Chicago*. Chicago: Univ. of Chicago Press, 1992. Originally published in 1922.
———. "The Mob-God." *Little Review* 2.3 (May 1915): 45–46.

Heller, Adele, and Lois Rudnick, eds. *1915, The Cultural Moment: The New Politics, the New Woman, the New Psychology, the New Art & the New Theatre in America*. New Brunswick, NJ: Rutgers Univ. Press, 1991.

Henderson, Alice Corbin. *The Sun Turns West*. Santa Fe, NM: Writers' Editions, 1933.

Herrmann, David G. *The Arming of Europe and the Making of the First World War*. Princeton, NJ: Princeton Univ. Press, 1996.

Hoftstadter, Richard. *The Age of Reform: From Bryan to FDR*. New York: Vintage, 1955.

Howe, Frederic C. *The Confessions of a Reformer*. New York: Scribner's, 1925.
———. *Why War*. New York: Scribner's, 1916.
———. "Democracy or Imperialism—The Alternative That Confronts Us." *Annals of the American Academy of Political and Social Science* 66 (July 1916): 250–258.

Howells, William Dean. "The Irish Executions." *The Nation* 102 (May 18, 1916): 541.

Hueffer, Ford Madox — see Ford Madox Ford.

Hughes, Glenn. *Imagism & the Imagists: A Study in Modern Poetry.* Stanford, CA: Stanford Univ. Press, 1931.

Hulme, T. E. "Lecture on Modern Poetry." Appendix 2 in *T. E. Hulme,* by Michael Roberts, 258–270. London: Faber & Faber, 1938.
———. "Romanticism and Classicism." In *Speculations: Essays on Humanism and the Philosophy of Art,* edited by Herbert Read, 111–140. London: Routledge & Keegan Paul, 1936. Originally published in 1924.

Hunt, Violet. *The Flurried Years.* [London]: Hurst & Blackett, [1926].

Hutchins, Patricia. *Ezra Pound's Kensington: An Exploration, 1885–1913.* Chicago: Regnery, 1965.

Hutchison, Hazel. *The War That Used Up Words: American Writers and the First World War.* New Haven: Yale Univ. Press, 2015.

Ickes, Harold L. "Who Killed the Progressive Party?" *American Historical Review* 46.2 (Jan. 1941): 306–337.

Irwin, Inez Haynes. *The Story of the Woman's Party.* New York: Harcourt, Brace, 1921.

Jolas, Eugene. *The Man from Babel.* New Haven: Yale Univ. Press, 1998.

Joll, James. *The Origins of the First World War.* Second edition. London: Longman, 1992.

Jones, P. Mansell. "The First Theory of the 'Vers Libre.'" *Modern Language Review* 42.2 (Apr. 1947): 207–214.

Jones, Peter, ed. *Imagist Poetry*. London: Penguin, 1972.

Kahn, Gustave. "Le Vers Libre." Preface to *Premiers Poèmes*. Third Edition. Paris: Mercure de France, 1897.

Kalaidjian, Walter, ed. *The Cambridge Companion to American Modernism*. Cambridge: Cambridge Univ. Press, 2005.

Kazin, Michael. *War against War: The American Fight for Peace, 1914–1918*. New York: Simon & Schuster, 2017.

Keegan, John. *The First World War*. New York: Knopf, 1999.

Kellogg, Paul U. "The Fighting Issues: A Statement by the Editor of the *Survey*." *Survey* 37 (17 February 1917): 572–576.

Kendall, Tim, ed. *Poetry of the First World War: An Anthology*. Oxford: Oxford Univ. Press, 2013.

Kenner, Hugh. *The Pound Era*. Berkeley: Univ. of California Press, 1971.

Keynes, John Maynard. *The Economic Consequences of the Peace*. New York: Harcourt, Brace and Howe, 1920.

Koetggen, Julius. *A German Deserter's War Experience*. New York: Huebsch, 1917.

Kramer, Dale. *Chicago Renaissance: The Literary Life in the Midwest, 1900–1930*. New York: Appleton-Century, 1966.

Kreymborg, Alfred. *Troubadour: An Autobiography*. New York: Liveright, 1925.

Kremer, J. Bruce, comp. *Official Report of the Proceedings of the Democratic National Convention, Held at Saint Louis, Missouri, June 14, 15 and 16th, 1916*. Chicago: [n.p.], 1916.

La Follette, Robert M. *"Old Bob" La Follette's Historic U.S. Senate Speech against the Entry of the United States into the World War: Delivered in the United States Senate on April 4, 1917*. Madison, WI: Progressive Pub. Co., 1937.

————. *The Political Philosophy of Robert M. La Follette, as Revealed in His Speeches and Writings*, compiled by Ellen Torelle. Madison, WI: La Follette Co., 1920.

————. *La Follette's Autobiography: A Personal Narrative of Political Experiences*. Madison, WI: La Follette Co., 1913.

Lamont, Thomas W. "The Effect of the War on America's Financial Position." *Annals of the American Academy of Political and Social Science* 60 (July 1915): 106–112.

La Motte, Ellen N. *The Backwash of War: The Human Wreckage of the Battlefield as Witnessed by an American Hospital Nurse*. New York: Putnam's, 1916.

Lansing, Robert. *Papers Relating to the Foreign Relations of the United States: The Lansing Papers, 1914–1920*. Two vols. Washington: DC: Government. Printing Office, 1939.

————. *War Memoirs of Robert Lansing, Secretary of State*. Indianapolis: Bobbs-Merrill, 1935.

Larkin, Jim. "The Irish Rebellion." *Masses* 8.9, "Preparedness Number" (July 1916): 20–22.

Larson, Erik. *Dead Wake: The Last Crossing of the Lusitania*. New York: Crown, 2015.

Lieven, Dominic. *The End of Tsarist Russia: The March to World War I and Revolution*. New York: Viking, 2015

Lindberg-Seyersted, Brita, ed. *Pound/Ford: The Story of a Literary Friendship*. New York: New Directions, 1982.

Link, Arthur S. "That Cobb Interview." *Journal of American History*

72.1 (June 1985): 7–17.

Lipmann, Walter. *Drift and Mastery: An Attempt to Diagnose the Current Unrest*. New York: Mitchell Kennerly, 1914.

Longenbach, James. *Stone Cottage: Pound, Yeats, and Modernism*. New York: Oxford Univ. Press, 1988.

Lowell, Amy. *Pictures from the Floating World*. New York: Macmillan, 1919.
———. "A Letter from London." *Little Review* 1.7 (Oct. 1914): 6–9.

Luhan, Mabel Dodge. *Movers and Shakers*. New York: Harcourt, Brace, 1936.

Lynch, Frederick. *Through Europe on the Eve of War*. New York: Church Peace Union, 1914.

MacMillan, Margaret. *The War That Ended Peace: The Road to 1914*. New York: Random House, 2013.

Marchand, C. Roland. *The American Peace Movement and Social Reform, 1889-1918*. Princeton, NJ: Princeton Univ. Press, 1972.

Marek, Jayne E. *Women Editing Modernism: "Little" Magazines and Literary History*. Lexington: Univ. Press of Kentucky, 1995.

Masters, Edgar Lee. *Across Spoon River: An Autobiography*. Urbana: Univ. of Illinois Press, 1991. Originally published in 1936.
———. Spoon River Anthology. New York: Macmillan, 1916.

May, Ernest R. *The World War and American Isolation, 1914–1917*. Cambridge, MA: Harvard Univ. Press, 1959.

May, Henry F. *The End of American Innocence: A Study of the First Years of Our Own Time, 1912–1917*. New York: Columbia Univ. Press, 1992. Originally published in 1959.

McGerr, Michael. *A Fierce Discontent: The Rise and Fall of the Progressive Movement in America, 1870–1920.* New York: Oxford Univ. Press, 2003.

Mencken, H. L. *My Life as an Author and Editor.* Edited by Jonathan Yardley. New York: Knopf, 1993.
———. *Prejudices: First Series.* New York: Knopf, 1919.
———. *A Book of Prefaces.* New York: Knopf, 1917.
———. "Civilized Chicago." *Chicago Sunday Tribune*, 28 October 1917.

Middleton, Christopher, ed. "Documents on Imagism from the Papers of F. S. Flint." *The Review: A Magazine of Poetry and Criticism* 15 (April 1965): 36–51.

Mohr, Anton. *The Oil War.* New York: Harcourt, Brace, 1926.

Monroe, Harriet. *A Poet's Life: Seventy Years in a Changing World.* New York: Macmillan, 1938.
———. "New Banners." *Poetry* 8.5 (Aug. 1916): 251–253.

Monroe, Harriet, and Alice Corbin Henderson, eds. *The New Poetry: An Anthology.* New York: Macmillan, 1917.

Morel, Edmund D. *Truth and the War.* London: National Labour Press, 1916.

Morrison, Mark S. *The Public Face of Modernism: Little Magazines, Audiences, and Reception, 1905–1920.* Madison: Univ. of Wisconsin Press, 2001.

Nadel, Ira B., ed. *The Letters of Ezra Pound to Alice Corbin Henderson.* Austin: Univ. of Texas Press, 1993.

Nathan, George Jean, and H. L. Mencken. *The American Credo: A Contribution Toward the Interpretation of the National Mind.* Revised and Enlarged Edition. New York: Knopf, 1921.

National Women's Party. *Campaign Text-Book of the National Woman's Party, 1916*. Washington, DC: Columbian Printing, 1916.

Nearing, Scott. *The Making of a Radical: A Political Autobiography*. New York: Harper & Row, 1972.

Neilson, Francis. *How Diplomats Make War*. New York: Huebsch, 1915.

Olson, Liesl. *Chicago Renaissance: Literature and Art in the Midwest Metropolis*. New Haven, CT: Yale Univ. Press, 2017.

Papers Relating to the Foreign Relations of the United States. The World War, 1914–1918. Twenty vols. Washington, DC: Government Printing Office, 1928–1933.

Patmore, Brigit. *My Friends When Young: The Memoirs of Brigit Patmore*. London: Heinemann, 1968.

Peattie, Elia W. *The Book of the Fine Arts Building*. Chicago: Ralph Fletcher Seymour, 1911.

Perloff, Marjorie. "The Avant-Garde Phase of American Modernism." In *The Cambridge Companion to American Modernism*, edited by Walter Kalaidjian, 195–217. Cambridge: Cambridge Univ. Press, 2005.

Peterson, H. C., and Gilbert C. Fite. *Opponents of War, 1917–1918*. Madison: Univ. of Wisconsin Press, 1957.

Pinchot, Amos. *History of the Progressive Party, 1912-1916*. Edited by Helene Maxwell Hooker. New York: NYU Press, 1958.
———. "The Courage of the Cripple." *Masses* 9.5 (Mar. 1917): 19–21.
———. "American Militarism." *Masses* 6.4 (Jan. 1915): 8–9.
———. "The Failure of the Progressive Party." *Masses* 6.3 (Dec.

1914): 9–10.

Pinkerton, Jan, and Randolph H. Hudson, eds. *Encyclopedia of the Chicago Literary Renaissance*. New York: Facts on File, 2004.

Pondrom, Cyrena N., ed. *The Road from Paris: French Influence on English Poetry, 1900–1920*.
Cambridge: Cambridge Univ. Press, 1974.
———. "The Book of the Poets' Club and Pound's 'School of Images.'" *Journal of Modern Literature* 3.1 (Feb. 1973): 100-102.

Pound, Ezra. *Selected Prose, 1909–1965*. Edited by William Cookson. New York: New Directions, 1973.
———. *Personae: The Collected Poems of Ezra Pound*. New York: Boni & Liveright, 1926.
———. *Pavannes and Divisions*. New York: Knopf, 1916.
———. *Gaudier-Brzeska: A Memoir*. London: John Lane, 1916.
———. "Extract from a letter." *Poetry* 7.6 (March 1916): 321–322.
———, ed. *Catholic Anthology, 1914–1915*. London: Elkin Mathews, 1915.
———. *Cathay: Translations*. London: Elkin Mathews, 1915.
———. *Des Imagistes: An Anthology*. New York: Boni & Liveright, 1914.
———. "Ford Madox Hueffer." *New Freewoman* 13.1 (15 Dec. 1913): 251.
———. "A Few Don'ts by an Imagiste." *Poetry* 1.6 (March 1913): 200–205.
———. "Status Rerum." *Poetry* 1.4 (Jan. 1913): 125.

Powell, E. Alexander. *Fighting in Flanders*. Toronto: McClelland, Goodchild & Stewart, 1915.

Pratt, William. *The Imagist Poem: Modern Poetry in Miniature*. New York: Dutton, 1963.

Prince, Sue Ann, ed. *The Old Guard and the Avant-Garde: Modernism in*

Chicago, 1910–1940. Chicago: Univ. of Chicago Press, 1990.

Proceedings of the National Negro Conference, 1909: New York, May 31 and June 1. [N.p.]: [n.p.], [n.d.].

Putzel, Max. *The Man in the Mirror: William Marion Reedy and His Magazine.* Cambridge, MA: Harvard Univ. Press, 1963.

Rascoe, Burton. *Before I Forget.* New York: Literary Guild, 1937.

Reed, John. *The War in Eastern Europe.* New York: Scribner's, 1916.
———. "At the Throat of the Republic." *Masses* 8.9 (July 1916): 7–12.
———. "The Traders' War." *Masses* 5.12 (Sept. 1914): 16–17.

Rudwick, Elliott M. "The National Negro Committee Conference of 1909." *Phylon Quarterly* 18.4 (4th Qtr., 1957): 413–419.

Ruhl, Arthur. *Antwerp to Gallipoli: A Year of War on Many Fronts— and behind Them.* New York: Scribner's, 1916.

Russell, Bertrand. *Justice in War Time.* Second edition. Chicago: Open Court, 1917.

Russell, Charles Edward. *Bare Hands and Stone Walls: Some Recollections of a Side-line Reformer.* New York: Scribner's, 1933.

Sandburg, Carl. *Always the Young Strangers.* New York: Harcourt, Brace, 1953.
———. *Chicago Poems.* New York: Holt, 1916.

Sanger, Margaret. *Woman and the New Race.* New York: Brentano's, 1920.

Sassoon, Siegfried. *Memoirs of an Infantry Officer.* New York: Penguin, 2013. Originally published in 1930.

Scott, Thomas L., Melvin J. Friedman, and Jackson R. Bryer, eds. *Pound/The Little Review: The Letters of Ezra Pound to Margaret Anderson*. New York: New Directions, 1988.

Seymour, Ralph Fletcher. *Some Went This Way: A Forty Year Pilgrimage among Artists, Bookmen and Printers*. Chicago: Ralph Fletcher Seymour, 1945.

Simonds, Frank H. "1914—The End of an Era?" *New Republic* 1.9 (January 2, 1915): 12–13.

Sims, William Sowden, and Burton J. Hendrick. *The Victory at Sea*. Garden City, NY: Doubleday, Page, 1920.

Sinclair, May. *A Journal of Impressions in Belgium*. New York: Macmillan, 1915.

"Sinking of the Lusitania." In *The Story of the Great War*, by Francis J. Reynolds et al., 3:152–164. New York: Collier, 1916.

Smith, Alson J. *Chicago's Left Bank*. Chicago: Regnery, 1953.

Smith, Angela K. *The Second Battlefield: Women, Modernism and the First World War*. Manchester, UK: Manchester Univ. Press, 2000.

Smith, Carl S. *Chicago and the American Literary Imagination, 1880–1920*. Chicago: Univ. of Chicago Press, 1984.

Smith, D. I. B. "Ford Madox Ford and Modernism." *University of Toronto Quarterly* 51.1 (Fall 1981): 61–77.

Solomon, Barbara Probst, ed. *America—Meet Modernism: Women of the Little Magazine Movement*. New York: Great Marsh Press, 2003.

Spinney, Robert Guy. *City of Big Shoulders: A History of Chicago*.

DeKalb: Northern Illinois Univ. Press, 2000.

Starrett, Vincent. *Born in a Bookshop: Chapters from the Chicago Renascence*. Norman: Univ. of Oklahoma Press, 1965.

Stearns, Harold E. *The Street I Know*. New York: Lee Furman, 1935.
———. *America and the Young Intellectual*. New York: George Doran, 1921.
———. *Liberalism in America: Its Origin, Its Temporary Collapse, Its Future*. New York: Boni & Liveright, 1919.

Steffens, Lincoln. *The Autobiography of Lincoln Steffens*. New York: Harcourt, Brace, 1931.

Stephens, James. *The Insurrection in Dublin*. New York: Macmillan, 1916.

Stevens, Doris. *Jailed for Freedom*. New York: Boni & Liveright, 1920.

Stevenson, David. *Armaments and the Coming of War: Europe, 1907–1914*. Oxford: Oxford Univ. Press, 1996.

Storer, Edward. *Mirrors of Illusion: With an Essay*. London: Sisley's, [1909].

Tagore, Rabindanath. "The Tryst." *Poetry* 3.3 (Dec. 1913): 79–81.

Tanselle, G. Thomas. "The 'Friday Literary Review' and the Chicago Renaissance." *Journalism Quarterly* 38.3 (Sept. 1961): 332–336.

Tarbell, Ida M. *All in the Day's Work: An Autobiography*. New York: Macmillan, 1939.

Thompson, John A. *Reformers and War: American Progressive Publicists and the First World War*. Cambridge: Cambridge

Univ. Press, 1987.

Tietjens, Eunice. *The World at My Shoulder*. New York: Macmillan, 1938.

Tuchman, Barbara W. *The Guns of August*. New York: Macmillan, 1962.

Turbyfill, Mark. "Whistling in the Windy City: Memoirs of a Poet-Dancer." Typescript. Chicago: Newberry Library Modern Manuscripts, Midwest.MS.Turbyfill.

Turner, John Kenneth. *Shall it Be Again?* New York: Huebsch, 1922.

Vorse, Mary Heaton. *A Footnote to Folly: Reminiscences*. New York: Farrar & Rinehart, 1935.

Walling, William English. *The Socialists and the War*. New York: Holt, 1915.
———. *Progressivism—and After*. New York: Macmillan, 1914.

Walton, Mary. *A Woman's Crusade: Alice Paul and the Battle for the Ballot*. New York: St. Martin's Griffin, 2015.

Watson, Steven. *Strange Bedfellows: The First American Avant-Garde*. New York: Abbeville, 1991.

Wells-Barnett, Ida B. "Lynching: Our National Crime." *Proceedings of the National Negro Conference, 1909*: New York, May 31 and June 1, 174–179. [N.p.]: [n.p.], [n.d.]. Reprint, " 'Lynching is color-line murder': the blistering speech denouncing America's shame," *The Guardian* (Manchester, UK), 17 April 2018; https://www.theguardian.com /world/2018/apr/27/ida-b-wells-barnett-national-negro-conference-chicago-speech.

West, Rebecca. "Imagisme." *New Freewoman* 1.5 (15 Aug. 1913): 86–87.

Whalan, Mark. *American Culture in the 1910s.* Edinburgh: Edinburgh Univ. Press, 2010.

Wharton, Edith, ed. *The Book of the Homeless (Le Livre des Sans Foyer).* New York: Scribner's, 1916.

———. *Fighting France: From Dunkerque to Belfort.* New York: Scribner's, 1915.

Whelpton, Vivien. Richard Aldington: *Poet, Soldier and Lover, 1911–1929.* Cambridge, UK: Lutterworth Press, 2014.

White, William Allen. *The Autobiography of William Allen White.* New York: Macmillan, 1946.

Whitlock, Brand. *Belgium: A Personal Narrative.* Two vols. New York: Appleton, 1920.

Williams, Albert Rhys. *In the Claws of the German Eagle.* New York: E. P. Dutton, 1917.

Williams, Ellen. *Harriet Monroe and the Poetry Renaissance: The First Ten Years of Poetry, 1912–22.* Urbana: Univ. of Illinois Press, 1977.

Williams, William Carlos. *The Autobiography of William Carlos Williams.* New York: New Directions, 1951.

Wilson, Edith Bolling. *My Memoir.* Indianapolis: Bobbs-Merrill, 1939.

Wilson, Woodrow. *Selected Addresses and Public Papers of Woodrow Wilson.* Edited by Albert Bushnell Hart. New York: Boni & Liveright, 1918.

———. *The New Freedom.* Garden City, NY: Doubleday, Page, 1913.

Woolley, Lisa. *American Voices of the Chicago Renaissance*. DeKalb: Northern Illinois Univ. Press, 2000.

Yeats, William Butler. *Introduction to The Oxford Book of Modern Verse, 1892–1935*. New York: Oxford Univ. Press, 1937.
———. *Michael Robartes and the Dancer*. Churchtown, Ireland: Cuala Press, 1920.

Zweig, Stefan. *The World of Yesterday: An Autobiography*. New York: Viking, 1943.

Magazines

Blast
The Egoist
The Little Review
The Masses
The New Freewoman
Others
Poetry: A Magazine of Verse
The Seven Arts

Websites

"9 poets of the first world war." Imperial War Museum. https://www.iwm.org.uk/history/9-poets-of-the-first-world-war.

Anderson, Margaret. "Elizabeth Jenks Clark Collection." Beinecke Library.
https://beinecke.library.yale.edu/collections/highlights/elizabeth-jenks-clark-collection-margaret-anderson.

"Chicago and the Midwest." Newberry Library.
https://www.newberry.org/chicago-and-midwest.

Deutsch, Abigail. "100 Years of Poetry: The Magazine and War: A historical look at the role of poetry in wartime." Poetry Foundation.
https://www.poetryfoundation.org/articles/69902/100-years-of-poetry-the-magazine-and-war.

"Documents of World War I." Mt. Holyoke International Relations. https://www.mtholyoke.edu/acad/intrel/ww1.htm.

Green, Michelle Erica. "Margaret Anderson and the Little Review." The Little Review—Making No Compromises with the Public Taste. http://www.littlereview.com/mca/mca.htm.

"Historical Documents of the Woodrow Wilson Administration (1913–1921)." Office of the Historian, United States Department of State. https://history.state.gov/historicaldocuments/wilson.

"The Journals." Modernist Journals Project.
https://modjourn.org/journal/.

"Online Collections." Jewish Museum Berlin.
https://objekte.jmberlin.de.

"The Poetry of World War I." Poetry Foundation,
https://www.poetryfoundation.org/articles/70139/the-poetry-of-world-war-i.

"Women of Protest: Photographs from the Records of the National Woman's Party." Library of Congress Digital Collections.

https://www.loc.gov/collections/women-of-protest/articles-and-essays/historical-overview-of-the-national-womans-party/.

"Woodrow Wilson: Related Documents." The American Presidency Project. https://www.presidency.ucsb.edu/people/president/woodrow-wilson.

"World War I Centennial: Commemorating the Great War." National Archives. https://www.archives.gov/topics/wwi.

"World War I Document Archive." Brigham Young University Library. https://wwi.lib.byu.edu/index.php/Main_Page.

"World War I Poets: From Apollinaire to Sassoon." Poetry Foundation. https://www.poetryfoundation.org/collections/101720/world-war-i-poets.

NOTES

Excerpts of essays, letters, etc., have for the most part been edited for length.

1 Sherwood Anderson, *Sherwood Anderson's Memoirs*, ed. Paul Rosenfeld (New York: Harcourt, Brace, 1942), 199.

2 Margaret C. Anderson, *My Thirty Years' War: An Autobiography* (New York: Covici, Friede, 1930), 45.

3 William Butler Yeats, *Introduction to The Oxford Book of Modern Verse, 1892–1935* (New York: Oxford Univ. Press, 1937), xi.

4 Jackson R. Bryer, " 'A Trial-Track for Racers': Margaret Anderson and the *Little Review*" (Ph.D. diss., University of Wisconsin–Madison, 1965), 14.

5 Woodrow Wilson, First Inaugural Address, 4 March 1913, The American Presidency Project, University of California at Santa Barbara, https://www.presidency.ucsb.edu/node/207576.

6 Arthur Ficke quoted in Harriet Monroe, *A Poet's Life*, 253.

7 Teddy Roosevelt quoted in William Jennings Bryan, *A Tale of Two Conventions* (New York: Funk & Wagnalls, 1912), 253–254, 278.

8 Harriet Monroe, *Introduction to The New Poetry: An Anthology*, ed. Harriet Monroe and Alice Corbin Henderson (New York: Macmillan, 1917), v–vi. In her memoir, Monroe has this to say about the anthology: "My anthology, *The New Poetry*, led the way, was the first of the twentieth-century collections which now fill four five-foot shelves of our poetry library. Alice and I began it together a few months before she was taken ill and went to Santa Fe for her long fight with the world's worst enemy. . . . In these days of high charges for the use of poems, it seems incredible that no poet or publisher received a cent for the loan of poems in our 1917 edition;

indeed they were all delighted to serve with us in this experimental appeal to a most uncertain public; and when our book became a 'best seller in the poetry field' . . .the long procession of anthologies general and special began with a rush, to confirm our faith that there would be a public for modern poetry" [Harriet Monroe, *A Poet's Life: Seventy Years in a Changing World* (New York: Macmillan, 1938), 387].

9 Henry L. Mencken, "Civilized Chicago," *The Chicago Sunday Tribune*, 28 October 1917, Section S, p. 5.

10 Harry Hansen, *Midwest Portraits: A Book of Memories and Friendships* (New York: Harcourt, Brace, 1923), 95–99.

11 Sherwood Anderson, *Memoirs* (New York: Harcourt, Brace, 1942), 230.

12 Floyd Dell, *Homecoming 12* (New York: Farrar & Rinehart, 1933), 217.

13 Amy Lowell, "Vernal Equinox," *Poetry* 6.6 (Sept. 1915), 275.

14 Edgar Lee Masters, *Across Spoon River: An Autobiography* (1936; Urbana: Univ. of Illinois Press, 1991), 139–141.

15 Ralph Fletcher Seymour, *Some Went This Way: A Forty Year Pilgrimage among Artists, Bookmen and Printers* (Chicago: Ralph Fletcher Seymour, 1945), 139–143.

16 Harriet Monroe, *A Poet's Life: Seventy Years in a Changing World* (New York: Macmillan, 1938), 222–223, 240–248.

17 For a list of *Poetry*'s guarantors see *Poetry* 1.1 (Oct. 1912), 29–30, https://www.poetryfoundation.org/poetrymagazine/browse?volume=1&issue=1&page=35. Full disclosure: Edward Ryerson's grandson, known as Ned, was my ninth grade English teacher in Cambridge, Massachusetts—a man who encouraged in me a love

of modern poetry as well as an obsession with clear, precise writing.

18 Monroe, *A Poet's Life*, 249–253. The circular Monroe sent out can be seen in its entirety in Harriet Monroe, "These Five Years," *Poetry* 11.1 (Oct. 1917), 33–41.

19 Monroe, *A Poet's Life*, 283–286.

20 Monroe, *A Poet's Life*, 258–260, 268.

21 George Creel, *Rebel at Large: Recollections of Fifty Crowded Years* (New York: Putnam's, 1947), 368.

22 Amos Pinchot to E. W. Scripps, 11 Sept. 1914, Amos Pinchot Papers, Library of Congress, box 225; quoted in John A. Thompson, *Reformers and War: American Progressive Publicists and the First World War* (Cambridge, UK: Cambridge Univ. Press, 1987), 43.

23 Ray Stannard Baker, *American Chronicle: The Autobiography of Ray Stannard Baker* (New York: Scribner's, 1945), 249–254.

24 William Allen White, *Autobiography* (New York: Macmillan, 1946), 423–428.

25 Frederic C. Howe, *The Confessions of a Reformer* (New York: Scribner's, 1925), 240–244.

26 Ida B. Wells-Barnett, "Lynching Our National Crime," in *Proceedings of the National Negro Conference 1909: New York, May 31 and June 1* ([n.p.]: [n.p.], [n.d.]), 174–179; reprint, " 'Lynching is color-line murder': the blistering speech denouncing America's shame," *The Guardian* (Manchester, UK), 17 April 2018; https://www.theguardian.com/world/2018/apr/27/ida-b-wells-barnett-national-negro-conference-chicago-speech.

27 W. E. Burghardt Du Bois, *The Souls of Black Folk: Essays and*

Sketches (Chicago: McClurg, 1909), 39–40, 116–118, 124–126.

28 Harry Hansen, *Midwest Portraits*, 212.

29 Floyd Dell, *Homecoming: An Autobiography* (New York: Farrar & Rinehart, 1933), 181, 184, 194, 218–219.

30 Harry Hansen, *Midwest Portraits*: (New York: Harcourt, Brace, 1923), 105.

31 In fact, the *Dial* was founded by Ralph Waldo Emerson.

32 Margaret C. Anderson, *My Thirty Years' War* (New York: Covici, Friede, 1930), 13–30.

33 Harry Hansen, *Midwest Portraits*, 99.

34 Eunice Tietjens, *The World at My Shoulder* (New York: Macmillan, 1938), 17-20.

35 Rebecca West, "Imagisme," *New Freewoman* 1.5 (15 Aug. 1913), 86.

36 T. E. Hulme, "Romanticism and Classicism," *Speculations: Essays on Humanism and the Philosophy of Art*, ed. Herbert Read (1924; London: Routledge & Keegan Paul, 1936), 132.

37 F. S. Flint, "Imagisme," *Poetry* 1.6 (March 1913), 198–200.

38 Ford Madox Hueffer (who has not yet changed his name to Ford Madox Ford) uses this expression in his poem, "On a Marsh Road (Winter Nightfall)," *Collected Poems* (London: Max Goschen, 1914), 135.

39 Ezra Pound, "A Few Don'ts by an Imagiste," *Poetry* 1.6 (March 1913), 200–205.

40 Edward Storer, "An Essay," *Mirrors of Illusion* (London: Sisley's, [1909]), 106–110.

41 F. S. Flint, "The History of Imagism," *Egoist* 2.5 (Saturday, May 1, 1915), "Special Imagist Number," ed. Richard Aldington, pp. 70–71. (In 1919, Ford Madox Hueffer legally changed his last name to Ford.) See, also, a slightly different point of view from Frank Flint—a piece found among his private papers, which according to Christopher Middleton, "appears to be a draft for his 'History of Imagisme.' It illustrates the point Flint made in a letter to Harriet Monroe, dated 22 March 1916; here he said of the six other contributors to *Some Imagist Poets* that they 'are no longer associated with him.... Our quarrel with Mr. Pound is, you see, both a private and an artistic one.'" In this piece, tentatively titled "The Bottle-Green Guide Fragment" (placed in brackets in the original), Flint writes about the dinners which gave rise to the Imagist movement:

> The bottle-green guide who touts for credulous Americans outside the Louvre will take you, if you are fool enough, to some odd picture in an out-of-the-way corner and announce with much triumph and mystery that he is the only guide who shows you that. Mr. Pound's method was the same.... [He] came and listened to all we had to say on the theory and practice of verse ... but he added nothing of any value to the discussion. Most of the members of the group were pretty widely acquainted with French theory, and Mr. Pound had simply nothing to teach them; but he took very much. He took away the whole doctrine of what he later on called Imagisme" [Christopher Middleton, ed.,"Documents on Imagism from the Papers of F. S. Flint," *The Review: A Magazine of Poetry and Criticism*, no. 15 (April 1965): 39–40].

For a full discussion of the controversy between Pound and F. S. Flint over the meetings at the Tour Eiffel restaurant and the "invention" of Imagism, see Helen Carr, *The Verse Revolutionaries: Ezra Pound, H.D. and the Imagists* (London: Jonathan Cape, 2009), 765–770.

42 Ezra Pound, "A Retrospect," in *Pavannes and Divisions* (New York: Knopf, 1918), 95–96.

43 John Gould Fletcher, "*Vers Libre* and Advertisements," *Little Review* 2.2 (April 1915), 29–30.

44 Ford Madox Hueffer [Ford], "Vers Libre," in *Thus to Revisit: Some Reminiscences* (New York: Dutton, 1921), 185–214. After the First World War, Ford Madox Hueffer legally changed his last name from Hueffer to Ford. To avoid confusion, his last name, when it appears as the author of sections of this narrative, is always given as Ford, though in the endnotes, depending on publication date, it will be listed as in the original document.

45 Harry Hansen, *Midwest Portraits*, 111

46 Sherwood Anderson, *Memoirs*, 197–198, 248–249.

47 According to Inez Haynes Irwin, this is "the 47 Suffrage banner which Inez Milholland bore in the first Suffrage procession in New York" [Inez Haynes Irwin, *The Story of the Woman's Party* (New York: Harcourt, Brace, 1921), 203].

48 Mrs. R. M. La Follette, *La Follette's Magazine*, May 1912, in Robert M. LaFollette, *The Political Philosophy of Robert M. La Follette*, comp. Ellen Torelle (Madison, WI: LaFollette Co., 1920), 342–344.

49 Inez Haynes Irwin, *The Story of the Woman's Party* (New York: Harcourt, Brace, 1921), 3–5. For more about Alice Paul, see Mary Walton, *A Woman's Crusade: Alice Paul and the Battle for the Ballot* (New York: St. Martin's Griffin, 2015).

50 Doris Stevens, *Jailed for Freedom* (New York: Boni & Liveright, 1920), 63, 68. Appendix 4 of Stevens' book (pp. 354–371), titled "Suffrage Prisoners," opens with the following note: "Scores of women were arrested but never brought to trial; many others were convicted and their sentences suspended or appealed. It has been possible to list below only those women who actually served prison sentences although more than five hundred women were arrested during the agitation." There follows a list of 168 names, with brief biographical details; I highly suggest that the reader download the book, now in the public domain, and read through the entire list. These women, and all others who struggled for years for women's rights, deserve our lasting gratitude.

51 Frederic C. Howe, *The Confessions of a Reformer* (New York: Scribner's, 1925), 232–235.

52 Eunice Tietjens, *The World at My Shoulder* (New York: Macmillan, 1938), 21–25.

53 Margaret C. Anderson, *My Thirty Years' War* (New York: Covici, Friede, 1930), 32–33, 35–39.

54 Sherwood Anderson, "The New Note," *Little Review* 1.1 (March 1914), 23.

55 DeWitt C. Wing.

56 Margaret C. Anderson, *My Thirty Years' War* (New York: Covici, Friede, 1930), 39–42, 44–45.

57 Eunice Tietjens, *The World at My Shoulder* (New York: Macmillan, 1938), 63–68.

58 Ben Hecht, *A Child of the Century* (New York: Simon & Schuster, 1954), 233–235.

59 Ben Hecht ["The Scavenger"], "The Mob-God," *Little Review*

2.3 (May 1915), 45–46.

60 Mark Turbyfill, "Whistling in the Windy City," TS (Chicago, Newberry Library Modern Manuscripts, Midwest.MS.Turbyfill), 10–18.

61 Harriet Monroe, *A Poet's Life* (New York: Macmillan, 1938), 317–321.

62 Rabindanath Tagore, "The Tryst," *Poetry* 3.3 (Dec. 1913), 79–81. Note (p. 113); note: "The great Oriental poet who has just received the Nobel prize for literature, may fitly open our Christmas number. *Poetry*, having introduced Mr. Tagore's lyrics to American readers a year ago, is now the first magazine to present his translation of a group of narrative poems. No one can question the 'idealistic tendency' of this poet's work; the recognition by the Swedish academy of its artistic and spiritual beauty opens another door between East and West, and leads occidental nations into a comparatively unknown province of oriental art"; https://www.nobelprize.org/prizes/literature/1913/tagore/biographical/.

63 In 1919, Ford Madox Hueffer legally changed his last name to Ford.

64 Harriet Monroe, *A Poet's Life* (New York: Macmillan, 1938), 321–322.

65 Ben Hecht, *A Child of the Century* (New York: Simon & Schuster, 1954), 247.

66 Margaret C. Anderson, *My Thirty Years' War* (New York: Covici, Friede, 1930), 58–60.

67 Harriet Monroe, *A Poet's Life* (New York: Macmillan, 1938), 323–325.

68 Eunice Tietjens, *The World at My Shoulder* (New York: Macmil-

lan, 1938), 23, 24, 29–30, 31–32, 35–36.

69 Floyd Dell, *Homecoming: An Autobiography* (New York: Farrar & Rinehart, 1933), 232, 242–243, 222.

70 Eunice Tietjens, *The World at My Shoulder* (New York: Macmillan, 1938), 38–39, 42–44.

71 Harriet Monroe, *A Poet's Life: Seventy Years in a Changing World* (New York: Macmillan, 1938), 377–381.

72 Eunice Tietjens, *The World at My Shoulder* (New York: Macmillan, 1938), 45–47.

73 Edgar Lee Masters, *Across Spoon River: An Autobiography* (1936; New York: Urbana: Univ. of Illinois Press, 1991), 338–340.

74 Ford Madox Ford, *Return to Yesterday* (New York: Liveright, 1932), 410.

75 Ezra Pound, "Status Rerum," *Poetry* 1.4 (Jan. 1913), 125. In 1919, Ford Madox Hueffer legally changed his last name to Ford.

76 [Ezra Pound, ed.], *Des Imagistes: An Anthology* (London: The Poetry Bookshop, 1914; also New York: Boni & Liveright, 1914); also published as vol. 1, no. 5, of the *Glebe* (Feb. 1914), a little magazine edited by Alfred Kreymborg.

77 Ford Madox Hueffer [Ford], "Les Jeunes and Des Imagistes," *Literary Portraits—XXXV, Outlook* 33.849 (9 May 1914), 636–637.

78 Ford Madox Hueffer [Ford], "Les Jeunes and Des Imagistes (Second Notice), *Literary Portraits—XXXVI, Outlook* 33.850 (16 May 1914), 683.

79 Ezra Pound, "Extract from a letter," *Poetry* 7.6 (March 1916), 321–322.

80 Harriet Monroe, *A Poet's Life*, 257 fn.

81 Ezra Pound, "Credo," *Pavannes and Divisions* (New York: Knopf, 1918), 103. Regarding Pound's and Yeats's "visionary poetics," see James Longenbach, *Stone Cottage: Pound, Yeats, and Modernism* (New York: Oxford Univ. Press, 1988), 22–23, 49–54, 79–82, 226–238, 241–244. For Ford's influence, see also D. I. B. Smith, "Ford Madox Ford and Modernism," *University of Toronto Quarterly* 51.1 (Fall 1981), 61–77.

82 Ford Madox Ford, "Those Were the Days," Foreword to *Imagist Anthology 1930* (New York: Covici, Friede, 1930), 13, 18–19; dated New York, August 1, 1929.

83 Douglas Goldring, *South Lodge: Reminiscences of Violet Hunt, Ford Madox Ford and the English Review Circle* (London: Constable, 1943), 47–48. Ford's description of Pound can be found in Ford Madox Ford, *Return to Yesterday* (New York: Liveright, 1932), 373.

84 Ford Madox Ford, "Ezra: Personae: The Collected Poems of Ezra Pound," in *Pound/Ford: The Story of a Literary Friendship*, ed. Brita Lindberg-Seyersted (New York: New Directions, 1982), 83–84 [82–87]; this book review originally appeared in the *New York Herald Tribune Review of Books* (9 January 1927).

85 Ezra Pound, "Ford Madox (Hueffer) Ford; Obit," in *Selected Prose, 1909–1965*, ed. William Cookson (New York: New Directions, 1973), 461–462 [461–463]; first appeared in *The Nineteenth Century and After*, August 1939.

86 Bryher [Winnifred Ellerman], *The Heart to Artemis: A Writer's Memoirs* (New York: Harcourt, Brace, 1962), 161–162.

87 Ford Madox Ford, *When Blood Is Their Argument: An Analysis of Prussian Culture* (New York: Hodder & Stoughton, 1915), 168.

88 Frank Harris, *England or Germany?* (New York: The Wilmarth

Press, 1915), 34.

89 Ford Madox Ford, "What the Orderly Dog Saw," *Poetry* 9.6 (March 1917), 293–294.

90 Ray Stannard Baker, *Seen in Germany* (New York: McClure, Philips, 1901), 6–8, 51–55, 65.

91 John Maynard Keynes, *The Economic Consequences of the Peace* (New York: Harcourt, Brace, 1920), 10–12.

92 Stefan Zweig, *The World of Yesterday: An Autobiography* (London: Cassell, 1943), 151–154.

93 Harold E. Stearns, *The Street I Know* (New York: Lee Furman, 1935), 109, 111–12

94 John Cournos, *Autobiography* (New York: Putnam's, 1935), 268–276.

95 J[ulius] Koettgen, trans., *A German Deserter's War Experience* (New York: Huebsch, 1917), 1–4.

96 H[enry] N[oel] Brailsford, Belgium and "The Scrap of Paper" (London: *The Independent Labour Party, 1915*), 1–2.

97 Harriet Monroe, *A Poet's Life* (New York: Macmillan, 1938), 341–345.

98 Woodrow Wilson, Message on Neutrality, 19 August 1914, The American Presidency Project, https://www.presidency.ucsb.edu/node/206513.

99 Woodrow Wilson, Second Annual Message, 8 December 1914, The American Presidency Project, https://www.presidency.ucsb.edu/node/207586.

100 Woodrow Wilson, Address to Naturalized Citizens at Convention Hall, Philadelphia, 10 May 1915, The American Presidency Project, https://www.presidency.ucsb.edu/node/206560; note: "The audience included four thousand newly naturalized citizens. This speech attracted great attention because in it no reference was made to the sinking of the Lusitania, three days before."

101 The so-called Iron Chancellor of the German Reich, Otto von Bismarck (in power 1871–1890), is often quoted as having said that "the whole of the Balkans is not worth the bones of a single Pomeranian grenadier."

102 Read, for example, this typical declaration by the Volkstimme, one of the German Socialist Party organs: "All must set aside the alms and purposes of their party, and bear in mind one fact—Germany, and in a larger sense all Europe, is endangered by Russian despotism. At this moment we all feel the duty to fight chiefly and exclusively against Russian despotism. Germany's women and children must not become the prey of Russian bestiality; the German country must not be the spoil of Cossacks; because if the Allies should be victorious, not an English governor or a French republican would rule over Germany, but the Russian Tsar.

Therefore we must defend at this moment everything that means German culture and German liberty against a merciless and barbaric enemy" [footnote in original].

103 Henry Noel Brailsford, The Origins of the Great War (London: Union of Democratic Control, [1914]), 3–5.

104 For a riveting and impressionistic account of the war in the East, see John Reed, The War in Eastern Europe (New York: Scribner's, 1916).

105 Frederic C. Howe, Preface to Why War (New York: Scribner's, 1916), vii–ix.

106 John Reed, "The Traders' War, *Masses* 5.12 (Sept. 1914), 16–17.

107 Scott Nearing, *The Making of a Radical: A Political Autobiography* (New York: Harper & Row, 1972), 105–107.

108 [Margaret C. Anderson], "Armageddon," *Little Review* 1.6 (Sept. 1914), 3–4. 378

109 Brand Whitlock, *Belgium: A Personal Narrative*, 2 vols. (New York: Appleton, 1920), 1:123–126.

110 J[ulius] Koettgen, *A German Deserter's War Experience*, 8–10.

111 "It wasn't. This was only the first slender trickling. The flood came three days later with the bombardment of the city" [Sinclair's note].

112 "Of all the thousands and thousands of refugees whom I have seen I have only seen three weep, and they were three out of six hundred who had just disembarked at the Prince of Wales's Pier at Dover. But in Belgium not one tear" [Sinclair's note].

113 May Sinclair, *A Journal of Impressions in Belgium* (New York: Macmillan, 1915), 117–120.

114 Irvin S. Cobb, Paths of Glory (New York: Doran, 1915), 41–42.

115 "This condition has somewhat improved since above was written" [note in original].

116 Amy Lowell, "A Letter from London," *Little Review* 1.7 (Oct. 1914), 6–9.

117 Margaret C. Anderson, *My Thirty Years' War* (New York: Covici, Friede, 1930), 60–62.

118 Florence Kiper Frank, "The Moving-Picture Show," *Little Review* 2.5 (August 1915), 11.

119 Albert J. Beveridge, *What Is Back of the War* (Indianapolis: Bobbs-Merrill, 1915), 3–7; note: "written at The Hague, December 26–27, 1914."

120 Edith Wharton, *Fighting France: From Dunkerque to Belfort* (New York: Scribner's, 1915), 18–24.

121 Richard Harding Davis, *With the Allies* (New York: Scribner's, 1914), 86–95.

122 J[ulius] Koettgen, *A German Deserter's War Experience*, 65–67.
123 E. Alexander Powell, *Fighting in Flanders* (Toronto: McClelland Goodchild & Stewart, 1915), 86–89, 115–118.

124 J[ulius] Koettgen, *A German Deserter's War Experience*, 68–69.

125 Mildred Aldrich, *A Hilltop on the Marne: Being Letters Written June 3–September 8, 1914* (Boston: Houghton Mifflin, 1915), 166–170.

126 J[ulius] Koettgen, *A German Deserter's War Experience*, 72, 124–125.

127 Eugen Wiener, Individual and Group Photographs, Online Photograph Collection, Jüdisches Museum Berlin, http://objekte.jmberlin.de/object/jmb-obj-182977 and http://objekte.jmberlin.de/object/jmb-obj-160127.
Individual photo credit: W. Gerlich's Photograph Studio, Neuruppin; Eugen Wiener as a soldier in uniform, c. 1914; Jewish Museum Berlin, Inv. No. 2000/285/94; donated by Peter Sinclair, formerly Peter Jacob.

128 See *Fashion and Persecution: The Fate of Jewish Clothiers in the Nazi Dictatorship on the Premises of Today's Justice Ministry*, vol. 2 of Re-

membrance, Reflection, Responsibility ([n.p.]: [German] Federal Minstry of Justice and Consumer Protection, [n.d.]; see also Meinhard Jacobs, "Mit Marlene Dietrich Befreundet: Die Familien Jacob und Weitz," in *Jüdische Familien in Groß Glienicke: Eine Spurensuche*, edited by Sonja Richter, Winfried Sträter, and Dieter Dargies (Potsdam, Germany: Groß Glienicker Kreis, 2011), 7–8.

129 E[llis] Ashmead-Bartlett, "The Battle of Nieuport-Dixmude," *Some of My Experiences in the Great War* (London: Newnes, 1918), 60–76.

130 Death Notice for Eugen Wiener, Online Imprint Collection, Jüdisches Museum Berlin, http://objekte.jmberlin.de/object/jmb-obj-520964; note: "In the upper left corner an iron cross is printed, as Eugen Wiener was the owner of this order."

131 Arthur Ruhl, *Antwerp to Gallipoli: A Year of War on Many Fronts—And behind Them* (New York: Scribner's, 1916), 75–76, 100–101.

132 J[ulius] Koettgen, *A German Deserter's War Experience*, 179–182, 186–187.

133 Mary Heaton Vorse, *A Footnote to Folly* (New York: Farrar & Rinehart, 1935), 119–124.

134 Robert Dunn, *Five Fronts: On the Firing-Lines with English-French, Austrian, German and Russian Troops* (New York: Dodd, Mead, 1915), 83–90; 122; 129, 135–136; 138–141.
    Two places in Galicia mentioned here, Przemysl and Radymno, now lie a few miles from the Polish-Ukraine border. Their names now have an eerie resonance, as just ten days after I put the final edits to rest on this manuscript, Russian tanks rolled into Ukraine, and there was yet another European war for the world to deal with. As Dominic Lieven writes at the beginning of *The End of Tsarist Russia*, "As much as anything, World War I turned on the

fate of Ukraine" [New York: Viking, 2015, p. 1]. That story is still being written.

135 Ford Madox Ford, *Return to Yesterday* (New York: Liveright, 1932), 378.

136 Bertrand Russell, *Justice in War Time*, Second Edition (Chicago: Open Court, 1917). 14.

137 *Norman Angell, The British Revolution and the American Democracy: An Interpretation of British Labour Programmes* (New York: Huebsch, 1919), 271.

138 Violet Hunt, "What the Civilian Saw," *Poetry* 9.6 (March 1917), 295.

139 Richard Aldington, "The Zeppelins over London," *Little Review* 2.8 (November 1915), 4.

140 Rihoku, referred to in the poem, is the Japanese name for the Chinese general Li Mu; Rihaku, who wrote the piece, is the great poet Li Po. See Richard Sieburth, *Ezra Pound: Poems and Translations* (New York: Library of America, 2003), 254 fn.

141 Ford Madox Hueffer [Ford], "From China to Peru," *Outlook* 35.907 (19 June 1915), 800–801.

142 William Allen White, *The Autobiography of William Allen White* (New York: Macmillan, 1946), 512, 513–514, 514, 516, 520.

143 Amos Pinchot, Advertisement, "Do the People Want War?" 28 Feb. 1917, Amos Pinchot Papers, Library of Congress, box 15; quoted in John A. Thompson, *Reformers and War: American Progressive Publicists and the First World War* (Cambridge, UK: Cambridge Univ. Press, 1987), 167. According to Alfred Kazin, "this ad appeared in various newspapers," including the *New Republic* of 3 March 1917—placed by the Committee for Democratic Control—

and "a galley proof is located in Amos Pinchot Papers, box 73" [*War against War: The American Fight for Peace, 1914–1918* (New York: Simon & Schuster, 2017), 332–333 fns 1, 18].

144 Woodrow Wilson, Third Annual Message, 7 December 1915, The American Presidency Project, https://www.presidency.ucsb.edu/node/207590.

145 John Reed. "At the Throat of the Republic," *Masses* 8.9, "Preparedness Number" (July 1916), 7–12.

146 Harold Stearns, *Liberalism in America: Its Origin, Its Temporary Collapse, Its Future* (New York: Boni & Liveright, 1919), 80–81, 82–86, 87–88.

147 Emma Goldman, "Preparedness: The Road to Universal Slaughter," *Little Review* 2.9 (Dec. 1915), 7–11.

148 Margaret C. Anderson, *My Thirty Years' War* (New York: Covici, Friede, 1930), 69–70.

149 Emma Goldman, *Living My Life* (NY: Knopf, 1934), 530.

150 Margaret C. Anderson, *My Thirty Years' War* (New York: Covici, Friede, 1930), 70–73.

151 Emma Goldman, *Living My Life*, 531.

152 Margaret C. Anderson, *My Thirty Years' War* (New York: Covici, Friede, 1930), 73–75.

153 Ellen N. La Motte, "Pour La Patrie," *The Backwash of War: The Human Wreckage of the Battlefield as Witnessed by an American Hospital Nurse* (New York: Putnam, 1916), 115–125.

154 Richard Aldington, *Life for Life's Sake: A Book of Reminiscences* (New York: Viking, 1941), 186–190.

155 Robert Graves, *Goodbye to All That*, revised edition (1929; London: Cassell, 1957), 52, 78, 105–106.

156 Henri Gaudier-Brzeska to Ezra Pound, in Ezra Pound, *Gaudier-Brzeska* (London: John Lane, 1916), 63–64.

157 Henri Gaudier-Brzeska to Mrs. Olivia Shakespear, *Gaudier-Brzeska*, 75–79.

158 Henri Gaudier-Brzeska to Ezra Pound, *Gaudier-Brzeska*, 69–70.

159 Gaudier-Brzeska's death notice as quoted in Ford Madox Ford, *Thus to Revisit* (New York: Dutton, 1921), 183.

160 William Dean Howells, "The Irish Executions," *Nation* 102 (May 18, 1916): 541.

161 Woodrow Wilson, "American Principles," Address delivered at the First Annual Assemblage of the League to Enforce Peace, 27 May 1916, The American PresidencyProject, University of California at Santa Barbara,
https://www.presidency.ucsb.edu/node/206570;
also in *Woodrow Wilson, Selected Addresses and Public Papers of Woodrow Wilson*, ed. Albert Bushnell Hart (New York: Boni & Liveright, 1918). 124 [121–125].

162 Jim Larkin, "The Irish Rebellion," *Masses* 8.9, "Preparedness Number" (July 1916), 21.

163 James Stephens, *The Insurrection in Dublin* (New York: Macmillan, 1916), 1–97.

164 Harriet Monroe, "New Banners," *Poetry* 8.5 (Aug. 1916), 251–253.

165 Margaret C. Anderson, *My Thirty Years' War* (New York: Covici,

Friede, 1930), 102–106.

166 Margaret C. Anderson, *The Little Review Anthology* (New York: Horizon Press, 1953), 124–125.

167 Margaret C. Anderson, *My Thirty Years' War* (New York: Covici, Friede, 1930), 135–137, 139–141.

168 John Milton Cooper, Jr., *The Vanity of Power: American Isolationism and the First World War, 1914–1917* (Westport, CN: Greenwood Publishing, 1969), 192–193.

169 T[homas] W[att] Gregory, "Wilson and the War: An Account of His Attitude as Seen by His Attorney General," *New York Times*, 29 January 1925, p. 18; quoted by C. Hartley Grattan, *Why We Fought* (1929; Indianapolis: Bobbs-Merrill, 1968), 202, 343.

170 Carl Sandburg, "Old Timers," *Poetry* 10.6 (Sept. 1917), 298.

171 Randolph Bourne, "The War and the Intellectuals," in *The War and the Intellectuals: Collected Essays, 1915–1919*, ed. Carl Resek (1964; Indianapolis, IN: Hackett Publishing, 1999), 3–14. This essay first appeared in *Seven Arts* 2.2 (June 1917), 133–134. Harold Stearns says this about Bourne: "I think many of my readers will agree with me that the untimely death of Randolph Bourne [in the influenza pandemic] was an irreparable loss to American liberalism. He was about the only one of the younger American writers and essayists who did not let himself be beguiled by the hypocrisies and shibboleths of the war. His criticism of American policy in the war and his predictions of where it would lead us read today like uncanny prophecy" [Harold Stearns, *Liberalism in America: Its Origin, Its Temporary Collapse, Its Future* (New York: Boni & Liveright, 1919), 15].

172 "The incident is described by George Creel, Wilson's Director of Information, in his autobiography, *Rebel at Large*, p. 155. Creel's testimony is supplemented by Gilson Gardner's account of the

'Sunrise Conference' in the spring of 1916 at which Wilson tried to persuade the Speaker of the House, the Democratic Floor Leader, and the Chairman of the House Foreign Affairs Committee that the time had come for the United States to get into the war. These revelations suggest that the President was more war-minded throughout the whole period in question than he allowed his pacifist friends to believe. Gardner's story appeared in *McNaughton's Magazine*, was reprinted by Harry Elmer Barnes in *The Genesis of the World War*, and retold by Gardner in *Lusty Scripps*, pp. 194–196" [this is the original note by Max Eastman, *Love and Revolution* (New York: Random House, 1964), 33].

173 Max Eastman, *Love and Revolution* (New York: Random House, 1964), 32–36.

174 Scott Nearing, *The Making of a Radical: A Political Autobiography* (New York: Harper & Row, 1972), 107–108.

175 The German Ambassador in Washington (Count Johann von Bernstorff) to the Secretary of State (Robert Lansing), 31 January 1917, Document 92, FRUS, 1917, *Supplement 1, The World War* (Washington, DC: U.S. Gov't. Printing Office, 1931), 97–100, https://history.state.gov/historicaldocuments/frus1917Supp01v 01/d92.

176 Count [Johann Heinrich von] Bernstorff, *My Three Years in America* (New York: Scribner's, 1920), 370–371.

177 Woodrow Wilson, Address to a Joint Session of Congress on the Severance of Diplomatic Relations with Germany, 3 February 1917, The American Presidency Project, https://www.presidency.ucsb.edu/node/206606.

178 Robert M. LaFollette, *"Old Bob" La Follette's Historic U.S. Senate Speech against the Entry of the United States into the World War: Delivered in the United States Senate on April 4, 1917* (Madison, WI: Progressive Pub. Co., 1937), 23–28; for original, see *Congressional*

Record 55 (65th Congress), 223–234.

179 Frederic C. Howe, *The Confessions of a Reformer* (New York: Scribner's, 1925), 36–39.

180 Telegram from the Ambassador in Great Britain (Walter Hines Page) to the Secretary of State (Robert Lansing), London, 5 March 1917 (received March 6), *FRUS, 1917, Supplement 2, The World War*, 2 vols. (Washington, DC: U.S. Gov't. Printing Office, 1932), 1:516–518.

181 William Sowden Sims, *The Victory at Sea* (Garden City, NY: Doubleday, Page, 1920), 5–7. Note: "Rear-Admiral Sims, USN, was commander of the American naval forces operating in European waters during the Great War."

182 See telegram from the ambassador in Russia (Francis) to the Secretary of State, 14 March 1917 (received March 15), Document 2, *FRUS, 1918, Russia*, 3 vols. (Washington, DC: U.S. Gov't Printing Office, 1931), 1:1-2, https://history.state.gov/historicaldocuments/frus1918Russiav01/d2.

183 Edith Bolling Wilson, *My Memoir* (New York: Bobbs-Merrill, 1939), 130–132.

184 Arthur S. Link, "That Cobb Interview," *The Journal of American History* 72.1 (June 1985), 7; this article includes a detailed analysis of the entire episode, though it doesn't include the interview itself.

185 Frank Cobb's account of Woodrow Wilson's ruminations, as quoted in John Chamberlain, *Farewell to Reform: The Rise, Life, and Decay of the Progressive Mind in America* (1932; Chicago: Quadrangle, 1965), 295–296.

186 Edith Bolling Wilson, *My Memoir* (New York: Bobbs-Merrill, 1939), 132–133.

187 "[I]n forty years, America had made so vast a stride to empire that the world of 1860 stood already on a distant horizon somewhere on the same plane with the republic of Brutus and Cato, while schoolboys read of Abraham Lincoln as they did of Julius Caesar. Vast swarms of Americans knew the Civil War only by school history, as they knew the story of Cromwell or Cicero, and were as familiar with political assassination as though they had lived under Nero. The climax of empire could be seen approaching, year after year, as though Sulla were a President or McKinley a Consul" [Henry Adams, *The Education of Henry Adams: An Autobiography* (Boston: Houghton Mifflin, 1918), 367]. For the declaration of war, see "Joint Resolution declaring that a state of war exists between the Imperial German Government and the Government and the people of the United States and making provision to prosecute the same," *Statutes at Large*, 65th Congress, Chapter 1; the vote on the war resolution was as follows: Senate, April 4: Yeas – 82, Nays – 6; House, April 5: Yeas – 373, Nays – 50, Not voting – 9 (*Congressional Record*, 65th Congress, 1st session, 55:261, 412–413).

188 Jane Addams, *The Long Road of Woman's Memory* (New York: Macmillan, 1917), 137.

189 Norman Angell, *The British Revolution and the American Democracy: An Interpretation of British Labour Programmes* (New York: Huebsch, 1919), 272–273.

190 Jane Heap, "The War, Madmen!" *Little Review* 190 3.9 (March 1917), 15; this was the first issue of the *Little Review* published in NYC.

191 Richard Aldington, "The Road," *Egoist* 5.7 (Aug. 1918), 97–98; reprinted in Richard Aldington, *The Love of Myrrhine and Konallis, and Other Prose Poems* (Chicago: Pascal Covici, 1926), 89–92.

192 Eunice Tietjens, *The World at My Shoulder* (New York: Macmillan, 1938), 69.

193 [Margaret C. Anderson], "Surprise!" *Little Review* 3.10 (April 1917), 25.

194 Hazel Hutchison, *The War That Used Up Words: American Writers and the First World War* (New Haven: Yale Univ. Press, 1915), 204.

195 Stanley K. Coffman, *Imagism: A Chapter for the History of Modern Poetry* (Norman: University of Oklahoma Press, 1951), 46.

196 Margaret C. Anderson, ed., *The Little Review Anthology* (New York: Horizon Press, 1953), 349–350.